INGMAR BERGMAN

Ingmar BERGMAN

Magician and Prophet

MARC GERVAIS

McGill-Queen's University Press
Montreal & Kingston • London • Ithaca

© McGill-Queen's University Press 1999
ISBN 0-7735-1843-6 (bound) ISBN 0-7735-2004-x (pbk)
Legal deposit fourth quarter 1999
Bibliothèque nationale du Québec

Printed in Canada on acid-free paper

This book has been published with the help of a grant from
Concordia University.

McGill-Queen's University Press acknowledges the financial
support of the Government of Canada through the Book
Publishing Industry Development Program (BDIDP) for its
activities. We also acknowledge the support of the Canada
Council for the Arts for our publishing program.

Canadian Cataloguing in Publication Data

Gervais, Marc, 1929–
    Ingmar Bergman: Magician and Prophet
    Includes bibliographical references and index.
    ISBN 0-7735-1843-6 (bound). ISBN 0-7735-2004-x (pbk).
    1. Bergman, Ingmar, 1918– Criticism and interpretation.
    I. Title.
    PN 1998.3.B47G47 1999   791.43'0233'092   c99-901002-6

This book was typeset in 10.2/14 Electra
Design: David LeBlanc

Frontispiece: Svensk Filmindustri

CONTENTS

FOREWORD

As I write this, Ingmar Bergman continues to be a very close friend and, at times, a very valued artistic collaborator. To be sure, there were those other years a few decades ago, when our sharing of our lives, both personally and professionally, was intense. So, when I think of his movies, for example, how do I approach them? For me – and I've mentioned this a few times in past writings – it tends, of course, to be a series of very personal things: intuitions about his past, painful or joyful memories, a capturing of moments, of a nuance, or of a sight or a sound, a sense of wonder, a searching for *the* answer, a cry for wholeness. And emotions, of course: good ones, and bad ones, terror, exaltation, love, hate, the mystical, the mundane.

Marc Gervais, I'm reasonably certain, would never claim to have had those kinds of close personal encounters with the subject of his book! And yet he never seems to abstract from these Bergman wellsprings as, time and again, in his own way, he returns to what he calls the "magical Bergman moments." Blessedly, his book is never free of them. And, especially in certain privileged instances, he brings a bit of magic of his own, explaining in great detail and in terms proper to film art, how Ingmar Bergman goes about creating these moments so that they become intensely personal to the viewer as well. One does not have to be a film professional to benefit from this, and readers will feel enriched in their understanding of the complexities of film.

But the book goes well beyond this. I would never describe myself as a professional culture scholar, so it was quite wonderful to discover to what an amazing extent those intense filmic moments have enjoyed a relevance well beyond the personal: for over fifty years they have served as artistic incarnations, nothing less, of mainline western culture as it has evolved since World War II. Marc Gervais brings his impressive knowledge and understanding of this shared culture – philosophy, art, theology, history, literature, the theatre, and the cinema – to serve a huge task: to demonstrate *how* the Bergman works are direct, specific, almost formal reflections, criticisms, extensions of that culture, in what might be called an ongoing, never-resolved conversation that has no parallel in the history of world film. As with the rest of us, Bergman is the product of a rich and often contradictory mixed heritage from the past. And Gervais spells this out clearly, as the culture and Bergman's movies have evolved through "post-war existentialism, deconstruction, postmodernism." To understand his films in this perspective is to help understand ourselves in our evolving culture.

All of this may sound a bit threatening, or at least (academically) heavy. But have no fear, dear reader: the Ingmar Bergman movies take on an added richness and delight as the book easily unfolds before us, a joy to professionals, I am sure, but also for any of us who love film and culture. I use words like "delightful" and "fresh" because, unlike most writers on culture, Marc Gervais, while trying to be fair and objective, never forsakes the richly human dimension, neither Bergman's nor his own. He does not mask his own enthusiasm, hopes, or disappointments: it's as if we can hear ourselves laughing or (almost) crying with him as he recalls over fifty years of "Bergman" experiences. And, ultimately, the reader comes to share the Gervais enthralment at the achievement of an artist who has indeed become a prophet of our times, enhancing our understanding of those times as he ceaselessly struggles to achieve wholeness and ruthless honesty, while revealing the cost and the personal vulnerability.

I find myself immensely touched by this situating on the broad cultural stage of Ingmar Bergman, a man I know so well, and who, in spite of what at times has been a sense of overwhelming complexity, ambiguity, even futility, has never ceased struggling to arrive at some kind of ultimate love, meaningfulness, immensity, the mystical.

And perhaps this too is part of the magic, an essential aspect of each one of us, and of our contemporary culture as it continues to evolve.

LIV ULLMANN

PREFACE

Power is where it all starts, a power to mesmerize seldom matched in the annals of film history. One remembers those special moments, those images of beauty, innocence, or spiritual devastation, the mystery of the silences, the enchantment, or the terror of the nature sounds, or the withering dialogues verging on the primal scream – and all of it set to rhythms echoing our heartbeats. Ingmar Bergman's ability to seduce, enthral, and subjugate us, and to drive us deep within our innermost selves, is unquestionably the first factor in a complex, powerful artistic equation.

Speak of a Bergman movie and you find yourself speaking of poetry, of heightened experience, "the magic of art." But beware: this is not magic dedicated to the flight from reality. Rather, it is a force driving us beneath, beyond, above the mundane, to explore those regions of our personal lives we might otherwise choose to leave unconfronted. Experiencing his movies we hear vaguely recognizable echoes; we grope for familiar terms of reference that have their origins in the experiences and memories unique to and yet shared by each one of us.

That is one aspect of Ingmar Bergman's cinema – one, sadly, that is often taken for granted or even dismissed in the strange "revenge of the intellect upon art" that Susan Sontag used to speak about.[1] The analyst/critic, sidestepping precisely those areas where art cannot be reduced to the categories imposed by his or her methodology, hurries on to what is "really important": the elucidation, from the carefully selected *appropriate* data chosen from the vast complexity of interwoven elements, of his or her interpretation of the "Bergman themes." As if, in truth, the mesmerizing power of Bergman's art did not represent an extraordinarily rich achievement, setting Bergman apart from the vast majority of his peers. Without it none of the rest would matter, for no

---

1 Susan Sontag, *Against Interpretation and Other Essays* (New York: Farrar, Straus & Giroux, 1966) 7.

one would feel the *need* to pursue, to make the work meaningful in terms of our culture.

That leads us to the other side, so to speak, of the Bergman film experience – the effort, not to say the industry, of cultural appropriation that surrounds his movies in such widespread fashion. There certainly were admirable film directors before Bergman hit the international scene in the late fifties. But somehow their works were not seen as *directly* participating in the great debates of our times. The Soviets of the mid 1920s, the French experimentalists of a little later, the neo-realists of the late 1940s, some of Chaplin's films – we all have our candidates as stirring exceptions, and certain writers about film did insist on treating the cinema as a serious aspect of the culture. But for whatever reason, very few film directors have succeeded in doing what certain other artists (especially writers) have taken for granted through the centuries: to engage explicitly in the great conversation of the time, to be part of the *Zeitgeist*, the *Weltanschauung*, to express their work directly through the very ideas articulated by people consciously involved in the culture of their times.

More than anyone else, Bergman changed that. After his "metaphysical" films of the latter 1950s, movies would indeed be accepted as capable of dealing with anything within our culture, yes, to the point of exploring life philosophically, sometimes even in the language of philosophy. A new audience was being created, admittedly far smaller than that programmed to consume the box office mega-hits, but a substantial one nonetheless, made up of men and women delighted to find in films an appeal to intelligence, to their culture, in the language used by the educated contemporary world, language one would encounter in literature, in the theatre, even (can you imagine) in the college classroom.

Underlying all of this, of course, was something far more significant: Bergman was bringing his "magic" to bear on the questions and answers that have always lain deepest in our western culture, exploring the very possibility of their finding expression in the ways of perceiving and in the understandings of contemporary culture. There was something in the Bergman films – and this is what made the experience so vital – that made us confront these Great Questions with a flesh-and-blood relevance and intensity. No safe erudite abstractions here, but life-blood experience shot through with thought. We felt compelled to explore personally, to find a personal meaningfulness – but always in terms of our culture, that same culture consciously reflected in the films. (I find myself speaking about the past, but of course that is misleading: the beat goes on for how many new Bergman viewers, and for veterans periodically returning to renewed Bergman experiencing.)

The overall Bergman film story has been a remarkable one. Bergman has been one of the privileged reflectors of the culture of the second half of our century, evolving with that culture, echoing it, extending it in its dizzying convolutions. Though many of his fellow Swedes initially did not accept this view (only recently, for example, have advanced studies on Bergman begun to appear from his own country), many in the rest of that "special" world audience were quick to recognize in Bergman a prophet of our times, a significant cultural figure. And so the books and articles and theses proliferated.

And so, too, yet another book on Bergman – and with it, you may be sure, the *need* to explain why. What does this book hope to achieve that has not already been done to death? Well, I suppose that "research" proposes not only the discovery of new material or the presentation of a brand new theory explaining this or that phenomenon; sometimes there is a need for a new synthesis, a capturing of a rather vast phenomenon from a broader point of view, or from a perspective insufficiently explored.

If this work proves worthwhile it will be because it succeeds in doing precisely this kind of thing, adding fresh insight into, on the one hand, the "Bergman power and magic" and, on the other, into Bergman's amazingly prescient and relevant role in western culture as it has evolved since World War II.

By lingering repeatedly on a series of powerful and haunting moments, and then, in section 2, through a thorough descriptive analysis of one particular "Bergman moment," I shall try to come to grips with the "Bergman magic." One "moment" hardly constitutes all of Bergman's filmic output, to be sure. But it can prove highly revelatory in showing us how Bergman achieves that peculiar effect which audiences find so mesmerizing. We are dazzled by the "object," as it were. But much more, a veritable benign (or not so benign) Pandora's Box of connotations is thereby opened: "poetry" and its limitlessness takes over. And that happens over and over again, in so many different ways in film after film, as Bergman weaves his patterns.

So for the first pole, ever a beacon. But there is another pole, to be sure: Bergman's *involvement in the culture.* In spite of the general recognition I mentioned earlier on, the cultural relevance of Bergman's output has, as far as I know, never been adequately highlighted. By relevance I mean the manner in which his movies have reflected, related to, engaged in, or furthered the mainline philosophical-cultural evolution in the West, from the days of postwar existentialism to present-day deconstruction and postmodernism. If by "prophetic" one means the interpretation of the signs of the times, then Bergman's forty years of intense activity as a film director reveal to what an amazing extent he has indeed been just that, a meaningful and relevant voice in the last half-century's global conversation, as men and women, in their efforts to cope with reality, continue to shape what we call western culture.

A few more situating remarks are in order.

FILM DIRECTOR, BUT MUCH MORE

Ingmar Bergman's work as a film director ended in 1983–84. This study by and large covers the movies that he has *directed*, though with passing references to other creative things he has done – especially in terms of some recent developments. The aspects of his work that do not belong to the strictly movie-directing activity point to an ongoing prodigious activity still in full flight as Bergman enters his eighties. His theatrical output goes on seemingly unabated, and many of his productions are seen in various of the world's theatre capitals, thereby extending the realization that Bergman is one of the greatest theatrical figures of the last half-century. But Bergman also writes film, television, and radio scripts, plays, short novels, critical autobiographies; and he is still busy directing operas, television dramas, radio plays.

I have been fortunate enough to see some half-dozen of his productions in Stockholm at Sweden's Royal Dramatic Theatre (Kungliga Dramatiska Teatern, usually referred to simply as the "Dramaten": Sweden's national theatre, it is surely one of the finest theatre companies in the world). Bergman served as its artistic director from 1963 to 1966, a post he held at several other theatres earlier on. And I have read most of his written work (in translation) and seen many of his television interviews. Inevitably some of this surfaces in this study; but, given a good dose of realistic inhibitions (both linguistic and geographic), and feeling the lack of direct experiencing of so much of this work, I make no claims of treating it adequately. The good news here, however, is that more and more serious research is being brought to bear on the non-filmic areas. Knowledgeable Swedes such as Mikael Timm are trying to capture the total artist as he shifts back and forth from one artistic enterprise to another, from one medium to another, complete with the inevitable interrelating and mutual influencing occasioned by all of this. A large group of Swedish university film specialists, really a new breed, are now exploring in great detail areas of Bergman hitherto unstudied. Exciting, substantial stuff, to be sure – all of which points to the fact that while much has already been done on Mr Bergman, much still remains to be explored.

ACKNOWLEDGMENTS

It has been a joy working with McGill-Queen's University Press. And for that I have to thank a multitude, beginning with the editor-in-chief, Philip Cercone, and Joan McGilvray, who heads the practical-creative side of things. The look of the book owes much to Susanne McAdam and to David LeBlanc. Maureen Garvie and I must be on the same wave length: how else explain the almost total agreement between writer and editor? And then there was Professor/editor John Zucchi, who brought me into the fold, and who guided and inspired me unfailingly.

The book is filled with photographs and written excerpts from the films. Throughout, as you encounter them, you will find them credited gratefully – especially Ingmar Bergman himself and Andrew Sinclair for the long script excerpt from *The Seventh Seal*.

The list of the many other people who contributed so much in one way or another is a long one: Claire Valade, Maj-Britt Piehler, Pauline Macfarlane, Agnes Jacob, Ramin Mahjouri, Elspeth Cochrane, Christine Shields, Mary Jane Stikeman. One would love to try to do justice to each one, and to others not even mentioned.

Concordia University deserves a special word or two, not only for its generous grant for the publishing of the book but for putting up with me for so many years. Opportunities for research, for interacting with valued colleagues, and for developing my own way of relating to and teaching movies – that has been my life in our Department of Communication Studies. And the students, generations of them, making it all so meaningful, important, fun. With them, I suppose I should add a big thank you to Fred and Ginger as well, and to Ingmar and Federico, François and Jean-Luc, Katherine and Cary, Hitch and John Ford, Woody Allen, and how many others.

And my fellow Jesuits? Little did I understand their dedication to culture, the adventure of the mind, the "listening to the Spirit at work in the Universe" when I joined the ranks. Their encouragement of my work has been a constant, no matter when, no matter where. My chief debt, of course, is to my own Jesuit Community (Loyola) here in Montreal. And, in terms of this book, add *Jesuiterna*, that lovely group of "S.J."'s in Stockholm.

Which brings me to Scandinavia: Norway and Per Haddal, Pål Bang Hansen, Bitten Linge, and Nils Klevjer Aas, it's Film Institute (especially Jan Erik Holst and Stine Oppegaard), Denmark and Lissy Bellaiche, Finland and Aito Mäkinen – only a few who have made me experience the Nordic reality so enrichingly. Sweden, of course, plays the main role: personal friends such as Nils Petter and Ulla, Lars and Monika, Susanne, Alvar and Inge. Through them, among many others, I believe I have learned to appreciate a wonderful people, the place, the culture. I should name a few of the more immediately (professionally) involved in the making of this book: Nils Petter Sundgren, Jannike Åhlund, Mikael Timm, Monika Tunbäck Hanson, Jan Aghed, Stig Bkörkman, Jan Olof Ullen, Lars Åhlander, Örjan Roth-Lindberg, Astrid Soderbergh Widding, Carl Henrik Svenstedt, Micha Leszcylowski, Kjell Grede. And of course the Swedish Institute and the Swedish Film Institute. How diminished this book would be had it not been for Elisabet Helge, the ever capable, welcoming, delightful Queen of the Film Stills.

One would love to go on. I shall merely mention some of Ingmar Bergman's close collaborators to whom I feel indebted in many ways: Bibi Andersson, Gunnel Lindblom, Agneta Ekmanner, Erland Josephson, Max von Sydow, Sven Nykvist.

Could this book have been written without David Eley, friend, colleague, fellow Jesuit, a gentle man whose generosity and practical help have been invaluable? Or without the relentless urgings of Michel Buruiana, a dynamo of inspiration and lover of culture, and of Paul Almond, artist, friend, mentor in so many things? Liv Ullmann's contribution has been immense, something indeed obvious to anyone reading this book. Had it not been for her, the vitally essential Epilogue would not exist, and the book would be without the ever-so-relevant "post–*Fanny and Alexander*" years.

Finally, to be sure, there is Ingmar Bergman. Not only for his many gracious gestures over the years, but well beyond that: his work has been part of me these last forty-five years or so. The debt is immense. Enough said.

Well, almost. I think I should end on a more truly Bergmanesque note. Memories, dreams … How could I not mention a childhood home filled with music, an open house to so many people of varied backgrounds, a mix of interests in culture, politics, the human condition … and my grandmother, partner in crime, conniving with me as we sneaked out time and again for another afternoon of delight at the Granada, home of movie double bills. Maybe it all started there.

INTRODUCTION

Starting out on this kind of book, inevitably one feels the need to point readers in the right direction, disabusing them of false expectations. And so one informs them on matters such as just what one is up to, the methodology employed, and perhaps the problems arising from one's approach, given the context of what at the moment the "correct," or at least fashionable, way may be to deal with such matters.

What follows, then, are a number of considerations which do not constitute the main point of this book but which may well be judged as essential if one is to feel at ease with the reading. Some of them are somewhat interrelated, some perhaps not. Or perhaps all of this should best be judged as a necessary evil, to be endured before the book "really begins."

THE STRUCTURING OF THIS BOOK

The book is divided into two sections.

Section 1, the longer, more formalized and organized part, could stand on its own. It treats of Bergman *qua* witness/prophet of the cultural flow of the times, following his films chronologically, and pausing at appropriate times to reflect on various key aspects of our evolving culture, underlining the vital link with the particular film(s) under discussion. The intention is *not* to write a survey that covers each film in its plot and character and "themes": that has been done sufficiently often, and sometimes very well.

While this broader cultural and artistic purpose is being served, I frequently highlight certain *moments*, to be sure, doggedly determined not to overlook what I have been calling the Bergman "power" and "magic." And as for the "special moment" already promised in the preface, that has been chosen from *The Seventh Seal*, for reasons soon to be seen. We'll be returning to it frequently as the book unfolds. The initial idea was to give that privileged moment much more complete filmic description and analysis when I came to

The Seventh Seal in its proper chronological order. But somehow that plan was not working well, in the sense that the structure of the book was becoming lopsided: it seemed to stop with *The Seventh Seal*, getting side-tracked for too long a time, and then start up again. Wiser heads prevailed, and I have relegated the privileged formal treatment of that moment to a special section of its own, created for that purpose.

It soon became evident, however, that there were other matters of relevance that I felt should find their way into the book, but which really could not be accommodated logically and comfortably within section 1 – things such as momentous recent developments that force me to change my initial cultural situating of Bergman based on his final "official" movie-directing effort, *Fanny and Alexander.*

Hence the emergence of section 2 in its present form, a hodgepodge of somewhat disparate elements which, on the one hand, lend some credibility to certain more abstract and more general statements that I dare to make in section 1 (about the films as they relate to the culture), and, on the other, bring a new, updated understanding of the Bergman of today in terms of his overall cultural evolution.

THE STRAWBERRIES AND MILK MOMENT

Time and again I experience the need to protest that the strawberries and milk scene, which is given such prominence in this book, is merely one among many possible choices for preferential treatment, almost apologizing for my selection because I know full well how this might colour the totality of Bergman's work in hues that could ultimately prove misleading. Bergman unquestionably communicates with power and conviction and complexity in this particular sequence. But had I chosen other moments, how equally powerful, perhaps, but how different the communication might have proven to be.

To some, "my" privileged moment may not even appear to be the most important in that film. *The Seventh Seal* is rich in mesmerizing moments of many kinds, from the cosmic opening of sea, sky, and cliffs and the chess game with Death, to the final dance of death against the horizon, followed by the little family's journey down the road of life (which matches any Chaplin epilogue). And what of those horrific visions of tavern torture and witch burning and faces distorted by angst or decomposing in pestilence, in overwhelming contrast to Jof's vision of the Madonna and Child in a sunlit glade?

And I am recalling a few privileged segments from only a single Bergman movie, one of his finest to be sure but not even, perhaps, *my* favourite "Bergman." Countless other moments from many of the forty or so other features he has directed could be cited … The lovely segment I refer to is, for example, by no means the Swedish master's most breathtaking nature scene. One need recall but some others of his 1950 movies to be convinced of this: *Summer Interlude, Waiting Women, Summer with Monika, Lesson in Love, Smiles of a Summer Night, Wild Strawberries, The Virgin Spring*. Indeed, Swedish nature has entered the universal film iconography.

And what about Birgitta's (Doris Svedlund) surrealistic dream prior to her suicide in *Prison* (1948–49), or Rut's (Eva Henning) enchanting, semi-neurotic early morning ritual that opens *Thirst* (1949), or Bertil's (Birger Malmsten) Hitchcockian nightmare of murdering his wife in a moving train in the same film? One remembers the astonishing force of Marie (Maj-Britt Nilsson) in *Summer Interlude* (1950) as she curses the god who has allowed her lover to die. On it goes, as in the stunning expressionism of the clown Frost's (Anders Ek) bearing of his wife Alma (Gudrun Brost) through the ranks of jeering soldiers in a Calvary reenactment in *Sawdust and Tinsel* (1953). The same year gives us the very antithesis as three generations of one family celebrate a picnic in *Lesson in Love*, with the earthly paradise stroll of Marianne (Eva Dahlbeck) and David (Gunnar Björnstrand), stunning in its celebration of the life (and love) force. And how could one pass over Isak's (Victor Sjöström) nightmares in *Wild Strawberries* (1957), or the concluding dream revelation as old Isak, hand in hand with Sara (Bibi Andersson), returns to a vision of his parents? Or the overwhelming vengeance of Töre (Max von Sydow), Kurosawa-like in its ritualized violence, and the response, at the end of *The Virgin Spring* (1959), as the miraculous spring washes away the horror.

Once one begins in this vein it is difficult to stop: Karin's (Harriet Andersson) visions in *Through a Glass Darkly* (1961); Tomas's (Gunnar Björnstrand) spiritual death in *Winter Light* (1961–62); the almost unendurable suffocation scenes of Ester (Ingrid Thulin) in *The Silence* (1962) and of Agnes (Harriet Andersson) as she dies in *Cries and Whispers* (1971); the bewitching beauty of Alma (Bibi Andersson) and Elisabet (Liv Ullmann) and its ruthless deconstruction in *Persona* (1965); the utterly haunting puppet rendition of the Pamina scene of Mozart's "Magic Flute" in *Hour of the Wolf* (1966), taken up again in the delightful communal celebration of that opera eight years later in *The Magic Flute* (1974); Eva's (Bibi Andersson) pathos-ridden ultra-romantic moment with Andreas (Max Von Sydow) in *A Passion* (1968), and his literal filmic disintegration before Anna's (Liv Ullmann) eyes at the end of the same movie; the endless, brilliant variations of man (Erland Josephson) and woman (Liv Ullmann) and marriage going beyond anything yet seen in the cinema in *Scenes from a Marriage* (1972); Charlotte's (Ingrid Bergman) inspiring and deeply moving demonstration of Chopin's "Prelude No.2 in A Minor" that all but destroys her daughter Eva (Liv Ullmann) in *Autumn Sonata* (1977); the Swedish family Christmas, the hocus-pocus semi-horror of magic land, and the Dutch Master formalism in *Fanny and Alexander* (1982) – a few reminders, only a few, out of literally hundreds I could delightedly come up with, of Bergman segments of almost incomparable richness and intensity and breadth. The sheer abundance of such powerful instances is attested to by each viewer's own list of choices, often so different from those of other Bergman viewers.

One's enthusiasm, to be sure, can be spent in what could become little more than an exercise in nostalgia. But these bright moments do much more, illuminating different, what might even seem contradictory, facets of the Bergman sensibility. And they are to be found all through his career, especially once he enters the 1950s. Each moment standing by itself has its own peculiar magic, its own exploration or illumination or extension of reality, the product of all kinds of operative choices in Bergman's ever-evolving cinematic practice. One must add that, when seen as part of the whole functioning text of the film of which they are but one segment, they communicate with even greater richness, nuance, and complexity some aspect of Bergman's relating to the human condition.

More than that, however, each of these segments takes on the role of one more formalized communication by an artist in a vital, ongoing conversation with his culture, renewed and progressing through film after film. For all their variations in style and content, their abrupt shifts in tone and approach, Bergman's films form a radically evolving but consistent personal vision of life; they are the product of what is incontestably one sensibility. Bergman, it is not excessive to claim, is the archetype of the film director *qua auteur*. And all who know his work, whether they enjoy it or not, are in agreement on this point.

This last statement risks triggering a film-theory war, I must admit. For a significant number of film and communications theory specialists today, it smacks of the outmoded, an implied rejection of what today has been decreed to be uniquely significant. For some, it even makes *Bergman* a highly undesirable specimen, something *passé*, irrelevant. This is a serious matter, raising questions about the validity of this book, and (what is considerably more important) the very validity of Bergman as an artist. As such it merits consideration, a digression, perhaps, but one that is essential in dealing with this book's approach.

THE HUMANITIES APPROACH AND ACADEMIC CORRECTNESS

Academic studies, it won't come as a surprise, are subject to patterns of change like just about everything else: what was fashionable a few decades ago may not be so today. Particular fields are more or less taken over by succeeding orthodoxies in a game of ever-evolving displacements.

One of the privileged areas of communication studies, for example, analyses culture. It is called, appropriately enough, cultural studies, which means, inevitably, that it spills over into movies. But there is a problem: a very limited understanding of culture has taken over as the dominating orthodoxy. It and only it tends to be proclaimed as relevant in the study of culture. So what, in this area, has become politically or academically correct? However astonishing, considering what has been going on in the world, Freud and Marx tend still to exercise an overwhelming influence, through the evolved methodologies and insights of brilliant theorists such as, say, a Lacan or an Althusser and their followers. The political/ideological, the psychological/psychoanalytical, gender studies, and their ilk – these determine the more or less exclusive focus. Too often anything else is dismissed as irrelevant today: thus the radical reduction of culture in that tightly limited but dominant discourse.

"Art," "artist," "cinema" – such notions tend to be banished as outmoded remnants of an outdated ideology or philosophy of life. Books, refereed journals, seminars, curricula, a whole industry entrenches this understanding, and along with it an "official," highly specialized vocabulary, style of writing, codes, icons. We are speaking here of a kind of intellectual enclosure, often characterized by energy and amazing results – all, of course, within rigidly adhered-to parameters, built on the conviction, it would seem, that this approach alone is "scientific" and "objective."

By the way in which I have described the situation it may be divined that I do not share such convictions – though I admit that this field of exploration is giving us a profoundly enriched understanding of certain aspects of film and culture, and, what is more, that many of its basic insights have become part of my own overall mix. As this particular study moves on, I shall be coming back to these considerations. Suffice it to say for now that for myself and so many others in the field – and that goes as well for the huge majority of non-professional human beings – culture is a vastly more complex reality. The culture we share is the product of a vertiginous ongoing evolution; it is not the product of the last forty nor even of the last one hundred years but of millennia. In the West that means all that Judaeo-Christian-Greco-Roman-medieval-postmedieval-modernist stuff, not to mention the terribly ignored Celtic and contemporary native indigenous and heaven knows what else.

My approach then might best be described, though vaguely, as Christian humanist sobered by a heavy dose of critical realism. What goes with that is a whole series of ways of understanding and experiencing life – including the consciousness, doubt, call it the ever-renewing dialectic created by these understandings at play with the contemporary reductive systems summarily described above. In other words, the spirit informing this book is that which animates the liberal arts – but the liberal arts as struggling to be enriched by, or to arrive at some kind of synthesis with, the anti-liberal-arts contemporary movements. And that means that notions such as "art" and "artist," however threatened, are seen as highly relevant and profoundly meaningful. And even that movies can be art, and film directors can be artists, working from a vision of the universe.

In our acutely self-conscious and pluralistic world, I suppose there can be no single, all-embracing, all-revealing approach. We have our various disciplines and methodologies; we try to be true to them, to understand their origins and their implications and potentialities and limitations, while admitting that they are all part of the larger view. So this book has the pretention of trying to relate, at least to some extent, to the larger view, as expressed in the breadth of what we call western culture. Inevitably many of my terms of reference will prove partial, limited. And since the big labels mean different things to different persons, I shall whenever using them try to explain what I understand by them.

AUTEURISM

This may be a good reason for returning to the beleaguered notion of *auteur*. At the risk of repeating what is common film knowledge, let's go back to the 1950s, when François Truffaut and many of his young colleagues at the *Cahiers du Cinéma* – a number of whom, of course, were to become distinguished film directors themselves, a vibrant component of the *nouvelle vague* – espoused a method of coming to grips with film by centring the creative focus strictly on the film director, the film director as *auteur*. Ideally, the director should also be the writer; and the film should be an expression of the director's sensibility and vision, the product of his or her creativity, much in the manner that a novel is seen as the creation of the one who writes it. This applies, of course, only to worthwhile movies, movies that have, shall we say, certain cultural ambitions.

And like novels, these movies in both their content and style can be seen as making up a consistent universe, the director's, as he or she relates to the world we all live in. The *auteurists* enormously advanced the film analysis enterprise by insisting that the whole mise en scène – the way a director organizes a scene, chooses film language, and so on – is an essential and meaningful part of this communication. (Thus it was that certain "non-intellectual" Hollywood directors such as Hitchcock, Welles, Ford, and Hawks were elevated to the status of *auteurs*.)

In a giddy moment Truffaut went so far as to affirm that the worst film of a genuine *auteur* is far more interesting than the best work of someone who is not an *auteur* but merely a gifted cog in the filmmaking machine. Each critical approach, to be sure, has its own special pitfalls. Before long the lunatic fringe of auteurist criticism began engaging in a silly race to "discover" yet another hitherto unacknowledged *auteur* – with predictable results.

Inevitably, therefore, a reaction set in, especially regarding Hollywood filmmaking. Theorists were quick to point out the influence of writers, studios, producers, stars, genres, and so on, in the making of films. Bringing "auteurism" down to earth in this manner, of course, could only improve it as a methodology, helping save it from its own excesses and grounding it in a broader spectrum of data.

Nowadays, however, the major threat to auteurism comes at a far less "film practical" and far more "theory abstract" level, precisely from that post-Freudian, post-Marxist, gender studies mix that constitutes the reigning orthodoxy loosely grouped under the label of "cultural studies" touched on above. Just suppose, for an instant, that the only relevant approaches to film could be reduced to the following types of preoccupations:

1 How and to what extent the object or network or movie or TV program or media legislation or dominant style confirms or subverts the power of the dominant system or hegemony;

2 How the above confirms or subverts sexual stereotypes, feminist aspirations, gender preferences;

3 That post-Freudian insights alone reveal the "real content" of art, even of language itself;

4 How art itself, or the very concept of the artist, can have any relevance, since the artist (as Foucault would have it) is merely a hollow conduit condemned to pass on the predetermined signs, systems, patterns of the culture as controlled by the dominant power group. No freedom here, no real creativity.

If this really is the way it is, no wonder then that the shadowy, shifting "canon of great films" more or less universally accepted by film history (and traditional cinema studies) is attacked as the product of elitist dilettantism and as the imposition of subjective "good taste" divorced from the "really relevant

7

reality." "Artistic excellence" indeed becomes meaningless; the study of "good films" should be replaced by the analysis of films as a mass product whose content and style, etc., have been imposed by the ruling hegemony for its own advantage – or as a more or less masked projection of (or "against") the unconscious. Film studies in this context are far happier concentrating on film and TV genre products at their most banal and clichéd, typical uninspired products of the "machine" and thereby much more suited to this approach than are complex "works of art." Film masterpieces? great film artists? the *auteur* theory? Ingmar Bergman? – no need to spell matters out.

This digression on the *auteur* theory, then, has its own sense of urgency, its own *raison d'être* in the reaffirming of the validity of art. For it is precisely from the vantage point of film as the work of an *auteur* vitally relating to the culture, of a film director shaped by that culture, but blessed (or cursed) by his or her own individuality, mitigated freedom, whatever, that this book proceeds. Bergman does indeed become the reflector and, to an extent, the extender of western culture in its evolution – and not a mere conduit in a predetermined language game. He is seen as a poet incarnating in his own creations his personal appropriating of the ever-evolving *Zeitgeist* from the end of World War II to the present.

THEMES

Before proceeding it might be useful to reiterate what the task at hand is *not*: a study of the "Bergman themes" as such, as they weave their way through his forty feature movies. For years this territory has been thoroughly explored, and most of its veins have been mined with unwavering resolve. The themes certainly are "always there": they are essential, usually highly obvious, identifiable, and almost formally enunciated by Bergman in the films. Indeed, it is difficult to find any other director in the history of the cinema who can so obviously be tied in with such clearly articulated "themes."

There have been many studies of Bergman's films based on thematic analyses growing out of other disciplines, of course.[1] In Bergman's movies it is impossible not to be struck by these themes, already enshrined in our culture, which

1 Some first-rate examples: Robert E. Lauder, *God, Death, Art and Love* (New York: Paulist Press, 1989) (philosophical); Frank Gado, *The Passion of Ingmar Bergman* (Durham: Duke University Press, 1986) (psychoanalytical); Richard Aloysius Blake, *The Lutheran Milieu of the Films of Ingmar Bergman* (Evanston: Northwestern University, 1972) (theological) – and many more, a good number of which bring rewarding professional insight to bear on a body of work strong enough to be enriched by the process.

become almost autonomous elements to be integrated into each movie, becoming organic parts, so to speak, along with the other "materials" Bergman utilizes.

One should recall them briefly, at least from an overview perspective. There is, notably, the great debate centring on God or non-God, meaningfulness or nothingness, and the concomitant suffering, disintegration, or acceptance, whatever, with life as a journey, open to opposed possibilities, to metaphysical realities or the negation of such realities. Linked to it is the nature sub-theme, with its life force and earth paradise motifs, or, conversely, as metaphor for the coldness, harshness, or sterility of the human condition.

Even more omnipresent is the theme of love. Bergman here is almost in a class by himself: his films are nothing if not portraits of love in all its manifestations, from the most sterile and destructive to the most beautiful and life-fulfilling – images of tenderness, of hatred, of family and belonging, of soul-disintegrating aloneness. There tend to be constant patterns shooting through: for example, more or less ineffectual males irresistibly drawn to women stunning in their beauty (at least as incarnated by Bergman's cinema, to such an extent that many have insisted that he could not create such presences without being in love with the actresses). Of course the attractiveness can be ambivalent, its source life-giving or death-inflicting, the women at one with the universe or tragically alienated. And as Bergman's films evolve, the women tend to become, like the men in his movies, more complex, more true-to-life.

Bergman illuminates his experiences of love with psychological insight, not to say downright expertise. Indeed, analyses of the films, especially of their characters (often treated by the film analysts as if they were real people), have abounded for decades. Many years ago, for example, a friend of mine attended a congress of fellow psychoanalysts held in New York. The topic for study was Bergman's *Wild Strawberries*; the film was judged so rich in psychoanalytical insights that the professionals were stupefied when informed that Bergman was not himself a specialist in their field. "But how *could* … ?" Many of his films, in truth, seem structured on psychoanalytic therapy processes, as Bergman worshipper Woody Allen has so clearly understood, and commented one way or another in some of his films.

"Sub-thematically" speaking, the psychologist or psychoanalyst characters in Bergman movies tend to be cruelly caricatured, exposed more often than not as charlatans, abusers of vulnerability, highly neurotic or cold or empty. But whatever his relationship to the practitioners in the field, Bergman is deeply marked by psychotherapy's insights, and his films prove to be treasure-troves for Freudian symbol hunters. In that sense he is indeed a spectacular reflector of twentieth-century culture in one of its dominant currents.

Freud si, Marx no. Perhaps surprisingly, Bergman shows little interest in the equally significant aspect of twentieth-century culture (however discredited it may seem to have become these last years) – Marxism. Do not go to a Bergman movie to find anything resembling a Marxist analysis of society, however aware of that phenomenon Bergman undoubtedly is. Bergman's world is the Swedish middle class, by and large privileged in its education, its standard of living, and its sense of belonging to a society decidedly ultra-modern while still steeped in carefully adhered-to traditions. Indeed, that is one of his major appeals to his international audience, most of whom revel in his Swedishness while recognizing a reflection, *mutatis mutandis*, of their own social mores. It is the culture and rituals and artifacts of that world that find their own thematic expression in his movies. We not only see the architecture of the chateaux, city apartments, and town and country houses of his Swedes but we are also initiated into their concerns, problems, celebrations, ways of thinking. True, some of the films do confront a vague Nazism, or communism, or totalitarianism, or militarism. And a few times Bergman situates the action in working-class milieus, or in social-problem areas. The political, social, or ideological, however, are definitely of marginal occurrence. Beyond a doubt his cinema in its concerns and rituals belong to the Swedish middle class.

Culture leads nicely into art, and that brings us to another constantly reiterated Bergman theme: art and the role of the artist. Many of Bergman's main characters are artists or writers of one kind or another; incessantly the question of art's validity becomes a main focus. Is the artist a seer, or a charlatan? Is he merely a prestidigitator, a humiliated denizen of suspect worlds of marginal deviance, dabbling in pseudo black magic, or does he open our hearts and minds to beauty and truth?

The question progressively deepens and broadens out: what kind of communication is art? theatre? filmmaking? Is the artist a vampire, an exploiter of everyone he touches? In this world of ours is communication itself possible, or is it all absurdity, the revelation, ultimately, that all is nothingness? And so by this process, we come back full circle to the metaphysical, "meaning of life" thematic.

Anyone acquainted with Bergman's films readily recognizes the recurring patterns of such themes. They shift, they thrive on a rhythm of ebb and flow, of dialectical oppositions ever evolving, ever renewing. My favourite image encapsulating all of this would be a vortex spiralling downward and upward, expanding and constricting, its inward vitality feeding on conflict between varying oppositions. There is a definite evolution, it would seem; and yet nothing, no possibility, ever really disappears: the territory remains familiar.

FUNCTIONING TEXT

The study of these themes can, of course, prove highly enriching. It also creates limitless possibilities of distortion, of over-emphasis or over-simplification.

One problem is that themes tend to be unearthed almost exclusively from plot, character, and dialogue. In recent decades, however, developments in film theory and film analysis have made it possible to adopt a far more comprehensive approach. Some thirty or so years ago Jean-Luc Godard wrote that "the adventure of the contemporary cinema is the adventure of cinematographic language." As with most of Monsieur Godard's pronouncements, this can lead in any number of directions. In my own experience, it has come to mean that the most rewarding way to understand what a film *really* is up to is to fix one's attention on its film language – its sights and sounds, the texturing/structuring, its strategies, the way it is put together, the very cultural signs it uses or shapes, and so on – what Umberto Eco so aptly terms the artist's "operative choices."[2] A descriptive analysis of the "functioning text" made up of all these interwoven elements, however we may describe, categorize, or define them, can go a long way in giving us insight into just what that Bergman magic is, what goes into creating it, and how its power operates on us.

The conclusion to all of this: Bergman is best revealed as "prophet of his times" through analysis of his film language – indeed, of everything that goes into his films, "what results from the operative choices of the director or team."[3] These choices reveal in most nuanced and enlightening fashion where Bergman is leading us, where he situates himself in terms of the general culture. Looking at his operative choices, one discovers the obvious: not only is there "magic" and "power," but there is an identifiable Bergman context made up of consistent, shifting cultural concerns caught in an ever-spiralling whirl and an ever-renewing dialectic. And as these operative choices themselves change, they are subject to a clear evolution that echoes, relates to, pushes forward the overall cultural evolution.

And as for the themes, this study all but takes their existence for granted: they are a given, something Bergman works on, reincarnating them through his creative sensibility. Which is not to say that I shall not be adverting to them in any way; rather, it will often happen from a different point of view – as pre-existing icons of the culture, elements, yes, in the overall functioning text. In other words, the objective is to decipher how Bergman's treatment of these themes and of the other elements within the context of the "whole functioning

2 *L'Oeuvre ouverte* (Paris: Editions du Seuil, 1965), the French translation of Umberto Eco's extraordinary study on contemporary art and literature, *Opera Aperta* (Milan: Bompiani, 1962).

3 Ibid. This notion of operative choices will become clearer as the book proceeds.

text" of his films reflects, comments, extends the main cultural movements of the times. One stands further back, as it were, in an attempt to discern the over-all interplay: are we really dealing here with a poet of the *Zeitgeist*?

CULTURE, METHODOLOGY ... BUT *CAVEAT LECTOR*

A few more cautionary statements are in order. First – and in spite of the abundance of articulated cultural themes in his movies – Bergman is not to be understood as an "intellectual" filmmaker: his mind does not function according to the rhythms and logic of those who engage in discursive and systematic reasoning. He reads a great deal; but he is not a student of intellectual treatises. His is essentially a poetic language, proceeding from intuition and feeling. Time and again he attributes his sources of inspiration to childhood memories, dreams, a certain sight or sound or movement. In a 1997 interview with Gunnar Bergdall, once again insisting on the affinity of film to music, he agreed with Stravinsky's contention that "you can never understand music." And so with film, with its pulse and rhythm, because it goes beyond understanding, straight to the emotions. It is only during the process of advanced elaboration, when writing the carefully planned final stages of the script, that the cultural or specifically philosophical reflections or references find their thought-out articulation as part of the whole filmic text. They are snippets, citations, suggestions charged with emotion, part of a far more complex totality, and certainly not the blueprint for a kind of intellectual discourse.

Secondly, as I play Bergman off certain aspects of the evolving culture, I fear giving the impression that it is he who is situating himself this way (my way) *deliberately*. Bergman may be aware somewhere down deep, intuitively, but I feel certain that he does not *plan* things in this specific manner.

Finally – and this may seem like a digression – when writing on Bergman, one may well be tempted to abandon ship out of the fear of being swamped by the quantity of often brilliant writings by Bergman himself, or by Bergman's own words in countless interviews. One thinks of his two autobiographies and personal assessments of his work,[4] the highly autobiographical character of so many of his films (especially of his last feature, *Fanny and Alexander*), and the three subsequent movie scripts he has written, *The Best Intentions* (directed by Bille August), *Sunday's Children* (directed by his son Daniel), and *Private*

---

4 Bergman, Ingmar, *The Magic Lantern*, English translation of *Laterna Magica* (London: Hamish Hamilton, 1988). This autobiography was followed in 1990 by *Bilder*, translated into English and published in 1994 under the title *Images: My Life in Film* (New York: Arcade). This is really a companion to the first book, with a greater emphasis given to the films themselves.

Confessions (directed by Liv Ullmann). Add to that some of his television work.

In speaking about artists – and this has been said often enough – such material can prove problematic. Bergman is constantly evolving in his attitudes about life, and his attitudes about his past work undergo similar shiftings. He has confessed, in addition, to a compulsion to adapt too cravenly to his interviewers in his desire to please them with the answer they are looking for. Undoubtedly he is exaggerating, one more instance of the Bergman self put-down, but his point is well taken. Thus, for example, he speaks one way to Vilgot Sjöman in 1961 about *Winter Light*,[5] then almost totally reverses himself, at least when referring to some of the theological content of the same film, in his mammoth 1970 interview *Bergman om Bergman*.[6] By 1990, however, in his book of reflections on his own films (*Images*), he criticizes himself for what he now understands as a false situation he was responsible for in 1970 when dealing with his three interviewers. It does not end here: in 1992, he explains to interviewers and in program notes that he felt the need to write the script for *The Best Intentions* to make up for what he felt was an unfairly severe portrait he drew of his father in his 1987 autobiography, *Laterna Magica*. The conclusion to all of this would seem to be a *caveat lector* … except that it is not a question of Bergman's lack of sincerity or of the desire to tell the truth, but rather of the intensity of the need of the moment experienced by an artist in the act of communicating himself to another. Or, as a friend put it, "Ingmar does give in to the needs of the novel he is creating on the spot at that moment" (conversation with Erland Josephson, 1994).

This in no way denies the enriching role of the writings and interviews in understanding the man and his work, as well as providing fascinating reading in themselves. My use of them, however, remains only incidental.

THAT PERSONAL TOUCH

The book adopts a deliberately cultivated personal tone. It is not just a question of trying to maintain an accessible, dare I say lively, approach, which may be reason enough in itself. But I am equally conscious that what I write springs from my own personal understanding: in order, freely and knowingly, to come to an understanding/judgment/whatever about what he or she is reading, the

---

5 Sjöman, Vilgot, L. 136: *Diary with Ingmar Bergman*. Translated by Alan Blair (Karoma: Ann Arbor, MI, 1978). Sjöman traces the evolution in 1961 of Bergman's *Winter Light* from idea to finished film.

6 Interviews with Stig Björkman, Torsten Manns and Jonas Sima, translated from the Swedish as *Bergman on Bergman* (London: Seeker & Warburg, 1973).

reader should know where I situate myself in terms of the culture – in a sense, what, given my background and experiences, I am all about, what shapes my approach to things. Besides, I have been around the Bergman phenomenon for a long time. I am delighted to think that this book might play its modest role in the expanding, ongoing "Bergman culture." Thus, while I may wax too often pedagogical, the book does not claim to be an "objective" reference to everything else pertinent that has been written on Bergman, nor does it go in for endlessly explaining or refuting other people's theories. The intent, deliberately and unashamedly, is to communicate my views (in so far as that is possible). And so, some may be delighted to know, there are scandalously few footnotes, in spite of the perverse habits growing out of academic training and profession.

But more than that: this is not an abstract, detached study of an object "out there," i.e., Ingmar Bergman's films. While that must be part of it, I nonetheless see the book as a living testimonial to someone whose movies have been immensely important to me, enriching, deepening, making me *feel*. The whole Bergman experience has meant value-for-me in both personal and professional terms. And so, reader, be warned: anecdotes, opinions, a wee attempt at humour tend to creep in, to help communicate what for me is still a living, thinking, feeling, vital experience.

And how can you write about poetry without writing "personally"? Bergman's movies still mean poetry to me. That fact, that experiencing, must not be totally reduced, proseified, embalmed within a system. There's always that danger: "systematic thought is nothing but poetry that has gotten frozen and … institutionalized."7

Besides, after a good number of years in the field, a time comes when many of us experience the desire, even the need, to witness to what we understand and feel about culture – and, really, about the life that we have been living. The writing becomes that personal witnessing, the sharing with others on that same journey.

7 Another footnote already, in spite of what I promised … thanks to Mark Edmundson in his richly thought-provoking *Literature against Philosophy: Plato to Derrida* (Cambridge: Cambridge University Press 1995), 38. Here he sets up – in rather extreme terms – one side of what he sees is the needed dialectic. Yes, both sides (poetry and systematic thought), it would seem, are necessary.

PRELUDE: SUMMER IDYLL

The scene was straight out of a Bergman film, or, to put it more precisely, a Bergman film of the 1950s. It was one of those blessed summer solstice days when even as far south as Stockholm the sun is rarely below the horizon. It would take a Wordsworth or a Keats to describe the countryside bathed in almost unending warm light, the earth exploding in bird sounds and flowers, and grass and foliage of every imaginable shade of green.

June 1968. I was strolling from my friends' home in Lidingö down a country dirt lane leading to the nearby Baltic seashore. It is strange to call this a suburb of Stockholm, but that's what it is, part of the archipelago that has found its way into the universal film imagination. Lidingö could be described as a kind of natural paradise sheltering the houses of artists, media types, and other (fortunate) Swedes. More like a forest surrounded by sea: but Stockholm itself is almost a city within a forest, and its innumerable waterways have earned its description as "Venice of the North."

Thirteen months earlier, in Cannes, a year before the legendary film festival collapsed in the May '68 uprising, I had met Kjell Grede, a young Swedish director whose first feature, *Hugo and Josefin*, had delighted a number of critics. Here, some of us thought, resided a special talent – a judgment that has looked pretty respectable, what with Grede's two most recent films (at time of writing), the magnificent *Hip Hip Hurrah!* and *Good Evening, Mr Wallenberg*.

So, drinking in the Swedish summer, I was on my way to brunch at the home of Kjell Grede and his wife (at that time), Bibi Andersson. Bibi, of course, already had her bedazzled fan club among discerning Bergman *aficionados* scattered around the world. To make sure I wouldn't feel let down, the Andersson-Grede home lay dutifully/beautifully nestled among trees and tall grass on land gently sloping to the Baltic, affording a water vista broken here and there by other islands of the archipelago.

I was trying, with true Canadian sophistication, to conceal my sense of enthralment over what could be called a homecoming to a place I had never been to before. We sat outside in the tall grass chatting and eating amidst nature's sights and sounds. After good British/North American bacon and eggs, it was time for dessert Swedish style. Wide bowl in hand, and totally unaware of the moment of revelation she was re-orchestrating for this particular wayfarer, Bibi set about picking berries which, true to form, were growing in profusion around us. (The Swedes make a point of letting things grow semi-wild, not trimming them ruthlessly *à la française*.)

Bibi filled the scooped-out wooden dish with the berries, covered them with milk, and handed me the bowl. I was transfixed. Was this a movie repeating itself, or actually becoming reality? Was I living out a fantasy? I heard myself asking, "Would you do that again, please?" Bibi looked at me quizzically. Then, a smile, a ripple of laughter: "Oh, yes, I remember now."

Revelation indeed. A decade earlier (1957), thanks to Ingmar Bergman and a Bibi in her late teens, I had been granted one of those flashes of insight we all should hope to experience. I was watching my first Bergman movie, *The Seventh Seal*, which also proved to be Bergman's first major international film success, a film that was to enjoy a prodigious art house and university world distribution lasting decades. Midway through comes a much-needed moment of respite when the weary Knight (Max von Sydow) is resting alone in a glade, concentrating on his chessboard. A short way off, in long shot, a young mother, Mia, and her infant child, Mikael, are observed by the Knight as they play in the tall, sun-dappled grass. All is quiet except for the occasional sound of a cuckoo and other bird chirps, the gurglings of baby Mikael as he totters about, and his mother's happy laughter. The scene smacks of a Madonna and Child late-medieval painting. In the background, tethered to a tree and swishing his tail, is a plump, contented horse, one of Bergman's life fertility symbols (as we'd learn to recognize). Indeed, the whole scene breathes life symbols – soft sun, blue skies, nature's gentle sounds, the works.

The Knight approaches, and for almost the first time in the film there is a smile on his face. Mia nonetheless senses his troubled state; and Bergman takes his time, with restrained camera movements and relaxed cutting, letting the scene play out as the Knight, almost in spite of himself, his tension for the moment forgotten, bares his soul to this simple peasant girl. Soon they are joined by Jof, Mia's juggler/seer/poet husband. The parents, unself-consciously in love, play with their infant. In the midst of this little (holy) scene, Mia hands the Knight a bowl of wild strawberries and a bowl of milk, for that is all she has to offer. No small offering, as it turns out; for Bergmanians would soon get to know that that was indeed Bergman's symbol *par excellence* for the poignantly short Swedish summer in the archipelago, and more too: for the earth's fruitfulness, young love, the life force itself.

As Jof plays the lute, softly singing a love song to Jesus Christ and spring-time, the Knight raises the scooped-out dish in a gesture straight out of the offertory, consecration, and communion ritual of the Christian Mass. Medium close-up of the Knight's face and of the raised hands holding the bowl of milk as, his face radiating peace and fulfilment, he says softly:

I shall remember this moment. The silence, the strawberries and milk, your faces in the light. Mikael sleeping, Jof with his lute. I'll try to remember what we have talked about. I'll carry this memory between my hands as if it were a bowl filled to the brim with fresh milk. And it will be an adequate sign – it will be enough for mc.[1]

The Seventh Seal may have been situated in fourteenth-century Sweden but to us, a North American audience in the late fifties, it was *today*. And the Knight's pilgrimage, through a countryside devastated by a post-Crusades Black Death, rampant evil, and religious fanaticism, felt strangely relevant to our own apocalyptic times, haunted as we were by images of the death camps and a cold war threatening nuclear holocaust. Thus, when the Knight is blessed with that little moment and its gift of meaningfulness and peace (at least for a time), all of us felt in need of it – the Knight, and surely Bergman himself, and each one of us in the audience, whatever our backgrounds or circumstances.

Bergman is dealing here with deep, deep things, with what might be termed the spontaneities imbedded in the human matrix. There are things that antedate any particular human culture, things we are so organically one with that we spontaneously resonate to them. They are simply part of us, or part of what we as human beings living on this earth and in this universe belong to. (This, I know, is a huge, highly contested kind of affirmation; and we shall be coming back to it, especially in the final section.)

So that is all part, surely the deepest part, of what underlies our reacting to a scene such as this one. But there are other factors also in play: on the one hand, the culture which I share with others, on the other, my own personal interacting with that culture. Each of us in experiencing a film brings a unique, complex network woven of background, aptitudes, sensitivities, understandings, particular needs of the moment – whatever it is that goes into making each of us a person at a given moment. This rather obvious fact has to be borne in mind when analysing a film. Whatever claims we may make about being "objective" when describing film language, when trying indeed to arrive at an "objective" analysis of the sights and sounds that make up the film, the

1 *Four Screenplays of Ingmar Bergman* (New York: Simon & Schuster, 1960), 176.

fact remains that the very perception of the film is itself heavily charged with subjectivity. Dudley Andrew is quite right, it seems to me, when, in exposing the naiveté of claims to objectivity put forward by certain practitioners of film semiotics, he insists on the interplay between object and subject in the film experience, between what is up there on the screen or coming out of the sound system, and my own personal antennae and decoders.

The subtleties of Andrew's phenomenological approach to film analysis are beyond the terrain proper to this essay.[2] Suffice it to say that there are networks of reasons why I, for example, as a film studies teacher, choose to give a particular course, use a particular film, analyse a particular sequence, follow a particular method of analysis, and so on. The very things I "really" see and hear in a movie, those things I consider relevant and to which I therefore assign privileged status, are the fruit of a personal conditioning that grows out of the life I have lived.

Andrew's idea of situating the whole process within the context of culture brings a wonderful understanding to what is highly complex. The process boils down to this:

1   Bergman (let us choose him as the obvious example), the product of his culture but also of his own individuality interacting with that culture, makes a movie, which, of course, is his way as an artist of communicating his life experience and understanding.

2   I, the product of my own culture (which substantially shares in Bergman's), experience the film. Given my own individuality, I accept and decode it in my fashion.

3   I may choose to talk or write about the film; and what results will be of necessity a somewhat altered "film." The optimistic way of assessing this phenomenon is to say that the culture is thereby being enriched: Bergman's film can never be just "Bergman's film"; it becomes part of a culture that is ever vitally expanding. All of which may (or may not) be nice for Mr Bergman. Anyway, it is quite consoling for the film critic and for the intelligent filmgoer who like to be part of the vital process.

4   And so (if we wish), the next person, reading or hearing me, will have his or her experiencing of the film further reshaped – and on and on it goes, for that is the way of culture.

2   These assumptions seem to underlie all Andrew's theoretical work. See especially his *Film in the Aura of Art* (Princeton: Princeton University Press, 1984). I shall be returning to Andrew explicitly or implicitly in this work.

All of this – I mean both the "pre-cultural" power and appeal of what is going on in the scene and the cultural factor as well – may help to explain what the real me was experiencing in that crucial moment in *The Seventh Seal*. As Max-the-Knight recited those beautiful words and performed that lovely ritual act, Bergman was intoning a hymn of profound affirmation of the meaningfulness and goodness of life. And for me at that particular moment in my life it had considerably more specific personal overtones. Max's enlightenment was being transposed onto me: as never before I was realizing that all manner of currents of activity I was engaged in could indeed be "as one," facets of one "organic whole" – film, art, the religious and philosophical search for meaning, the power of beauty and heightened reality, love, life itself. (I spare the reader all kinds of more personal stuff, the point, I hope, having been made with sufficient clarity.)

Charged words, the above, and chosen deliberately. Most lives are blessed, I think, with turning points, or, perhaps more accurately, with moments in which we reach a higher plateau of consciousness, recognition, insight, self-integration, organic wholeness, whatever. That strawberries and milk moment was not one I likely would forget … And here, ten years later (1968) – in real life, real live Sweden, and real live Bibi Andersson! – I, weary pilgrim from the cultural and political upheavals of the 1960s, was being offered the bowl of milk-covered berries … .

As I smile at the recollection, I have to admit that this is (shamelessly) endowing with a huge burden of personal connotations what was a charming Lidingö brunch. In a way Ingmar Bergman had been setting me up through my ten years of viewing his 1950s movies (for after *The Seventh Seal*, in North America, we began seeing not only the movies that followed but prior ones as well). Visiting Sweden for the first time was in a way coming home to a privileged part of my life. And while I was "really seeing" what I was seeing, I was experiencing Sweden in a special way, through a lens enchantingly. That Stockholm archipelago was already familiar territory, already charged with lovely mystical connotations, thanks to Ingmar Bergman's sensibility and insight and his ability to communicate these with artistry. And I must confess that it has, to my delight, continued to be that way with my experiencing of Sweden, as well as of many other professional and/or personal things – even if (as we shall see) Bergman himself was to evolve away from much of that 1950s way of relating and communicating.

The Lidingö strawberries and milk story has some obvious points of relevance. For one thing, it is a personal witnessing to the power of Ingmar Bergman as a filmmaker. He was indeed able to create a Sweden for me, and, in a sense, to bring me there. Beyond that, the Great Moment in *The Seventh Seal* has had a substantially enriching bearing on my life – no small achievement for what is after all "only a movie."

Inevitably the story also reveals quite a bit about this writer (me): it serves to bring the personal dimension up front. And by that very fact the reader is given insight into what I am all about. Remember the prefatory *caveat*: no matter how much they champion "objectivity," film critics/theoreticians/analysts are steeped (also) in subjectivity. Their judgments are subject to their own world view, education, orientation, psychological leanings, political ideology, riches, and limitations – in a word, their experience of life – even if in many instances they themselves may not be giving much evidence of any real awareness of their own *a prioris*, those things that may inhibit their coming to grips with the totality of the film, and therefore reduce their judgments within perhaps very narrow parameters.

Be that as it may … the strawberries and milk scene affords me (and many others, as it turns out) the opportunity of witnessing to the power of Bergman's cinema. Of the countless magnificent moments in Bergman's films, all of which could serve, this one enjoys privileged status for me, and I shall be returning to it. Not surprisingly, it will serve as the moment to be described and analysed at much greater length, in the final section of the book.

So on to section 1 and the attempt to capture Bergman's films as they evolve and interact with the mainline western culture, itself ever in a state of evolution. Culture, yes, but never abstracting from those filmic moments glowing with the Bergman magic. And, equally, never abstracting from that personal dimension where films become immensely relevant and life-enhancing, even if less lyrically so than at that strawberries and milk brunch in Lidingö.

PROPHET OF OUR TIMES

CHAPTER ONE

IN THE BEGINNING

Crisis   filming July 1945
                                            release February 1946

It Rains on Our Love   filming summer 1946
    (The Man with an Umbrella)   release November 1946

A Ship Bound for India   filming spring 1947
    (The Land of Desire)   release September 1947

Music in Darkness   filming autumn 1947
    (Night Is My Future)   release January 1948

Port of Call   filming spring 1948
                                            release October 1948

Prison   filming November 1948
    (The Devil's Wanton)   release March 1949

Thirst   filming January – February 1949
    (Three Strange Loves)   release October 1949

To Joy   filming July – August 1949
                                            release February 1950

This Can't Happen Here   filming July – August 1949
    (High Tension)   release October 1949

THE FIRST FIVE FEATURES

For a non-Scandinavian, seeing most of Bergman's first nine feature movies is no easy matter. In the late 1950s after *The Seventh Seal*, Bergman films began appearing in most major North American cities, and film institutes, cinémathèques, film clubs, or universities could manage to find a print of some of the movies, even of some of those preceding *The Seventh Seal* – but only as far back as *Summer Interlude*, initially released long before in Sweden, in 1951.

But what of those nine other, earliest (pre-*Summer Interlude*) features? In June 1992 at the Swedish Film Institute, Mikael Timm and I were watching Bergman's third feature, *A Ship Bound for India*. Made in 1947, it was the only "Bergman" still on my unseen list, even if four or five of the other eight of that batch I had only managed to see decades after they were made. So all in all there was a feeling of something like a sense of achievement. Every now and then as we watched Mikael would manifest some sign or other of delighted surprise ("You know, this is much better than I expected") as he guided me through the complicated spots, given my next-to-non-existent Swedish. I too was enjoying the film, an added reason for this being my ability to recognize moments, concerns, figurations that would reappear time and again in his later films. That, of course, is the blessing (or the curse) that goes with the territory when one specializes in one thing or another.

Not much has been written about most of these movies. Certainly for me the two Bergman autobiographies, with Bergman's own comments, assessments, and descriptions of various incidents surrounding their making have proven both delightful and enlightening, filling in some serious gaps in my knowledge of that period.[1] As I watched *A Ship Bound for India*, the academic in me was quite aware that this was, after all, a film made in 1947 by a young director trying to find the best way to bring each particular moment to filmic

1 Especially helpful in one way or another have been the already mentioned Frank Gado's *The Passion of Ingmar Bergman* (Durham: Duke University Press, 1986) and Peter Cowie's *Ingmar Bergman: A Critical Biography* (New York: Charles Scribner's, 1982), updated and republished in 1992 by Limelight Edition, New York. Old stand-bys are Jörn Donner's *The Personal Vision of Ingmar Bergman*, Indiana University Press (translated from the 1962 Swedish edition); Birgitta Steene's *Ingmar Bergman* (New York: Twayne, 1968); and Vernon Young's *Cinema Borealis: Ingmar Bergman and the Swedish Ethos* (New York: David Lewis, 1971). All my Cowie references are from the Scribner's edition.

life. So he was turning to certain esteemed models: there was a touch of real-istic detail, especially in the depiction of the docks and life on the little trawler (shades of neo-realism?), and a good dose too of brooding poetic impression-ism à la Marcel Carné of the '30s; and German expressionism's low-life nightspots cast their aura of decadent humanity and romanticism. What I was failing to identify was what Bergman probably was at least to a degree indebt-ed to, the mainline way of making movies in Sweden at that time.[2]

One thing, however, was clear enough: Bergman's energy, in *A Ship Bound for India*, is expressed in his concern for the young man (played by Birger Malmsten) and his difficult transition into adulthood, dominated as he is by his swaggering father, unable really to relate to his victimized mother, in love with the nightclub girl (Gertrud Fridh) the father callously has brought onto the boat to live in a *ménage à trois* (or is it *à quatre*?). Pervading all is a climate in which everyone dreams of freedom, of living another life, played out against the need for security, no matter how life-diminishing that may prove to be.

The five first Bergman features are by no means what one could reasonably term bad viewing, especially for those interested in Bergman movies. But as might be expected, all of them, like *A Ship Bound for India*, are uneven, smacking of lack of true mastery of film form even while showing flashes of artistic flair. Compared to Bergman's later work, they appear as hybrid cre-ations, all of them in fact originating from non-Bergman material; and even when Bergman does have a hand in writing, scripts are based on an already existing play by someone else. There is no great depth of insight, the charac-ters show little inner probing, and, indeed, no consistent filmic control is in evidence. This, of course, is exactly true to the real situation, that of a gifted and promising young theatre director trying his hand at what for him, profes-sionally speaking, is a new dramatic medium.

Melodrama is rampant, and situations some might describe as theatrical

2   This may be disputed, for Bergman himself and the film writers dismiss such an influence. The accepted wisdom is that the departure in the 1920s of Victor Sjöström and Mauritz Stiller for Hollywood brought the great early era of Swedish filmmaking to a close. Nothing truly memo-rable would happen in Sweden until Bergman, although an exception is made, up to a point, for Alf Sjöberg and Arne Sucksdorff. A few names such as that of Gustav Molander tend to surface in film histories of the two decades following the golden era, but with great diffidence. If we are to look for influences, so the opinion holds, we must turn to those already mentioned – Carné, the German expressionists, neo-realism, perhaps some Hollywood works, and, of course, the lone three Swedes, Sjöström, Stiller, and Sjöberg. I have no proof whatever to the contrary, yet I feel that serious and more sympathetic research – which in fact is already underway in Swedish uni-versities – will reveal that matters are not quite as simple as the prevailing opinion.

abound, with the usual preoccupation centring on a young man or a young woman going through a difficult time, at odds with parents in one way or another experienced as oppressive, or led astray by nasty, exploitative tempters. Institutional forces, be they state or church, only add to the misery with their bureaucratic dehumanization. For whatever reason, Bergman seems to be concentrating on social class types not at all part of his early upbringing. Further to the point, all of them are life's victims, or at least victims of a dreary Swedish grey world. In this he would seem to be echoing the mood of the *Fyrtiotalisterna*, a group of Swedish writers of the 1940s noted for their nihilism and apocalyptic despair (as Vernon Young puts it).3 Peter Cowie describes their vision dramatically, with humanity envisaged "as a lost entity, wandering vaguely on a dark plain, with neither purpose nor precedent."4 Or perhaps Bergman, who denies any connection with that group, is simply expressing the long-held feeling generated by an older, generalized, somewhat fatalistic, somewhat deterministic philosophy growing out of that oft-caricatured Scandinavian gloom and desperation that spawned, among others, the single greatest influence on Bergman the artist, August Strindberg. Indeed, the shadow of Strindberg overhangs Bergman's work; and that I shall simply take for granted, not exploring what has already been thoroughly documented.

Drifting through this world, in some of the films, are decidedly otherworldly, almost fantasy figures representing good or evil (*It Rains on Our Love*). In a number of the dark characters it is almost impossible not to detect devil figures, and there is gloom a-plenty. In *Music in Darkness*, Birger Malmsten, for example, is a suffering young pianist coping with blindness (is it fate?). *Port of Call* seems more consciously and consistently to aspire to a Swedish brand of neo-realism, especially in its depiction of the squalid port section of Gothenburg. And Marcel Carné's "poetic realism" (dark streets glittering with pessimism) is never far removed, as pointed out, in these early film-directing days.

However, one must be leery of overstating the case. There is a constant battle going on between good and evil. Always, there are figures representing love, sacrifice, an essential goodness. And whatever the fate of some of the characters may be, however grim the tone at times becomes, the central characters, the young man and/or young woman, do manage to come up with some kind of affirmation at the end: the movie lights up, literally, we see the sky; and just maybe, the Swedish summer is not far away. In a sense – and this seems highly paradoxical – the films can be seen as rather traditional moral tales, affirming

3 Young, *Cinema Borealis*, 26.

4 Cowie, *Ingmar Bergman*, 39.

values in keeping with mainline Swedish culture.

From the beginning, then, it is clear that Bergman's films rise out of a cultural undergrowth very serious in its preoccupations. It is difficult at this time, nonetheless, to discover evidence seriously substantiating what may seem my rather pretentious claim that Bergman is a "prophet of his times." True, the films do share in the generalized malaise experienced through Europe at the end of the war; and especially the French intellectual ferment of that time would play a significant role in shaping Bergman's film texts, as we shall see. The filmic influences mentioned above tended to be part of that cultural environment, and even Hollywood, in its film noir heyday, was manifesting similar symptoms. Add that to the grand cliché of Swedish gloom, and Bergman unquestionably emerges as a typical figure on the creative landscape. Bergman's, however, is hardly a significant voice in all of this. His conscious appropriation of the *Zeitgeist* is at this time no more appreciable or personal than is his mastery of filmic form.

In *The Passion of Ingmar Bergman*, Frank Gado[5] compares the plays or novels that were the bases of the first four film scripts with the finished movies themselves. He demonstrates how consistently Bergman shifts the centre of interest to the young male protagonists (usually played by Birger Malmsten), and he submits the various figures, situations, symbols, bits of dialogue, or plot and the like to be found in the Bergman films to a tight interpretation based on Freudian hermeneutics. One may have strong reservations about going all the way with Gado in this, but it is difficult to quarrel with his insight that all of this is highly revelatory of Bergman's own deep psychological tensions at that time. This means, from the perspective of the present study, that even in those relatively unformed early days when Bergman was handed the imaginative work of others to translate onto the screen, he nonetheless managed to put himself into the finished products, from the beginning making film a personal expression, revealing his own psyche and obsessions, his own relating to the culture.

That the protagonists tended to seem younger than Bergman himself (already in his latter twenties) is beside the point: he obviously identifies with them, he occupies their psychological space. But that should be no surprise. In 1944, before directing these movies, as a writer he did the same thing with the young protagonist of his first script, *Torment*, brilliantly brought to the screen by Sweden's finest film and theatre director of that time, Alf Sjöberg. In that movie, it is worth noting, Bergman goes back to his own high-school days at Stockholm's Palmgrenska Gymnasium. Little wonder, then, that after a

---

5 All references to Gado's book in this chapter are found in his two chapters "The Forties Films" (37–92) and "Playwright Bergman" (93–136).

while the more snide among Swedish critics began referring to Bergman as "the puberty crisis director" specializing in "delayed adolescence."[6] Suffice it to say that there was plenty of anguish expressed in these films; but it was the self-pitying, pouting outpouring associated with adolescence rather than the dark, ever-so-rationalized and philosophically fashionable stuff that was in the process of immortalizing Le Café Flore and Les Deux Magots into tourist icons on the Boulevard St-Germain.

However, this initial three-year output of five feature movies should not simply be dismissed. And not everyone treated them with scorn. For one thing, Bergman was demonstrating the kind of talent that enabled him to get the backing to go on making films, no small feat. Nils Petter Sundgren, Sweden's well-known film and culture critic, remembers them with affection. He is just about my age, and that means that we enjoy reminiscing (as a matter of fact, it was at his house I was staying in Lidingö that lovely strawberries-and-milk day): "I [Sundgren speaking] was just emerging out of adolescence when Bergman's films started appearing. They were really a young person's way of relating. He was expressing a lot of the things we felt at that age, and a lot of us enjoyed them."

As for me, trying to imagine those initial efforts through a misguided, clichéd reasoning process based on vague second-hand sources, I had succeeded in painting for myself a portrait of the young Bergman as a fiery film rebel out to challenge all things Swedish, cinematic or not – a 1960s cultural anarchist before the fact. These films, of course, destroy that image: they make much more sense as metaphors for the difficulties experienced by young people in coming to terms with adult life and society. Indeed, in a conversation with Mikael Timm and myself, Erland Josephson, himself a huge figure on the Swedish dramatic scene, and a friend and professional collaborator of Bergman's going back to their earliest professional days, insists, "we were not rebels in that sense at all. It didn't enter Ingmar's mind to want to try to change Svensk Filmindustri [the leading film company]. He only wanted to become part of it, to be given a chance." In those days he did what he was told: he made the movies he was lucky enough to be told to make.

PRISON AND THIRST

With *Prison* (sixth feature, 1948–49) and *Thirst* (seventh feature, 1949), Bergman begins to come into his own as a film artist. *Prison* (or *The Devil's Wanton*) is the first film he both wrote and directed. The budget was extremely low, and the shooting schedule impossibly brief (two-and-a-half weeks); but

6 Ibid., 49.

this may have been the trade-off that permitted him to have much more creative freedom than ever before. Here Bergman succeeds in creating his own world while at the same time getting closer to the characters he really understood – theatre folk, writers, actors, the very people he was associating with.

The problems dealt with are for a change very much those of his own age group, Sweden's thirty-somethings of that era, and the preoccupations – interpersonal relationships, artistic expression, and so on – reflect this. And Bergman's technical skill seems to leap forward. In a remarkable dream sequence, for example, the brilliance in execution, a kind of Bergman baroque bravura exploiting of Cocteau-esque surrealism (if I may be permitted a turn of my own) points to spectacular future achievements. Shortly before embarking on this film, Bergman, with money received from David O. Selznick for an adaptation of Ibsen's *A Doll's House* – nothing ever came of it – was able to buy prints of some German silent classics. Knowing that, one easily recognizes the atmosphere, sets, and so on reminiscent of films such as *The Cabinet of Doctor Caligari* and *The Three Penny Opera*. *Prison* is chock-full of memory, longings, guilt feelings, a sense of desperate Sartrian absurdity. More importantly perhaps, Bergman is indeed beginning to articulate his obsessional world with some thematic clarity and consistency, so much so that this film receives serious treatment in most studies on Bergman's cinema.

Thirst (*Three Strange Loves*) pushes the benign creative evolution yet further. Though not scripted by Bergman (Herbert Grevenius, a frequent early collaborator, adapted Birgit Tengroth's short stories), *Thirst* represents a kind of breakthrough, displaying a maturity and technical control as yet unseen in the director, who turned thirty-one during its filming.

The portrayal of the dazzling and neurotic Ruth is astonishing in its virtuosity, psychological sharpness, humanity, and depth. High marks must go to Eva Henning, who plays the role, but Bergman is masterful in guiding her through this performance while creating a world around her that is artistically convincing and thematically consistent. Birger Malmsten (Bertil) now looks as if he is in his thirties; and he is exploring the character in greater depth here as he portrays a rather desperate young husband trying to cling to a fragile rationality in the midst of a matrimonial maelstrom.

Here is a Bergman capable of executing a mise en scène that one can qualify as brilliant. The film opens with Ruth's waking up in a hotel room she shares with her husband in Basel: she glances at Bertil, compulsively lights a cigarette, wanders about the room, brushes her teeth, and so on – with most of this captured in one single spectacular shot as Gunnar Fischer's camera stalks her relentlessly. Later on, Hitchcock himself might chortle over the cinematic orchestration of a train passageway nightmare sequence as Bertil fantasizes (?)

that he is murdering his wife. And then there are those masterful tortured exchanges between the two in their small (*No Exit*) train compartment, trapped by space and by their love/hate bond.

In addition, Bergman, in a new kind of complex plot structuring (thanks in great part to Tengroth and Grevenius), seems completely at home in weaving what are essentially three stories, with shifts in time and in mental and geographic space, in memory and flashbacks, into an all but seamless tapestry, going from comedy to melodrama to pathos, from dream world to contemporary reality, from longing for happiness and fulfilment to defeated avowal of absurdity. Indeed, the film ends on the oft-quoted wisdom-of-desperation line: "The hell of living together is less unendurable than the hell of living alone."

Prison and *Thirst* usher us into a world where one would willingly linger. Suffice it to affirm for the moment that in these two movies one can justifiably draw attention to the first real signs of what would in succeeding years become a Bergman commonplace: a personal, artistic style, on the one hand, and on the other, ever-strengthening echoes of a dark pessimism sweeping European cultural life. And though Bergman himself feels he had no contact with the Swedish literary movement of the '40s that reflects this spirit,[7] it is safe to affirm, at least, that what was influencing those Swedish writers was also influencing Ingmar Bergman as he was entering his thirties – and as the world was ushering in the second half of the twentieth century.

It is not by accident, it would thereby appear, that of those initial nine movies, *Prison* and *Thirst* would be the first to achieve some degree of international distribution – of course, *after* the 1950s films which they antedate. Bergman's next feature, *To Joy* (his eighth, 1949/50), would also achieve limited international exposure, though still more belatedly.

TO JOY

To Joy may well be minor Bergman, but it is the product of someone who by now obviously has, to a great extent, tamed the movie-making monster. Consistency, flow, no undue straining after effect, no terrible need to imitate this style or that – *To Joy* reflects all of this, in addition to (as Bergman has stated) being very personal in nature.

There arc so many pluses: the radiant Maj-Britt Nilsson as the wife and mother, the legendary Victor Sjöström as the elderly symphony conductor, music bits from Mozart, Mendelssohn, Smetana, and the fourth movement of Beethoven's Ninth Symphony, and highly autobiographical material about

7 Ibid., 93.

Bergman's early days with his second wife, Ellen Lundström, in Halsingborg. Bergman is dealing with something he knows intimately and loves passionately, the world of artistic creation – his *raison d'être*, really – and about the experience he knew so well and so painfully, that of failed (marital) relationships. Something else very typical appears for the first time: Bergman's painting of the Swedish summer as a symbol of life and happiness.

If the film lacks stature, it may well be because of what has the feel of imposed melodramatic structuring, complete with appropriate characters, and an overweening desire to expose the struggling young artist (played by another Bergman regular of the early days, Stig Olin, obviously standing in here for Bergman himself) as a callow, self-centred male who nonetheless does achieve a measure of redemptive reintegration before the end of the film (and to the strains of the "Ode to Joy").

THIS CAN'T HAPPEN HERE

This Can't Happen Here is Bergman's ninth feature, released 23 October 1950. In point of fact, it was shot in July and August of that year, that is, after *Summer Interlude*, whose release was delayed over a year until the fall of 1951. Since the latter film, however, marks a new phase in Bergman's filmmaking, it fits far more conveniently into the next chapter, as film number 10, so to speak, whereas the earlier-released *This Can't Happen Here* makes an appropriate ending for phase 1.

With several households to support, Bergman was in dire straits financially. *This Can't Happen Here* is a job, no more, no less. It is a political thriller, dealing in international intrigue, Baltic style, with a strong cast headed by Alf Kjellin, Ulf Palme, and Swedish Hollywood star Signe Hasso. A well-made commercial film noir, it has received merciless treatment by Bergman himself, who sees it simply as a regrettable aberration forced on him by his need for money, and he wants no one to see it. Well, two or three things, it seems to me, should be noted here: *This Can't Happen Here* is by no means a bad film, and it demonstrates that Bergman was now a highly skilled technician capable of making a solid commercial (recipe) entertainment when he had a mind to. And because it in no way can be referred to as a recognizably "Bergman" film, it also demonstrates in comparison how immensely personal the films that followed it (and some that preceded it) really are.

So much, then, for phase 1, the first five or six years that saw the release of nine Bergman feature movies. The "prophet of our times" has not yet found his prophetic voice, though there are very serious and widespread mutterings, a steadily increasing reflection of the larger European mood. That, however, is not the whole story of those years, dedicated as they were by Bergman to a feverish outburst of play-writing. It is difficult to know exactly how many plays he wrote, particularly in the early period. Peter Cowie claims that there were probably twenty-three or twenty-four, seven of which saw the light of day. Cowie feels they shed little light on the films, but Frank Gado claims that no fewer than ten plays written by Bergman were presented either on the Swedish stage or over national radio before 1952 (more, therefore, than by any other living Swede at that time).[8] International critics have paid great attention to the excellent film that Alf Sjöberg directed from Ingmar Bergman's first filmscript, *Torment*, written as far back as 1944. The personal Bergman elements of the early directorial efforts are obvious, the adolescent problems and so on. But, says Gado, "the adolescent concerns addressed in their substance stand at a distant remove from the issues he would later confront. In contrast, the *plays* [emphasis], even when naive in their postulations, directly engage the Great Questions: the contest between God and the Devil, despair; the testing of life by the consciousness of death."[9]

In other words, in another medium, Bergman was beginning to reach out meaningfully to broader European cultural issues. The cinematic expression of that we shall be exploring in the following chapters.

8 Ibid., 22; Gado, *The Passion of Ingmar Bergman*, 93–7.

9 In this Gado receives implicit support from Birgitta Steene and Vernon Young.

CHAPTER TWO

SUMMER TEARS, SUMMER SMILES

Summer Interlude (*Illicit Interlude*)	filming April – June 1950 release October 1951
Waiting Women (*Secrets of Women*)	filming June – July 1952 release November 1952
Summer with Monika (*Monika*)	filming August 1952 release February 1953
Sawdust and Tinsel (*The Naked Night*)	filming February – June 1953 release September 1953
A Lesson in Love	filming July – September 1953 release October 1954
Dreams (*Journey into Autumn*)	filming June – August 1954 release August 1955
Smiles of a Summer Night	filming June – August 1955 release December 1955

SUMMER INTERLUDE

> I don't believe that God exists. And if He does exist I hate Him. More than that. If He were standing here before me, I'd spit in His face. I'll hate Him every day of my life. I'll never forget what He's done. I'll hate Him till I die.

So explodes the soundtrack of the film. The speaker's young lover (Birger Malmsten) has just died. In his hospital room, the youthful ballerina Marie (Maj-Britt Nilsson), looking at each one of us, or rather, just past our right shoulder(s), with flat deadened eyes, a deep inner look, recites in an incantatory voice these words almost straight out of a Sartre play or novel in their *prise de conscience* vis à vis the ultimate absurdity, death. Lurking behind her, the Seducer, the tragic romantic figure of her Uncle Erland (Georg Funkquist), softly calls her away to forget, to steel her heart, to stifle her soul.

Powerful stuff – and Bergman hardly paints the scene in neutral tones, with Marie walking down a long (death) corridor, in and out of shadow, the soundtrack echoing the beat of her heart. This is mitigated expressionism at its finest. And this is the articulation of a cultural current shaping the European sensibility, and communicated here not as an incidental aside, an immature posturing, but with passion and dramatic intensity. Here is a Bergman with a new mastery, a new maturity.

Poetry, integration of story, character, and theme, and that mastery of craftsmanship that produces mesmerizing moments and overall artistic consistency – this launches a period of film form achieved, in terms of filmmaking, both in the general classical sense and in that peculiar appropriation of film language to suit an artist's personal expression. *Summer Interlude* is the first Bergman film that belongs in the masterpiece category.

Bergman's Stockholm archipelago bursts upon the screen as never before, far beyond the timid hints appearing in *To Joy*. Nature is endowed with the connotations of beauty, brief young love, and even of life in its poignant brevity, a sign equally of the life force and the ability to resonate to a blessed existence. I am back, of course, to those moments, the ones that audiences have responded to in enchantment. *Summer Interlude* ushers in a whole period of films where nature will be so endowed. But nature will equally serve as the signifier of destruction and death, where a stark, austere reality with slate-grey skies, and shrilling winds agitating trees and sea, are always a possibility. There is no hiding the exuberance here of the creative élan.

Summer Interlude is a compendium of styles, references, and themes that cohere as an organic whole. The Swedish nature paradise, foreboding pathetic fallacy, old-style romanticism, expressionism, drab realism, young life, psychoanalytical probing, memory, existential anguish, absurdity, death, bitterness, exaltation, classical art – it is all there, and more.

The film is able to capture first love in its charm and pathos, set against the matchless beauty of a Swedish island in springtime. But with equal power Bergman communicates other levels of existence, other soul states. Later on (years later, the "present" in terms of the story), in a powerful scene of catharsis, Marie faces the spiritual death she has given herself to with its attendant despair. Alone in her dressing room after a night performance, the now prima ballerina is visited by her ballet master (Stig Olin) in full costume as the diabolical Coppelius. He – angel of nothingness or agent of therapy? – forces her to face the emptiness. Once that is done, the miracle occurs (psychoanalytical moment of recognition or onslaught of grace?). She wipes off the theatre paint, clean water pouring over a face literally coming back to life. It is so simple and clear: having finally come to terms with the past, she is free to give the diary about her beautiful, tragic summer of what seems so long ago to her newspaper reporter lover. And the film ends with him, backstage, gazing in rapture at her, the lead ballerina, celebrating life to the strains of Tchaikowski's *Swan Lake*. The life force, at least for now, has won over absurdity; but both experiences have been given splendid expression.

The wonder of it all is that Bergman manages to capture so many levels of experience, so many intricate shifts in time, in real and mental space. There is the rather grey, realistic world of the film's diegetical "today," symbolized by Marie's present-day lover, journalist David (Alf Kjellin), and by Marie's off-stage life. But there is also the enchantment of the dance, and the music of Delibes and Tchaikowski, with their transforming capabilities. Built on a series of flashbacks as Marie, now a prima ballerina well into her thirties, visits the island where in her youth she spent her summers, *Summer Interlude* transports us out to the island, through water and sea and shore scenery all flat and grey. As she walks to the great summer house, however, nature changes, a menacing expressionism gradually taking over – wind, cawing crows, a death-like old woman, overexposed branches darkening the sky, a land and sky-scape transformed into lifeless, ultra-contrasted blacks and whites. But then comes a further transformation into the first real treatment of Bergman's idealized summer paradise as Marie, entering the little camp that was her domain, recalls that earlier summer years ago, when she discovered love with Henrik – shimmering waters, wild strawberries, a beautiful sky with gentle, endlessly lingering light.

And there is Uncle Erland's romantic nihilism. As he plays Chopin in the grand and elegant summer-house salon, and drinks and dreams of possessing Marie (instead of her dead mother), he emerges as an ambivalently sympathetic death figure, the antithesis of the midsummer life force and its expression in the innocent love of Henrik and Marie.

Bergman resonates to every approach, and we are his accomplices. He makes the audience share his wisdom, his ability to sympathize with every level and yet to situate it in mature judgment. As never before, he has organized his feelings, emotions, ideas, and cultural awarenesses with such all-encompassing control and apparent ease that heart and mind are satisfied: this is indeed a story both traditional and yet very much in touch with the contemporary European spirit – if not with formalized precision, then at least in a vague, generalized fashion. *Summer Interlude* is a deeply moving, complex, intelligent film built on solid psychological insight. It faces the absurdity, the suffering cry of existentialist absurdity, squarely. On a note of very modest optimism, it says yes to life, in all its limitations and heartaches, even its mostly grey lived moments, because there are those other, transforming moments – gifts of nature, magic, art, love.

WAITING WOMEN

From 1950 to 1955 Bergman was to make seven features (not counting *This Can't Happen Here*, as mentioned in the previous chapter). These years have been referred to in a variety of ways, usually as Bergman's "rose period," or the "women's films." The movies indeed are lighter in tone than most of the others; and three are outright comedies. Women are the centre of action, the stronger characters, far more attuned to life's sources. This does not mean, of course, that Bergman's humour is limited to this period, and that women would not continue more often than not to be at the centre of things, right through to the end of his filmmaking career. Indeed, Bergman is acknowledged, in this male-dominated craft of film directing, as nonpareil in his rich filmic treatment of women.

As in *Summer Interlude*, all the films of this period are constructed as journeys in space and time – journeys, it is essential to note, to wisdom of one kind or another. To an extent, one might term that a constant in all his work. What is specific to this period, however, is that the journeys are now the fruit of maturity of thought and in expression, even if Bergman has not yet formally centred the quest on the metaphysical. That dimension may at times be felt, but it is still in a more or less submerged state.

Waiting Women is Bergman's first comedy, the kind of comedy, as in all of his work, that will wend its way close to the edge of the anything-but-comic. As in *Three Strange Loves*, he intertwines different stories, but this time through a structure that is simple and obvious. We are on an island in Stockholm's archipelago, and five women are gathered with their children on a summer evening in the Lobelius family summer home, waiting for their men. The youngest is secretly expecting her lover, with whom she will "escape" for her initiatory summer interlude, more or less with the complicity of some of the others. Her story is not really developed. The waiting mothers (the other four) decide to pass the time by each telling a personal love story, though the eldest remains silent, no doubt because what she would have to say would shatter anything approaching the spirit of comedy. And so we share in the stories, all of them revealing facets of the human comedy, the man-woman game, a Bergman kaleidoscope of the ways of love as experienced by the Swedish middle class.

The three episodes are self-contained, merging in a satisfyingly shared epilogue when all the husbands arrive in the sunlit Swedish summer night, and, with joy and affection and laughing children, the life force is reaffirmed. As Bergman goes from one story to the next he is permitted an outpouring of witty repartee and cinematic styles. Anita Björk's tryst with her former lover, Jarl Kulle, for example, is a light study of repression, frigidity, and desire, with wry comments. Its dominant tone is revealed as the two, lounging in the bath house, observe a fish swimming by lazily, and the man chuckles, saying one word: "Freud!" It ends in tragicomic farce when the husband returns, threatens suicide, and finally is calmed as all's well that ends well (more or less). The flashy middle episode relates the story of Maj-Britt Nilsson and her more than willing seduction in Paris by a young Swedish painter (Birger Malmsten), the complications, the birth of their child – a really baroque Bergman *tour de force*, this – and the eventual marriage. The final episode is high farce, Bergman managing to shoot almost the entire scene in an elevator, in total contrast, to be sure, to the previous episode. This marks the first pairing of one of Bergman's most brilliant teams, Gunnar Björnstrand and Eva Dahlbeck; and their bitter/sweet performances, as guided by Bergman through this period, are sheer adult delight. In fact they serve as a symbol of Bergman's graduating into a more adult world – with all that implies. It would be foolish, in *Waiting Women*, however, to seek philosophical profundities attuned to the existentialist debate of the mid-twentieth century. And yet ... in the broadest of senses, going back to the roots of classic comedy which delights in exposing human behaviour as rather absurd, growing as it does out of the limitations of the human condition in all its frailty, with its ridiculous posturings and mores, and its ultimate (tragic) promise of death, there may be a point of convergence. The comic spirit manages to have the last laugh. True to its religious origins, it celebrates and liturgizes what we might call the life force: we laugh, recognizing that force, that vitality, which, whatever the absurdities, insists that life goes on, and that human life and fertility and natural renewal – and love (even at times of the romantic kind) – are all part of the equation. This would indeed seem to have some connection with the existentialist dialectic that we shall be exploring at greater length in the next chapter.

SUMMER WITH MONIKA

Summer with Monika reveals a Bergman apparently bent on demystifying that life force, at least in its manifestations of the romantic spirit. There is scarcely a smile in this film, even though its major section is given over to the young lovers' long summer tryst in the Stockholm archipelago. Nature is there in quiet splendour, but thanks to Bergman's systematic choices in texture and rhythm, we no longer hear the heartbeat of the universe. The magic is gone. The film's creative energies are dedicated to capturing the instinctual Monika, part girl and part woman, more amoral than conscious, and ultimately destructive to herself and others. Although the treatment is not denuded of sympathy, Bergman has certainly succeeded in creating aesthetic distance in this portrayal of two young working-class people caught in a love affair that is judged unsentimentally and with little connivance on the filmmaker's part. A fine, controlled movie, *Summer with Monika* is rather sad, but not all pessimism, reaffirming the need of responsible living in the grey world of the proletariat, a world to which Bergman is not attuned. The dominant tone is clear enough, sounding the protest against the unfairness of life, so common to that period.

SAWDUST AND TINSEL

The next film embraces with a vengeance the absurdity pole of the great existentialist debate, pushing it further than ever before in Bergman's cinema. Experiencing it, one does not feel far removed from the French existentialist mood of the war and post-war eras, as exemplified by even the titles of works by Sartre and Camus: *La Nausée, L'Etre et le néant, Huis clos,* or *La Peste, La Chute, The Myth of Sisyphus.* In *Sawdust and Tinsel's* most absurdist moments, we are on the verge of entering the terrain of a Beckett or an Ionesco.

Here is a cinema of frontal attack upon any claims to rationality that might be attributed to the human condition. The sky is an unending slate-grey, and the expressionist visual techniques, with their repertory of over-contrasted exposures, grainy film stock, and looming off-kilter angles, communicate an image of a world unrelieved by meaning. Filled with grunts and wailing and shouting, rituals of absurd, directionless wandering, and unending cries of humiliation, this is indeed a slap in the face which the audience must endure and yet simultaneously enjoy in that vaguely shared connivance of perception that ferocious comic irony often achieves.

If *Summer Interlude* has its matchless moments, *Sawdust and Tinsel* displays its own bravura treasures of a far different order. Even the German cinema of the 1920s would be extremely hard-pressed to match the Way of the Cross endured by the clown Frost (Anders Ek) as he carries his naked, grotesque wife, Alma (Gudrun Brost), through the ranks of jeering soldiers after her frolicking in the sea with their fellows. Crude phallic cannons booming in rhythmic approbation, leering close-ups of men become images of cruelty and lust, Frost's Rouallt-like agonized face as he stumbles, bare feet bleeding on the merciless stones, with a cold metallic sun beating down on this denatured scene of absurd human pathology, and a soundtrack denuded of the natural, its silence implacable except for calculated percussion or horn effects – this is expressionism seldom excelled, if ever, in the history of the feature film.

One could pursue this line indefinitely with a description of the slightly less spectacular but downright ghoulish mise en scène backstage at the theatre, as the seductive, snake-like leading actor (Hasse Ekman) proceeds to have his way, cat-and-mouse, with a confused, only too willing Anne (Harriet Andersson), as the camera of Hilding Bladh (aided by a young Sven Nykvist, who, eight films and six years later, would replace Gunnar Fischer as Bergman's director of photography) prowls about, in and out of shadow, jarringly surprised by trick mirrors, jack-in-the-box masks, and other stage grotesqueries.

Indeed, *Sawdust and Tinsel* is the road of life as seen from the travelling-circus vantage point – a circus so dear to the German cinema of the '20s and so rich an absurdist metaphor for the human condition. The clown faces, nightmare artifacts, the wild animals – all are there, poeticizing, heightening (or lowering) human behaviour as instinctual and all but deprived of sanity. Through it stumble Bergman's pathetic lovers, the fat, dirty owner (Åke Grönberg) and his somewhat victimized circus rider (Harriet Andersson).

The theatre, revealed as one social step up from the circus, is mercilessly caricatured in the person of its arrogant and ironic director (Gunnar Björnstrand). And "normal life" has its dispiriting moment as well, as Albert, the circus owner, visits his estranged wife and their son in her little shop: there is no life here for the wanderer. But this is comedy; however absurd everything surely is, still, life must go on. And so the circus caravans roll on, Frost and Alma are still together, and Anne, the circus girl, and Albert, having survived her miserable tryst and his failure both at reconciliation with his wife and a subsequent suicide attempt, are reunited, surely sadder and perhaps a bit wiser, realizing that in this world they have no alternative.

And so Bergman's quintessential absurdist parable, much admired in the years after its release, even if, at the time, it alienated most of the Swedish intellectual establishment and the film-going public at large, takes its place among his most striking works.

It may be appropriate to repeat here that the Jean-Paul Sartre of the 1940s and early '50s looms large in this movie. It is not, of course, that Bergman is engaging in the practice of "professional philosophizing" and formally adopting the absurdist option of the then reigning existentialist debate. Suffice it to recall for now what is rather obvious – the dominant intellectual mood of this time, the result of the suffering, injustice, breakdown of values and institutions through the war years, the feeling of resentment and guilt, a kind of desperation accompanying the perception of generalized absurdity. The *philosophy* of "existentialism" grows out of that mood; and *mood* is its life blood, so to speak. How to integrate that into some sort of rational explanation of what existence is – that was the question. So Sartre's positing of the absurd as the basic and ultimate human situation captured part of the spirit of the times. Bergman, no intellectual but a highly intelligent and sensitive artist working in an art form that includes, as an essential part of its creative materials, the expression of words and ideas, could not have remained untouched by all of this, even in Sweden – or should one say *especially* in Sweden, where those involved in the cultural life, feeling rather out of the mainstream, were especially open to all currents, and very eclectic in their approach. Above all, it would be to a basic, motivated underlying mood that he would resonate, expressing it in his own work, through his own terms of reference. Whatever the reasons – personal experiences and upbringing, the psychological, social, political, moral, or metaphysical – that may have predisposed him to absorb these stimuli, he certainly was carried by the cultural flow, even if that current by no means encompassed the totality of his relationship to existence.

Thus, after *Summer Interlude*, *Waiting Women*, and in a sense, *Summer with Monika*, where a sense of the absurd is strong but is counteracted by the beauty and strength of the life force, what more natural than for the filmmaker to give full rein to the negative side, to create a film parable akin to Sartrian/Camus metaphors such as *Nausea*, *The Wall*, *No Exit*, or *The Plague*, *The Fall*, *Sisyphus*, indeed to be on the verge of engaging in Beckettian tragicomic gobbledygook?

Here, the smiles hurt, and the tears are cold and sterile.

A LESSON IN LOVE

In Bergman's next film, the smiles, not unexpectedly, are delightful and the tears, if any, warm. In this period of his life, it would seem, the awareness of absurdity cannot long triumph when faced with the vitality of the life force.

A Lesson in Love is all comedy, and a brilliant one at that. The situations surrounding the philandering gynaecologist, David (Gunnar Björnstrand), his wife, Marianne (Eva Dahlbeck), and her lover and ex-suitor (and David's good friend), the painter Carl Adam (Åke Grönberg), might very well in real life occasion a good deal of suffering. Here, however, they are treated farcically, from the appearance of the delightful revolving porcelain figurines that open and set the tone for the film to their reappearance at the end. Farce, yes, but high comedy farce, with large doses of romance. Once again there are journeys a-plenty, all of them swinging back and forth in time, playing their catalytic role in favour of wisdom and regeneration. The film veers from the sophisticated repartee of a weary middle-aged David being castigated by his latest mistress and patient (Yvonne Lombard), to the raucous Danish episodes centring on Carl Adam in his art studio, his almost-wedding with his model Marianne (sabotaged by best friend David), and a wild Copenhagen nightclub where all pretence of civilized behaviour is swept away, to perhaps Bergman's most beautifully filmed romantic interlude gathering generations of David and Marianne's family in the Swedish midsummer countryside.

I feel the need to pause on this last segment, for it adds to the life force of earlier films a dimension essential to an understanding of Bergman's world. Bergman gives us one glorious sunlit day as three generations of the Erneman family – David's parents, David and Marianne, and their two children, the elder of whom, Nix (Harriet Andersson), is going through a teenage feminine identity crisis – gather in Grandpa's bedroom early in the morning according to family ritual, to wish him happy birthday. The rituals continue, built around typical Swedish middle-class family mores: Grandpa, for example, is able to talk alone with Nix, sharing with her his love of life and his modest belief in God as source and final destination. Then comes the drive to the *de rigueur* picnic, with all of them finally seated or lying in the tall summer grass. The camera leaves the elders snoozing on the picnic blanket as David and Marianne stroll into the forest. At a lower level a short distance away the children can be seen throwing stones into the sea. David and Marianne are now in the midst of forest trees, the sun breaking through the leaves in dappled patterns. Hand in hand they continue to stroll to the usual benign Bergman sounds of nature: bird calls, a gentle breeze rustling those same leaves. Dag Wirén (not a Bergman regular) creates sheer enchantment with rich, soft string choral accompaniment; and Martin Bodin (also not a Bergman regular) fills the screen with his filmed light patterns as Marianne and David lie together in as tender a love scene as one can imagine. She talks of life, of her desire to have another baby.

Bergman crowns matters with a cut to the birthday ball that evening honouring old Professor Erneman. All is formal elegance as the three generations dance with the many guests. David and Marianne glide off to the inevitable porch outside the great room, savouring the magic of the moment – and permitting the audience too to savour an experience of immense beauty and depth.

I have lingered here on what for me rank as the loveliest of all the Bergman "life force" scenes because of their significance in his work at this time. As far back as *To Joy*, as we saw, he began to use elements of such scenes to express those moments that symbolize an almost idealized state of happiness and fulfilment. In *Summer Interlude* nature really comes into its own as an essential player, the essence of a blessed time in life, identified here with young love. *Waiting Women* pursues this more discreetly, adding to the nature iconography of trees, water, grass, skies, and birdsong the images of children and married life. *Summer with Monika* deromanticizes the notion with its more subdued, perhaps more naturalistic nature rendering, but not totally: that Swedish summer still is a dream to experience, even if we see it as just that, only a dream. *Sawdust and Tinsel* cruelly breaks the powerful evocation of life, denaturing nature, as it were, into lifeless icons of alienation. But nature comes back enchantingly in *A Lesson in Love*, encompassing all ages of life, even adding an echo of the divine to nature's almost sacred heartbeat.

Bergman sees the possibilities, the various facets of human experience. Within the films, in varying degrees, and sometimes between the films, he sets up a veritable dialectic. On the one hand is a sense of the absurd, a touch of the death of the spirit, on the other a life force containing within its smile the possibility of a mysterious meaningfulness. It is not quite that clear, of course, but through all the complexities, theatrics, and bravura figurations, that dialectic lends immense substance to Bergman's films of the 1950s.

DREAMS

Dreams is indeed, in Bergman terms, a journey into autumn. Gone is the Swedish summer magic, gone the celebration and the vitality. *Dreams* is a finely wrought intimist movie which in no way aspires to reflect vast world cultural movements. Bergman focuses tightly on the very human love problems of two women in the fashion world, one young (Harriet Andersson), the other approaching middle age (Eva Dahlbeck). Two portraits of pathos and suffering, the film further demonstrates Bergman's sensitivity and mastery in his cinematic treatment of women. Gunnar Björnstrand and Eva Dahlbeck, after their brilliant teamwork in the previous two films, serve Bergman magnificently; but here they switch partners, he playing the tragic diplomat who spends a rather innocent afternoon with the young model, and she the love-ravaged victim of a hopeless affair with a married man, Ulf Palme.

At one level *Dreams* is certainly a loving study of the female psyche. But it can also be seen as a study in social mores. And being a Bergman movie, it cannot avoid asking questions, at least implicitly, about life and love, ageing and dying, and the possibility or impossibility of happiness. To the extent that its spirit is afflicted by sadness and a touch of absurdity generated by what seems to be the universal frustration of all human aspirations to a happier life, one can see it as one more sign of a culture in a state of disenchantment. Modest in its ambitions, it is nonetheless a very well-made movie, a testimonial to Bergman's maturity of spirit – precisely the kind of maturity required to make his next film, surely one of his finest.

SMILES OF A SUMMER NIGHT

Bergman was thirty-seven when he directed his sixteenth feature film. *Smiles of a Summer Night* was released at the end of 1955; and when it won what counts as second prize ("*Prix spécial du jury*") at the Cannes film festival in May 1956, he was propelled for the first time into international attention. While only with the launching of *The Seventh Seal* would real international celebrity follow, for the *cognoscenti* the word was out: here indeed was a "new" film director worth watching. Most stunned of all were the Swedish film community, much to Bergman's future benefit in terms of greater creative freedom; he now would encounter financial willingness to invest in his projects.

Smiles is the perfect fusion of film and theatre, a triumphant exercise in the comedy of manners genre. Also, it truly represents a culmination point, the crowning of the "rose period." It is as if Bergman not only gathered together into one film the various experiences of love that had heretofore nourished his films but also categorized them in a pattern at once intellectually appropriated and fundamentally mystical. Even more significantly, the Bergman game is now obvious: under the guise of comedy, the quest for life's meaningfulness is now bidding for centre stage, the position it will occupy during the next creative phase. Indeed, *Smiles* could serve as the introduction to the Bergman films overtly dedicated to the Metaphysical Quest.

The stage may be set for that formalized thrust, but one cannot forget that *Smiles* is essentially *comedy*: brittle, frothy, constructed with the precision of a Swiss clock. Or say, rather, with the precision of a Comédie Française production combining two of its most illustrious playwrights, the eighteenth-century Marivaux, all elegance, witty repartee, and precious nuance of sentiment, and the later Feydeau, hilariously romping through love triangles, frantic characters popping in and out of boudoirs and closets, mistaken identities, and the rest. All of this is hardly surprising, since Bergman himself tells us (in *Images*) that his initial contact with the Comédie Française was nothing short of magical. *Smiles* reflects that, setting up outlandish characters in the finest comedy of manners tradition, the manners, in this instance, being decidedly Swedish upper and middle class. The fact, too, that the early silent Swedish cinema, especially through Mauritz Stiller, was hugely instrumental in transferring that essentially theatrical genre to the cinema – and how brilliantly that soon evolved in Hollywood's screwball comedy – no doubt played an important role, consciously or not.

Smiles delights in this contrived spectacle of the human comedy, the inevitable battle of the sexes, in which men in their pomposity are understood, endured, and eventually manipulated to their own advantage by a series of sparkling, strong, wise women far more attuned to the realities.

Bergman sets up human love as a series of stratagems; and indeed, the actress Désirée Armfeldt (Eva Dahlbeck) is his partner in manipulating the plot as she and her bed-and-chair-ridden mother (Naima Wifstrand) invite all the key characters for a summer weekend in the country at the mother's chateau (given her by a former lover precisely for not writing her memoirs!).

The occasion is a wonderful one for demonstrating the folly and absurdity of human behaviour and eliciting our laughter. No one is spared, be it the pompous lawyer and former lover of Désirée (with whom she is still secretly in love), Fredrik Egerman (played impeccably by Gunnar Björnstrand), Désirée's pompous soldier count and current lover (Jarl Kulle), scheming women, a desperate seminarian, Henrik, who is Fredrik's son, the ever-willing Egerman chambermaid (Harriet Andersson), or even Anne (Ulla Jacobsson), Fredrik's oh-so-innocent young and as yet untouched second wife.

That, however, is only part of it, a sparkling surface rippling over depths both exalted and tragic. Once we are moved out to Madame Armfeldt's chateau in the country, a new reality takes over the film – the spirit of romance, so much part of rebirth rituals at the roots of comedy (already alluded to) and so essential to Bergman's other comedies. It is the glorious Swedish summer, of course, with its sunlit nights causing human beings to dance to another kind of life rhythm. At regular intervals the plotting and scampering cease, and we are afforded moments of breathtaking loveliness and repose – an artificial punctuation, yet meditative and magical. Gunnar Fischer's camera captures stream and sky and earth, and faces of lovers in nature's paradise; and

Erik Nordgren's deep, soft romantic chords infuse all with a mystical beauty, the incarnation of a life force which proves irresistible.

Magic is in the air, no doubt about it. It is formalized in a (literally) bewitching banquet scene, all elegance and ritual, resonating with mysterious power. Madame Armfeldt presides, seated across the great table as she faces her guests, reciting a kind of incantation, casting a spell over their glasses filled with a wine enriched, so she suggests, by a drop of milk from a young mother and a drop of seed from a young stallion. All is silence as Fischer's camera hypnotically dollies in on each face in succession, revealing each guest's innermost truth: we hear each murmur the name of the true beloved. Bergman's art (or is it Madame Armfeldt's spell, or the nature magic of the Swedish summer night?) will soon resolve all the silly triangles. A kind of mystical order is imposed; and it is Frid (Åke Fridell), the chateau's lusty jack of all trades, who, Pan-like, has been pursuing the earthy Egerman maid Petra through field and haystack, who is endowed by Bergman with the mantle of poet and seer. Frid situates the lovers within their proper categories, corresponding to the three smiles by which the sun punctuates the summer night.

The first, "a smile so soft that one has to be very quiet and watchful to see it at all," is for young lovers. "There are only a very few young lovers on this earth. Yes, one can almost count them. Love has smitten them both as a gift and as a punishment." And of course Frid means Henrik, Fredrik's son, and Anne, Fredrik's young wife.

A little later there is the second smile, "for the clowns, the fools, the unredeemable ... [who] invoke love, call out for it, beg for it, try to imitate it, think [they] have it, lie about it, but don't have it." Frid and Petra know that this, for better or for worse, is their lot.

And finally, just as the sun slips back over the horizon, comes its third smile, "for the sad, the depressed, the sleepless, the confused, the frightened, the lonely" – for our two main characters, that is, Fredrik Egerman (who has just tried to kill himself) and Désirée Armfeldt. And maybe it's a soft landing after all, what with Désirée's mysterious little son, Fredrik, having finally found a daddy – and surely his real flesh-and-blood daddy at that.

All of this is recited within the context of nature's most ravishing and nurturing setting. Here indeed is the life force, smiling through the absurdity and tragedy, containing it, reaffirming and perpetuating humanity. Frid has the last word, after having been beaten by Petra into promising to marry her. His arms stretched out to the skies, he shares his happiness: "Ah, this is life! And there's none better!"

Well ... (there are hints) maybe yes and maybe no. For *Smiles* dares come perilously close to that "undiscover'd country from whose bourn no traveller returns." Time and again, our laughter is cut short – those anguished closeups of Fredrik (foreshadowing similar shots in *Winterlight*) as he recognizes the truth about his fantasy love for Anne and experiences premonitions about his own death; and Désirée herself, aware of the passage of time; Madame Armfeldt, so obviously approaching the end; the tortured, high-tension Sartrian couple of the count and his dazzling, desperate young wife; and our semi-tragic young lovers, the hopelessly idealistic Henrik and unprepared Anne. There are even two suicide attempts, one of them admittedly funny, but not so the other. Finally, there is that ancient chateau clock ringing out the hours with its circular parade of tiny medieval carved figures, seen in close-up. We recognize each as symbolizing this suffering character or that, except for one: Death, scythe and all, in his dark monk's habit, sensitive, no doubt, to the relentless passage of time, and waiting.

He is not allowed to play a "human" role in *Smiles of a Summer Night*, which is, after all, a comedy. But he is patient, and his cryptic message, never verbalized, is clear enough: "And, silly mortals, what about me?" In Bergman's next movie, which he was finally allowed to make precisely because of the unexpected success of *Smiles*, Death most certainly does reappear, actually controlling the game … almost.

CHAPTER THREE

THE LIGHT IN THE DARKNESS

The Seventh Seal	filming July – August 1956 release February 1957
Wild Strawberries	filming July – August 1957 release December 1957
Brink of Life (*So Close to Life*)	filming November – December 1957 release March 1958
The Magician (*The Face*)	filming February – August 1958 release December 1958
The Virgin Spring	filming May – June 1959 release February 1960
The Devil's Eye	filming October 1959 – January 1960 release October 1960

So we return to *The Seventh Seal*, the inspiration and catalyst for the "Summer Idyll" prelude, which will reappear for special study and demonstration in the final part of the book. Perhaps now is a good time to reiterate what has already been suggested: the "debt" of the sixteen previous films to *The Seventh Seal*. Just as it was the resounding international acclaim surrounding this film (and some of its successors, such as *Wild Strawberries*) that spurred distributors from various countries into buying the rights to earlier films (especially those from *Summer Interlude* on), so our own way of looking at and understanding them was enormously influenced by our already experienced understanding of those of the second half of the 1950s.

I have been trying to situate the earlier films from a particular point of view, that is, as participating or not participating in a mainstream Western European culture flow. I probably would not have thought of engaging in this sort of activity had I not first seen *The Seventh Seal* and some of the later ones. What I have been alluding to in the previous chapter are generally moments of a *subtext* that might easily be overlooked – or, perhaps more accurately, be seen as marginal. In *The Seventh Seal*, however, what was previously part of a subtext emerges clearly to the surface, dominant, formally enunciated, stage centre. Once that happens it becomes obvious that Bergman is very much the reflector of the larger issues informing European life. He is indeed a vital participant in that great cultural debate in his own fashion. Having understood that, one can then, looking at the earlier films, truly enjoy one's little moment of insight with an "Aha! Of course, that was what Ingmar was getting at all along!" At least, so it seems obvious to me.

This is a fascinating example of how culture functions, at least at the critical level. One of the things that surprised me when I "discovered" Bergman in the latter part of the 1950s was the realization that large areas of the Swedish literary and filmic elite were far from sympathetic with the kind of movies Bergman was making. They were nonplussed, downright annoyed, by the international acclaim as Bergman films began garnering key awards at prestigious international film festivals (Cannes, Berlin, and so on). Worse still (!), there were all those laudatory articles springing up in many parts of the world. Trust the French, too, to push matters over the edge by initiating a movement in international book-writing about Bergman films.

The simple fact would seem to be that Ingmar Bergman – if I may use the *de rigueur* phrase enshrined in early 1990s parlance – was not politically correct within his own immediate context, at least in the eyes of some of his Swedish contemporaries. Beyond that context, however, it was quite another matter.

Some more cultural situating, then. "Modernism" is one of those terms one almost has to apologize for using, simply because it encompasses so many phenomena and theories that it can come to mean any number of (often contradictory) things. As used here, I would describe it as an evolving dominant world view shaping much of the contemporary western sensibility, which progressively displaces the medieval and post-medieval belief in the God of the Bible, and its attendant Aristotelico-Thomistic understanding of the world: fundamental notions such as causality, authoritative standards concerning the good, the true, and the beautiful, and the role of the human intellect as attuned or not attuned precisely to grasping and understanding, at least up to a point, a reality that really does exist.

As this understanding partially disintegrates it is replaced by new beliefs, by a kind of secular liberalism exalting the possibilities of "rational" science. Historicism now replaces God as the absolute with a faith in human progress, in the perfectibility of humanity and society. Modernism replaces old creeds with new ones in a process of progressive displacement. As the nineteenth century evolves into the twentieth, Darwin, Marx, Freud become icons of the culture; and a little later, so does Einstein.

There is a downside to all of this: the loss of a certain sense of security, with a concomitant growing sense of crisis. Without the old absolute verities, humanity gazes into the abyss – unless, of course, the loss is replaced by the somewhat less reassuring faith in historical progress. Should *that* also break down, then indeed we are speaking of BIG crisis, growing out of the realization that our human condition is without direction, reason, whatever.

In twentieth-century Sweden the positive side of modernism was expressed with spectacular success in the organization of the mixed social/political/economic system called social democracy, which helped create a remarkable improvement in the material standard of living. But the downside was ever manifest, as elsewhere in Europe, only all the richer, growing as it did out of good old angst-ridden Scandinavian soil.

Many of Bergman's critics seemed to be wedded to a notion of a cinema whose sole relevance grew out of the socio-politico-economic understanding of life to which they were committed. And here was Bergman, studiously avoiding that reality, and, in terms "no longer relevant," pursuing his personal demons and giving in to his eclectic aestheticism – the epitome of bourgeois alienation.

I may be slightly caricaturing or at least oversimplifying the position of many anti-Bergmanians. But I believe it fair to affirm, nonetheless, that their secularist social-progress commitment was always subject to severe parochial limitations. There was, after all, a long and rich history in many parts of Europe (including Scandinavia) of grappling with areas of human experience simply not encompassed by the social, political, or ideological, growing precisely out of that profound reorienting occasioned by modernism.

Especially as World War II drew to a close, and the revelations of the hitherto undreamed-of horrors of the death camps were added to the nightmarish experience of the slaughter of millions and the general devastation in countless towns and cities, the optimistic side of modernism was subjected to extremely destructive contrary evidence. And the realization of possible nuclear holocaust was the last symbolic step, was it not, in an escalating manifestation of the human species' collective insanity. Human progress? Speak rather of the meaninglessness of human existence.

One clear response was the Sartrian brand of existentialism. For our present purposes it suffices to see in that phenomenon a privileged(?) expression of the generalized disenchantment. Surely, intoned Sartre – and in this indeed he was a prophet, a reader of the signs of the times – humanity has sufficiently demonstrated the futility of its credos and aspirations. Cast aside all the illusory codes and systems. There is nothing left for the conscious and honest individual except to re-create himself or herself by choosing within the limitations of human freedom whatever it is that experience indicates as the individual's way to live. But, Sartre insisted, during and right after the war, let there be no illusion: humanity must face the fundamental truth of death, and with it the negation of all aspiration. Hence the frustration: all is absurd. And hence too the only noble response to such a fate: to protest.

Bergman, working as he was in theatre and in film, could not be unaware of this cultural ferment, not in eclectic Sweden, interested in whatever was going on "outside." This particular state of mind (or this *mood*) Bergman certainly could relate to, philosophy or no philosophy. But that, of course, represents only one aspect of his cultural conditioning. He was also very much the (ambivalent) product of another powerful cultural force – his own Christian upbringing, his childhood and youth spent in the rectories of his father, a Lutheran pastor. The copious biographical (and autobiographical) material on Bergman has long revealed – it is now something of a cliché – his early rejection of his father, of the Established Lutheran Church, and of so much else that rebellious young men are wont to reject. What is equally obvious, however, is the extent to which the Christian ethos, its very structuring of the imagination, and its spontaneous understanding of life, were and would remain an integral part of his artistic sensibility.

This, it seems to me, is what makes Bergman especially interesting as a reflector of his times. Like many others in what we call the western world, he is very much a product of the spirit of modernism, but also of the older Christian tradition, even while, as many of his fellows, he rejects a large part of that tradition. Unlike so many artists, however, he neither hides that schizophrenic cultural legacy nor fails to come to grips with it. In his own person he represents an arena wherein is fought a cultural battle never completely resolved.

THE SEVENTH SEAL

How to describe *The Seventh Seal*? Let's give vent to verbal exuberance: it is a medieval fresco worked out in time. It is an apocalyptic vision of the ending of one civilization addressed to another (ours) on the verge of extinction. Here is a film filled with biblical quotations, morality play figures, religious symbols, archetypal images, medieval iconography, liturgical motets and rituals, various fourteenth-century social types – all of it indeed one vast tapestry of Europe's dying Middle Ages set to variations akin to the rhythms of music but shot through with intellectual ideas in a dialogue straight out of theatre, theology, and philosophy, the tone shifting from the lyrical to the ironic, from tragedy to comedy.

Bergman sets his characters as figures in a totally controlled chess game, their moves (actions and words) all part of a strikingly prearranged plan. But the game is a cosmic one, as immense as sea and sky and rock; and life and death are the stakes, nothing less. *The Seventh Seal* is full of dread, of omens signifying the end, its characters trapped among people driven to the kind of group frenzy only a perceived common doom can occasion. The Middle Ages are coming to a close in agonizing fashion, highlighted by the Black Death. All about is desolation, suffering, rotting corpses, physical manifestations of an imminent evil, a foreshadowing of doom – and people driven to desperation, most of them acting blindly, senselessly, following grossly superstitious rituals, official religion itself having become part of the corruption.

So the movie is pock-marked, to be sure, with pestilence-ridden victims, witch burnings, hysterical flagellants, mob torture. But time and again (and we began by referring to one such example), it is transfigured by visions of loveliness – tenderness, love, fellowship, communion, the Madonna with Child in a forest dell, moments of at-one-ness with the universe. And lots of humour.

The whole tapestry is contained within the parameters of Revelation and Death. *The Seventh Seal* opens with cosmic breadth – earth, sea, and sky, yes, and a large hawk (or is it an eagle, or even a dove?) soaring high, all of this further dramatized to the strains of a Carl Orf-like choir, with a reading from Revelations (the Book of the Apocalypse) announcing the catastrophes about to befall the earth when the seventh seal shall be broken and all will be revealed. And foregrounding all of this is a chess game played between a Knight and Death.

The movie ends on a similar note in the Knight's castle, his wife reading the same seventh-seal passage, and Death arriving to claim his victims. A hitherto mute girl, her face transfigured in quiet exultation and her eyes shining with special knowledge, repeats Christ's dying words on the Cross: "It is finished!" But not quite: in an epilogue we see Death leading six of his victims in a final dance far off on the horizon, as the little family (more about them later) make their innocent way down life's road, the storm now past and the sweet notes of a celestial choir floating down in benediction.

Admittedly, I have been weaving my own little baroque tapestry of suggestive details. Needless to conclude that there never has been a film quite like *The Seventh Seal*. Plot? Ah yes, for it seems that feature movies have the time-sanctioned duty of adhering to plot lines: they are subject to the laws of narrativity. (All through the history of the movies, to be sure, attempts of one kind or another have been made to subvert plot, but the plot resists, battered at times but ever triumphant, going about its job of capturing our interest, organizing the materials, and extending the art form in time, from one action to the next.) And so, too, for *The Seventh Seal*, which has its characters and its story and its incidents. In the waning years of the 1300s a Knight (Antonius Blok) and his Squire (Jöns), returning home from the Crusades, are nearing the end of their journey through plague-ravaged Sweden as they head north to the Knight's castle where he hopes to find his wife. Along the way, they are joined by, or briefly meet, a range of characters – a husband (Jof) and his wife (Mia) and their infant (Mikael), itinerant players, along with their venal partner (Skat); an abandoned, apparently mute girl who has attached herself to the Squire, having just been saved by him from a hate-filled defrocked seminarian (Raval). And there are assorted others: Plog, a dim-witted fellow and his strumpet wife (Lisa), village folk, soldiers, monks, a painter, a girl burned for witchcraft. The narrative wends its peripatetic way from one scene or action or encounter to the next, on the little band's way to their final destination.

More final perhaps than they actually intend. For there is another character who is part of the story in a special way; he is seen only by the Knight and sometimes Jof, and (fortunately) by the audience: Death. Frightening in his black monk's habit and cowl, with his dark flat eyes and white-makeup face, he is nonetheless rather gentle and sympathetic, with a nice ironic sense of humour. But he has, after all, come to do his job: to claim his victims. From a structural point of view, part of that job is also to continue at appropriate intervals his chess game with the Knight, for he has agreed to spare him and his companions as long as the game endures. Thus the film's overall structure and its various "real life" incidents are contained and punctuated by more or less regular resumptions of the chess game – and thereby, it would seem, by the intrusion of another level of reality. The end, as agreed upon, comes when the Knight loses, having sacrificed the game – and himself – in order to permit the little family to escape.

But while this brief résumé suggests the tone, feel, look, sound, and plot incidents of the film, there is another crucial factor in the equation that constitutes *The Seventh Seal* – one that certainly has not escaped notice. This is made up of the dialogue and a set of characters who are obviously also the director/writer's intellectualizers. Each character embodies a way of life, a distinctive philosophical point of view, so much so that *The Seventh Seal* can be experienced as an on-going philosophical debate – one laden with the resonances of the great existentialism debate raging through Europe at the end of World War II and into the mid 1950s when the film was made. Occupying centre stage is the Knight, a sort of tortured post-Christian desperately seeking rational proofs to reaffirm his dying faith in a God of Love who nonetheless permits the horrors they are all living through. At least, he prays, let me be given the opportunity to perform one significant act. His debating opponent, the Squire, the incarnation of a Sartrian existentialist, scoffs at this quest, affirming his own conviction of the absurdity of the universe and voicing his profound protest against the conscious experience of nothingness he must consequently endure. Complementing this opposition is Death, who has absolutely no answer to anything, counteracted by the little family of Mia, Jof, and Mikael, who resonate with love, life, a sense of the beauty of the universe. Clustered by symbols at once Christian and life-force embracing, they are clearly modelled on the Holy Family of Christian iconography. Finally, other characters – a noble wife, a mysterious mute girl, a witch, a renegade seminarian, a rascally actor, an artist, fanatical monks, superstitious and venal peasants and soldiers – represent what can be interpreted as different orders and aspects not only of society but of ways of relating to life.

The words are theatrical, yet with the ring of lived experience, totally artificial yet convincingly flesh-and-blood; they are rich in connotations, brilliant in their wittiness. Add terrifying, profane, scatological, sacrilegious yet biblical, holy, sacred. A unique kind of movie indeed.

From that vantage point *The Seventh Seal* can be seen as an extraordinary document reflecting the cultural debate, mid-1950s style – without ever losing its artistic quality as passionate, ironic, witty, aware, terror-laden, and thought-filled, and without its characters being deprived of their rich humanity (as they tended to be, say, in the Soviet cinema of the 1920s with its one-dimensional caricatures and grotesques and disincarnated symbols). Can anything be more representative of post-war Europe than life as a chess game between Man and Death, with the stakes nothing less than the meaningfulness or absurdity of existence? Death is indeed everywhere, not only as an actual character in the story but also in the journey of the protagonists through repeated scenes of suffering, torture, and plague. And a journey to what, if not ultimate destiny? The apocalyptic dimension keeps bursting through; we are made aware that the end (of something) is fast approaching.

The debate is carried on at many levels, in many modes. The Sartrian pole is brilliantly incarnated in Death, who reveals nothing (*ingenting*) – and nothingness. Imagine, in what one usually means by a movie, a dialogue interlude such as what follows. It breaks all "the rules"; yet it works brilliantly, thanks to Bergman's cinematic treatment. The Knight is kneeling in a confessional box, confessing his soul-state to what he thinks is a monk but is in reality Death, his face averted (though *we* know). We contemplate a dramatic Gothic painting, with light shining through the grill, working its criss-cross patterns on the Knight's tortured face:

DEATH: What are you waiting for?

KNIGHT: I want knowledge.

DEATH: You want guarantees?

KNIGHT: Call it whatever you like. Is it so cruelly inconceivable to grasp God with the senses? Why should He hide Himself in a mist of half-spoken promises and unseen miracles?

(*Death does not answer.*)

KNIGHT: … What is going to happen to those of us who want to believe but aren't able to? And what is to become of those who neither want to nor are capable of believing?

(*There is complete silence.*)

KNIGHT: Why can't I kill God within me? Why does he live on in this painful and humiliating way even though I curse Him and want to tear Him out of my heart? Why, in spite of everything, is He a baffling reality that I can't shake off? Do you hear me?

DEATH: Yes, I hear you.

KNIGHT: I want knowledge, not faith, not suppositions, but knowledge. I want God to stretch out His hand toward me, reveal Himself, and speak to me.

DEATH: But He remains silent.

KNIGHT: I call out to Him in the dark, but no one seems to be there.

DEATH: Perhaps no one is there.

KNIGHT: Then life is an outrageous horror. No one can live in the face of death, knowing that all is nothingness.

This is obviously a the tragic expression of 1950s Christian (or post-Christian) agnosticism. At the end of the scene Bergman adds an element that colours the discourse in decidedly existentialist hues:

(*The Knight raises his hand and looks at it in the sunlight which comes through the tiny window.*)

KNIGHT: This is my hand. I can move it, feel the blood pulsing through it. The sun is still high in the sky and I, Antonius Block, am playing chess with death.[1]

It is a nice touch, this act of wilful existentialist bravado in the midst of anguish, and it changes the mood. But the debate will rage on, with Jöns, the stoic, noble in his own way Squire, a far more Sartrian incarnation. Jöns acts according to his freely chosen code, his own lights, but in full awareness of the absurdity of everything, and ever in defiant protest against the human condition as he experiences it. So the Knight, who, after all, is the central character, the one representing humanity in the decisive chess game with Death, must struggle against himself, against Death, and against the Squire. And that, it would seem, is how Bergman sees himself and post-Christian western culture to boot – at least at this particular time of his life.

The debate continues off and on throughout the film, often in a detached, wry, even humorous fashion but often with painful intensity. Of course, this being Bergman, one can be sure that much of the debate will be transformed into moments of immense emotive power. This is never more poignantly demonstrated than in the scene in which the young woman who believes she is a witch is being burned at the stake, the two men standing beneath her in anguish over her suffering. The screen is enveloped in fire and smoke, through which we see terrifying medium shots of the brutalized girl and of the Knight and the Squire while a mournful and tragic music wails on wind instruments. Has anyone better demonstrated the problem of evil and suffering as it challenges western Christian notions of God's justice and love?

SQUIRE: So what does she see now? Tell me that.
KNIGHT: (*shaking his head*) She feels no more pain.
SQUIRE: You don't answer my question. Who watches over that child? Is it

---

1 The dialogue excerpts are taken from the English translation of Bergman's screenplay. See *Four Screenplays of Ingmar Bergman* (New York: Simon & Schuster, 1960), 150–1.

the angels, or God, or the Devil, or only the emptiness? Emptiness, my lord!
KNIGHT: No. This cannot be.
SQUIRE: Look at her eyes, my lord. Her poor brain has just made a discovery. Emptiness under the moon.
KNIGHT: No.
SQUIRE: We stand powerless, our arms hanging at our sides, because we see what she sees, and our terror and hers are the same. (*An outburst*) That poor child. I can't stand it, I can't stand it.[2]

There seems to be no resolution as to who is right, the Knight or the Squire. The Knight does indeed seem to be blessed with a moment of respite and fulfilment. A little later, after the setback occasioned by the witch-burning, he confirms his new state, it would seem, by deliberately sacrificing himself in the chess game in order to permit the little family to escape Death unnoticed – thereby fulfilling the Knight's wish to perform the "one significant act" that will put the lie to the total futility of human action, of existence itself. But is it really all settled? Near the end, the Knight's band – without Jof, Mia, and baby Mikael – have reached his castle, and they have been greeted by its lone remaining inhabitant, the Knight's wife, Karin, faithfully awaiting him. They are grouped about a great table as she reads passages (quoted in part at the beginning of the film) from the Book of Revelation, wherein are described some of the ills loosed upon the earth after the breaking of the seventh seal. They are interrupted by a booming knocking on the castle doors, and Death appears to claim his victims. As they stand or kneel to face the grim visitor, the debate between the Knight and his Squire is, in a manner, renewed, with the Knight seemingly having lost his serenity:

(*The Knight hides his face in his hands.*)
KNIGHT: From our darkness, we call out to thee, Lord. Have mercy on us because we are small and frightened and ignorant.
SQUIRE: (*bitterly*) In the darkness where You are supposed to be, where all of us probably are … In the darkness you will find no one to listen to your cries or be touched by your sufferings. Wash your tears and mirror yourself in your indifference.
KNIGHT: God, you who are somewhere, who *must* be somewhere, have mercy upon us.
SQUIRE: I could have given you a herb to purge you of your worries about eternity. Now it seems to be too late. But in any case, feel the immense triumph

2 Screenplay, Ibid., 186.

of this last minute when you can still roll your eyes and move your toes.

KARIN: Hush, hush.

SQUIRE: I shall be silent, but under protest.

YOUNG WOMAN: (*hitherto mute, now on her knees*) It is consummated.[3]

Are those final words by the two women the expression of at least part of Bergman's emotional response to the unending debate? *The Seventh Seal* is not limited to the articulation of the two opposed positions. Just as Bergman in *Smiles of a Summer Night* divided humanity into various groups of lovers, so he attempts a similar categorizing in *The Seventh Seal*. The smith Plog and his wife, Lisa, the rascally actor, Skat, the soldiers, the superstition-filled monks and the venal peasants – all seem more or less outside the pale of consciousness, freedom, and responsibility. Then there is the hopelessly damned Raval, dedicated to evil. And there is the blessed little family, free of all philosophical rationalizings, joyously attuned to life and seemingly predestined to experiencing certain sacred (Christian) realities beyond the reach of others. They escape the final Dance of Death and continue blessedly along life's journey. Two others escape Death's triumph, though we scarcely notice: Karin, the Knight's wife, and the young woman who was apparently mute. They seem to soar above the rest at Death's final visit. In a daring, one might even say mischievous, exercise of mise en scène, Bergman centres the final key moments of Death's visit to the castle on a hitherto rather minor (hitherto mute) character, the woman who was rescued by the Squire. The camera dollies in on her face, glowing in inner exultation. We do not know what it is that she is experiencing, but the dying Christ on the cross may be the key as she repeats his last words: "It is consummated." One thing we do sense: the two women are conscious of something the others ignore. And as Jof in the epilogue names off the participants in the Dance of Death which he sees out there on the horizon, the very alert among the audience realize that the two women have been spared. Jof points to the dark, retreating sky where summer lightning glitters like silver needles over the horizon:

JOF: I see them, Mia! I see them! Over there, against the dark, stormy sky. They are all there. The smith and Lisa and the Knight and Raval and Jöns and Skat. And Death, the severe master, invites them to dance. He tells them to hold each other's hands and then they must tread the dance in a long row. And first goes the master with his scythe and hourglass, but Skat dangles at the end with his lyre. They dance away from the dawn and it's a

3 Ibid., 200–1.

56

solemn dance toward the dark lands, while the rain washes their faces and cleans the salt of the tears from their cheeks.
(*He is silent. He lowers his hand. His son, Mikael, has listened to his words. Now he crawls up to Mia and sits down in her lap.*)
MIA: (*smiling*) You with your visions and dreams.4

What exactly Bergman is up to in resorting to such strategies is difficult to pin down. Perhaps the wisest surmise I have heard came from a friend who saw in the young woman's enraptured gaze the vision of further mysteries, further mystical experiences to be explored in later films.

And why not, since this is precisely what was to happen. In any case, the openness and complexity of *The Seventh Seal* have already been sufficiently demonstrated. It is obvious, it seems to me, that Bergman leans heavily on the side of a certain kind of affirmation of life and, perhaps, of meaningfulness. By ending on the little family's resumed journey on the road of life, for example, he has the audience leaving the cinema with minds and hearts uplifted. But Bergman is not unequivocally espousing a position here: everyone has his or her truth, and the whole filmic text, complete with its distanciation techniques, irony, and elements of mystification, becomes the arena for a contest between differing visions of life – and with that, different interpretations of the film. One might call it Round One in the existentialism debate, with Bergman setting up the question rather systematically, but not clearly affirming exactly where he stands (though his sympathies may well appear obvious).

One thing seems incontestable. Even though *The Seventh Seal* strays far from the secular social concerns of some of his fellow Swedes, Bergman really is consciously "reading the signs of the times" in terms of the larger, dominant European cultural debate.

WILD STRAWBERRIES

Were *Smiles of a Summer Night* and *The Seventh Seal* mere passing phenomena, streaking across world screens like short-lived comets, or would Bergman prove to be a permanent star in the film firmament? For those wonderful few who become involved in such concerns, *Wild Strawberries* would furnish a glorious answer. Shot in July and August 1957, it would in June 1958 win the Golden Bear, number-one prize at what may be the number-two movie event in the world, the Berlin Film Festival.

If film-lovers were canvassed to find out their "favourite Bergman," *Wild*

4 Ibid., 201–2.

57

Strawberries might well amass the most votes. It is undeniably a beautiful film, brilliant in its heartfelt intensity and intellectual depth, and as a cultural icon of its times. Contemporary viewers feel at home with its strong psychological understanding. From the perspective of this study, it is a kind of companion piece to its predecessor, *The Seventh Seal*, shifting Bergman's quest onto a different level, and further clarifying his articulation of concerns at once personal and broad-based.

The film unfolds in the journey mode typical of Bergman's work in his first fifteen years of film directing. This time round, Dr Isak Borg (played by the legendary Victor Sjöström, Bergman's greatest Swedish predecessor and film mentor) is the protagonist. Isak is seventy-five years old; he has created a reasonably comfortable space for himself, self-centred and surviving quite well, thank you. It is as if the Knight in the previous film had reached old age and been able to suppress all the Big Questions and existential anguish in favour of a grey, day-to-day existence in a state of spiritual semi-death. His journey to the University of Lund, where he is to be awarded an honourary doctorate (or "Doctor Emeritus") for his services in the practice and research of medicine, will of course be a journey into time, dream, history, the psyche. Accompanied by his half-estranged daughter-in-law (Ingrid Thulin) on the way to see her husband, Isak stops here and there, and remembers. It is in these moments that the suppressed reality, the existential anguish, surface.

Bergman's favourite narrative structuring has never been so unforced, so "naturally motivated"; in this film, it is reinforced by another strong structural grid, Isak's voice-over as he recounts and comments on various episodes. There is yet another powerful reinforcing sub-structuring: the movie could serve as a classical demonstration of the Freudian journey to sublimation and fulfilment, dream therapy and all. Never, indeed, has Bergman's psychoanalytical insight been served so obviously, so profoundly and sympathetically. I have already mentioned the amazement occasioned at a psychoanalytical congress some years ago precisely on that score. However harshly he may treat practitioners and their rationalizations in some of his films (e.g., *Three Strange Loves*), once one has seen *Wild Strawberries*, there is no escaping the recognition of how sensitive Bergman is to psychological insight and how indebted to it he is in the structuring of most of his films. In this he reveals himself a typical product of western culture in our age, marked for over a hundred years by the kind of (at least implicit) world view developed by Freud and those who have been influenced by him.

The structuring of *Wild Strawberries* as a journey through place, time, and the psyche harks back especially to *Summer Interlude*, and so does its visual stylization, covering an even broader range than that film. Once again two visual worlds, two extreme poles or kinds of reality, are set in opposition. They certainly are dialectically opposed in what they signify, but they do not exclude other gradations of reality in between.

As in *The Seventh Seal*, clusters of oppositions are set up in a variety of guises, many of them affording us heightened, vibrating "Bergman moments." So there is Isak's frightful nightmare of death near the beginning, shot in cruel expressionistic sharpness. In the latter part of the film he is assaulted by yet another expressionistic nightmare as his life is literally put on trial. In a similar vein but not as extreme are "real" sights and episodes such as flocks of screeching birds darkening the skies, the car encounter with the neurotic Alman couple, and the visit with Isak's mother, if not ice-cold then at least utterly self-absorbed.

This kind of clustering is tied in with death, with lovelessness, with indifference and suppressed memories of Isak's disastrous marriage. It is extended into the next generation in the person of Isak's son, Evald (Gunnar Björnstrand), like his father a doctor, who understands his relationship to life in true Sartrian terms. Denying love, he still feels a terrible need for his wife, Marianne, who insists on going through with a pregnancy he abhors. Bergman articulates this in a cold, withering, rain-swept scene as Evald, with death-mask face and flat voice, explains himself to Marianne:

EVALD: It's absurd to live in this world, but it's even more ridiculous to populate it with new victims, and it's most absurd of all to believe that they will have it any better than us.

MARIANNE: That is only an excuse.

EVALD: Call it what you want …

MARIANNE: You're a coward!

EVALD: Yes, that's right. This life disgusts me and I don't think that I need a responsibility which will force me to exist another day longer than I want to. You know all that, and you know that I'm serious and that this isn't some kind of hysteria, as you once thought.

MARIANNE: … I know that you're wrong.

EVALD: There is nothing which can be called right or wrong. One functions according to one's needs; you can read that in an elementary-school textbook.

MARIANNE: And what do we need?

EVALD: You have a damned need to live, to exist and create life.

MARIANNE: And how about you?

EVALD: My need is to be dead. Absolutely, totally dead.[5]

5 Ibid., 271–2.

At the other extreme is another world, it too finding its incarnation in breathtaking moments. Isak interrupts the journey to show Marianne the old Borg summer house where, as a very young man, in love with his enchanting cousin Sara (Bibi Andersson), he spent his holidays. Ah, the lovely Swedish summer, fields and trees and water captured in far more haunting fashion than anything in *The Seventh Seal*. Bergman creates an idealized world of joy, family, youth, laughter, love. All the elements already discussed as ingredients in the "life force" cluster are present, save perhaps the religious one. But in a more subdued, more "realistic" moment as Isak, Marianne, and three young student hitchhikers (a bouncy reincarnation of Sara – Bibi Andersson again – and her two feuding young suitors, one an atheist rationalist, the other a seminarian!) are seated about a table overlooking a lovely nature scene, that too is included. At table, food, wine, a sunlit field, youth, life – Isak suddenly begins reciting a Wallin hymn:

> ISAK: "Where is the friend I seek everywhere? Dawn is the time of loneliness and care. When twilight comes, when twilight comes …" What comes after that, Anders?
> MARIANNE: "When twilight comes I am still yearning."
> ANDERS: "I see His trace of glory and power. In an ear of grain and the fragrance of flower …"
> MARIANNE: "In every sign and breath of air. His love is there. His voice whispers in the summer breeze." (*Silence.*)[6]

We are back to the articulated moment of wholeness experienced in *The Seventh Seal*. But within a broader spectrum we are also back to serious philosophical dialectic informing the previous film: is existence meaningful? Is life worth living? To be sure, there is also the everyday "normal" life, neither desperate nor exalted – Isak's apartment in Stockholm, the car travelling along the country road on a greyish autumn day, the university ritual in Lund (treated ironically by both Isak and Bergman) – that medium zone whose ultimate degree of meaningfulness is being defined, one way or another, by the more intense realities, much as it was in *Summer Interlude* but with far greater consciousness and in greater depth.

Wild Strawberries moves beyond *The Seventh Seal* in two significant ways; or at least it is the occasion for two shifts in emphasis. First, the broad medieval fresco has been narrowed into a portrait of a few middle-class individuals living in the contemporary culture of the 1950s. In compensation, the protagonist

6 Ibid., 250.

is not merely a given, an artistic cypher to be manipulated by the artist, but rather a flesh-and-blood complex human being, analysed in depth from a rich contemporary (psychoanalytical) perspective.

The second divergence is perhaps even more significant as an instance of Bergman's plunging into his era's debate about the meaning of life. In *The Seventh Seal* he divided humanity into various fixed categories: the characters were blessed or not blessed, and pretty well remained as such from beginning to end. In *Wild Strawberries*, Bergman is refining that concept: without caricature, and in unforced manner, Isak begins as a dried-out human being awaiting death, freezing out others in a life essentially deprived of love. His voyage becomes a voyage toward discovery, enlightenment, a new, freed capacity to love and be loved. He makes his peace with his son and Marianne and the others. And we learn what has brought him to this point. In a remarkable example of psychoanalytical breakthrough at the end of the film, the elderly man lies in bed, telling us how, now, he often recalls a summer scene back in the days of his youth. We see him as old, but guided by the young Sara of that time: they walk through the sunlit fields listening to the youngsters at play at the water's edge. They reach a promontory, and Sara departs, leaving (old) Isak to contemplate his parents, off in the distance, fishing from the rocky shore, waving at him – a scene of warmth and affection, and precisely what he has lacked all through his life. In what is surely one of film history's most moving moments, the camera dollies ever so slowly into a huge close-up of Isak's face – Victor Sjöström's face in his farewell appearance in film – as it is slowly transformed into a gently smiling, sacred image bespeaking love and peace.

In *The Seventh Seal* the characters may well remain trapped by a kind of immutable predestination. In *Wild Strawberries* Bergman permits Isak to experience a radical transformation. There is a hint that even Evald is on the road to change, that the infernal cycle of spiritual death is broken. All of this represents a far more authentic expression of hope, both in Christian terms and along psychiatric therapeutic lines as well. Psychiatry and religion, it would seem, share this moment of profound affirmation of life. Psychiatry has identified the death forces with psychological pathology, and the life forces with psychic health. Religion has affirmed the meaningfulness of human existence in love of self, others, the universe. At this time, in other words, the affirmation of life is being formalized in very strong terms. And as for the dialectic of the times, the Sartrian vision is seriously undermined.

BRINK OF LIFE

The danger with the kind of approach espoused in this section is that it creates the impression that the film director is a consistent thinker working his way step by logically developing step to some kind of theoretical understanding, while developing stylistically in parallel fashion. It is good to repeat, then, that this was far from Bergman's creative reality. True, the later 1950s seem to have been very good years for Bergman. Artistically, he was directing his Malmö ensemble in a series of brilliant theatrical successes, and working with many of the same collaborators, he had become an international film celebrity. The creative energy and the output were at their peak, nothing short of amazing.

But Bergman, like so many Swedes, ever remained the eclectic. His directorial gifts in both theatre and film could, and did, serve many different cultural currents and attitudes. *Brink of Life* (*So Close to Life*) marks a change of pace: Bergman forsakes the overtly metaphysical to bring to the screen a scenario he wrote in conjunction with Ulla Isaksson from one of her short stories – and to fulfil a contractual promise. It stars three Bergman regulars, Eva Dahlbeck, Ingrid Thulin, and Bibi Andersson – they shared the 1958 Cannes Festival best-actress award – portraying three women in a maternity ward, each with a different attitude toward her own pregnancy, ranging from the sterility/absurdity pole to the life-force pole (as one might expect at this time).

Stylistically antiseptic, *Brink of Life* forsakes the cinematic bravura of its predecessors. And while it is more than adequately shot by Max Wilén and quite up to Bergman's professionalism in craftsmanship in general, it reduces the artist's canvas and its potential – a forerunner, perhaps, of Bergman's later television works. It is one of those Bergman films whose central reality is (exclusively) woman – a beautiful study of the female psyche, something Bergman was already noted for, served as he is by actresses who literally glow under his directorial guidance.

Brink of Life can be seen as a moral tale, affirming the value of life, almost a polemic against abortion. It certainly reflects Bergman in many ways, but even more Ulla Isaksson, a writer with strong ties to Christianity.

Although *Brink of Life* expresses a joyful affirmation of the life force, one senses, however, no passionate Bergman involvement in this film, which most agree is rather marginal within the context of his total output. And it is somewhat predicable, contributing little to the "great western cultural debate" Bergman now seemed embarked upon, except to reaffirm the "positive" pole of the dialectic.

THE MAGICIAN (THE FACE)

Before making *The Birds*, one of his most serious and profound works, Alfred Hitchcock does a "quickie" – *Psycho*. And John Ford inserts a delightful, self-indulgent caper, *Donovan's Reef*, between two of his most serious final works, *The Man Who Shot Liberty Valance* and *Cheyenne Autumn*. Many of film history's major film directors, it would seem, enjoy opportunities for creative fun, digs at themselves or their audience. In Bergman's case, add to this an essential eclecticism and a consciousness of ambivalence so deep that strong affirmation seems to set the pendulum in motion, a movement in the opposite direction denying or invalidating that affirmation – at least up to a point. After *Wild Strawberries* and *The Seventh Seal*, what?

The Magician continues the debate between Max von Sydow (Vogler) and Gunnar Björnstrand (Dr Vergérus), that is, between a doubt-ridden believer and a rationalistic scientific atheist of Sartrian hue. But what is this film, really?

The Magician, to put it baldly, is gothic horror and semi-farce, with a touch of *grand guignol* thrown in. We are hurtled once again into the back-lit world of *Sawdust and Tinsel*, to a creaky horse-drawn wagon against the dark horizon, containing a witch, scruffy actors, and road-show types … and Emmanuel Vogler – magician, Christ figure (Emmanuel means God-with-us), artist – charlatan? Gunnar Fischer's masterfully complex light-and-darkness effects, a camera eerily peering through darkened rooms, passageways, and attics in looming, off-centre angles – Bergman plays at expressionism, complete with plot/incident devices, tricks, surprises. Vogler may be defeated, exposed, humiliated, but we are never quite sure; and his outrageous *deus ex machina* triumph at the end is revealed as just that. Bergman's parody of his own eruption-of-grace-and-wholeness resolutions in the films of that period?

It is not, however, all fun and games. The angst is anything but funny, especially as portrayed by Vogler and his wife Manda (Ingrid Thulin). Existentialist cries of pain ring out: "One walks step by step into the darkness. The motion itself is the only truth"[7] – these words from an almost decaying, drunken actor who actually dies and whose corpse is dissected. And all of this in the midst of a comic sex romp in the manor's kitchen and bedrooms! As Peter Cowie[8] so beautifully puts it: "[Just as] there is a laugh behind every shiver, so there is a shiver behind every laugh."

The more deeply one analyses *The Magician*, the more bewildered one becomes – if one is seeking logical coherence, that is. For in almost any direc-

7 Ibid., 345.

8 In his excellent *Ingmar Bergman: A Critical Biography* (New York: Charles Scribner's Sons, 1983), 77.

tion one may travel, sooner or later one arrives at some kind of mystification. Meaning falls victim to the ironical, the sardonic, the mocking. Here is a clear manifestation of an attitude always ready to erupt, one that periodically does take over a Bergman film, warning us not to take too seriously certain affirmations he may seem to be making – or anything else connected with movie-making, for that matter. Push that one step further and one may (perhaps justifiably) feel that the very structuring and tone of the film, then, is in itself a sign of the world's absurdity, or the perfect antidote to works of analysis such as the present one. *Caveat lector.*

THE VIRGIN SPRING

In *The Virgin Spring*, Bergman returns to "high seriousness" with a vengeance, further refining his exploration of reality as he develops his filmmaking in a rather new direction – perhaps because he felt that his "metaphysical movies" begun with *The Seventh Seal* had reached a degree of formal perfection that was so easily recognizable as to verge on the predictable. An eclectic artist such as Bergman, it seems reasonable to assume, will soon distrust anything that he "does too well," anything that he feels smacks of the repetitive, the facile, the banal. Besides, Bergman was fully aware of what other filmmakers were doing, and very generous in his enthusiasms. Here is a man who for years had been collecting movies and who would eventually build his own little movie-viewing theatre on Fårö. In 1958 more and more films from a variety of countries were becoming available. Bergman, as he himself has stated, became acquainted with the work of Japanese film giant Akira Kurosawa; and that, as we shall see, did produce some effects.

Coincidentally or not, it is at this time that Sven Nykvist replaces Gunnar Fischer as Bergman's director of photography. Fischer's marvellously intricate lighting setups, his use of back light, intense light and shadow contrasts, and so on had enabled Bergman to achieve remarkable results. But now, it would seem, Bergman felt the need to go in another direction, to free himself, as it were, from the shooting restraints and general characteristics imposed by the Fischer method.

The Virgin Spring literally explodes upon the screen, a Swedish movie bursting with Kurosawa's Dionysian frenzy, propelled by a demonic force not at all typically Swedish ("My Kurosawa period," Bergman has laughingly called it).

Fischer's careful lighting effects are replaced by Nykvist's more natural use of available light and generally simplified light sources. The framing, too, is far more supple, less centripetal, less obviously pictorial. Thanks to that, Bergman is enabled to open out his mise en scène with a more naturally flowing movement of camera. The result is a greater feeling of "reality." In contrast, his previous work looks more static, more stagy – though by no means necessarily inferior.

Dionysian frenzy? In Kurosawa-like sweeping travelling shots – the camera and protagonists flashing by in parallel movement, but often separated by small trees and so on – Bergman propels us breathlessly into the action. With it come outbursts of choreographed physical violence, complete with elemental (almost "Japanese") grunts, groans, yells. Cinema had rarely witnessed a rape scene of such savagery, followed by an even more brutal, ritualized vengeance later on in the film.

The film world was stunned, shocked. And Hollywood would see fit to crown *The Virgin Spring* with its Academy Award for Best Foreign Film: now *this* was cinema.

It was not, however, merely an exercise of style, one master director entering another master's film world. Far beyond that – and in spite of Bergman's severe reservations in later years about this movie – *The Virgin Spring* emerges as one of the most explosive and intense explorations of evil in the history of the cinema. But that evil is presented within the mythic Christian pattern of innocence/evil/vengeance and then repentance/redemption. To put it more graphically, Bergman is surely one of those film directors who most closely approach Shakespeare's breadth (Kurosawa is another). In *The Virgin Spring* it is the Shakespearean intensity that we feel, of a Macbeth embracing the dark forces, succumbing to evil, and being overwhelmed by conscience – but with the essential difference that the protagonist, unlike Macbeth, achieves Christian forgiveness, reconciliation, at-oneness.

What classical philosophy calls the "problem of evil" is the challenge to all wisdom systems, the brutal rock against which any rational attempt at explaining the human condition may founder. In the post-war context it is precisely that which led a Sartre to proclaim the absurdity of existence. In a much more contained context, Bergman approaches the terrible reality in a Shakespearean spirit, with Samurai movie explosiveness but a Christian religious solution.

Perhaps in yet another strategic move to free himself from his "perfected form," he turned to Ulla Isaksson for the script; and it is her faith-affirming adaptation of a thirteenth-century ballad that serves as the base for his film. Max von Sydow incarnates Töre, the lord of a country manor. The world he lives in is a world of opposed forces, with witchcraft and pagan worship still very much factors to be reckoned with (as they were at that time in Sweden), and a dominant Christianity itself split, much as in *The Seventh Seal*, into two expressions, one rendered perverse in its fixation upon suffering, the other incarnating an affirmative, fertile, loving spirit. All of this is communicated beautifully in the first three scenes or sequences of the film, with clear, yet far less defined contrasts by Sven Nykvist's photography.

Bergman/Isaksson lead us from the relatively innocent but vaguely troubling existence of Töre's relationship with his wife and daughter, to the horror of the daughter's rape and murder, to Töre's terrible ritualized pagan vengeance, to the final reconciliation. And the film is once again organized through clusters of oppositions, even if in mitigated visual texture: the breathtaking nature of sunlit harvest fields, trees, birds, and laughter, versus crows, rocks, shadows, dead forests, fire and smoke.

Töre is torn between two ritualized imperatives: pagan vengeance, Christian repentance and forgiveness. At the end of the film the little house-hold goes on its Way of the Cross in a journey through these worlds to the sun-lit glade where the dirt-stained body of Töre's daughter is lying. Töre withdraws a short distance, totally lost, almost in despair. He raises his hands to heaven, those same blood-stained hands he had, Macbeth-like, tried to wash after slaughtering his daughter's killers. He falls to his knees, hands still held aloft in the archetypal priest gesture:

You saw it, God, You *saw* it! The death of an innocent child, and my vengeance. You permitted it, and I don't understand You … I now ask You for forgiveness. I don't know of any other way of reconciling myself but with my own hands. I don't know of any other way of life. And I promise You that as a penance for my sin, I will build a church for You, I will build it here of limestone and granite and with these my hands![9]

This is the moment, this is the archetypal crucial moment in the *Christian* existentialism pattern. When the consciousness of the horror of evil is so over-whelming, when the inherited values no longer mean anything, the human being is crushed, has nowhere to turn, and cries out to God in desperation. And the answer is overwhelming, gratuitous, beyond the rational, beyond merit, beyond human power and human codes: a spring gushes forth where the girl's body is lying, exercising its wondrous effect on every member of Töre's household. To the sound of the little stream and of a gentle celestial choir similar to the one heard in *The Seventh Seal*, a liturgy of reconciliation, wholeness, at-oneness is enacted: kneeling, their faces bathed in loving seren-ity, Töre and his wife hold their daughter, cleansing her face of blood and dirt with the fresh spring water.

9 See screenplay (Ulla Isaksson, *The Virgin Spring* [New York: Ballantine Books, 1960] 107).

For purposes of almost caricatural clarity, it is tempting to see the Squire and the Knight (from *The Seventh Seal*) and Töre (from *The Virgin Spring*) as three men facing the spiritual desolation and emptiness which were the heirlooms of World War II and of the cold war in the nuclear age. They live out the existentialist cycle in that their old ways of coping with life, with their terrible knowledge of themselves and with perceived senselessness, are no longer adequate: Jöns the Squire is a Sartrian, naming the emptiness, proclaiming the absurdity; the Knight struggles to renew his old faith, and though he does experience a moment that brings meaningfulness, in his demand for rational proof he is unable to live it fully, still racked by anguishing doubt. Töre is the one blessed by Grace: his desolation has been the occasion for a far deeper, truer contact with God.

We shall be returning to this notion of the Christian brand of existentialism when dealing with *Through a Glass Darkly*. However, since there is question here of Bergman's explicitly relating to his culture, an additional point growing out of *The Virgin Spring*'s perhaps most horrific scene helps further to understand the world Bergman was born into.

The two herdsmen who have raped and killed his daughter have unwittingly taken refuge with their little brother in Töre's manor. In a kind of prelude to Töre's slaughtering of all three, a wandering beggar monk speaks to the boy:

A certain stillness falls over the manor hall. Up at the table the two herdsmen drink and eat with their backs turned against the room. After a while, the beggar lifts his head and looks down at the boy who, with wide-open eyes and clenched hands, lies staring at the ceiling. The fire has decreased somewhat and doesn't burn as briskly as before. The boy's eyes follow the shadows of the many objects that hang from the ceiling. Some of the shadows tremble because of the wind that comes through the open vent. The boy clasps his hands even tighter together. He lies tense and motionless: only his eyes flicker with fear. The beggar suddenly begins to whisper in a monotonous and soothing voice, somewhat absently, yet with a strange hypnotic authority:

"Do you see how the smoke trembles there in the vent? As if it were moaning and frightened?" (The boy stares and nods silently).

"Yet it all goes out into the air, and out there it has all of space to wheel around in. But it doesn't know it. That's why it crouches and trembles in here under the sooty ridge of the roof.

"It's the same with human beings. They tremble and worry like a leaf in a storm – because they know and because they don't know" …

(The boy bites his hand in intensified fear.)

"You stand before a mountain of fear. It vomits fire like an oven, and at its foot a huge abyss opens. All kinds of colours blaze there: copper and iron, blue vitriol and yellow sulphur. The flames dazzle and flash and eat the rocks. All around them people are leaping and writhing – people who are as small as ants – because this is the oven which swallows murderers and violators." (The boy is wildly frightened: he wants to spring to his feet.)

[Says the] beggar (in a sudden change of mood which surprises even him): "But at the same moment when you think you are lost, a hand will grasp you and an arm will be placed around you and you will be taken far away where evil can no longer harm you."[10]

Here is a poetic image, to be sure, a product of the dark side of a certain Christian tradition – but more specifically, expressive of the dark side of an aspect of Lutheran sensibility familiar to both Ulla Isaksson and to Ingmar Bergman. Implied is a human helplessness, and the horror of human existence, fertile ground for the mood of existentialism, even if that mood far antedates the 1940s and '50s. But it is an existentialism, one must repeat, that is heavily shaped by Christian insight. And this may well explain why Bergman would subsequently be so adamant in rejecting *The Virgin Spring*: however rich it might prove in psychological insight and however adept at re-creating medieval Sweden, Bergman may well have had misgivings all along about the film's lacking a voice steeped in contemporary irony, the Christian affirmation ringing out so strong that it excludes the Sartrian pole of the existentialist dialectic. We may indeed be hearing far more of Ulla Isaksson's voice than Ingmar Bergman's.

Bergman would have ample opportunity to develop his own personal response through many films in the years to come.

THE DEVIL'S EYE

With over thirty years of hindsight, what was obvious from the beginning becomes overwhelmingly clear: *Through a Glass Darkly* demands discussion immediately after *The Virgin Spring* – especially in the context of the preoccupations of this study.

The Devil's Eye, then, shot only two months after the shooting of *The Virgin Spring* (off and on from October 1959 to January 1960), can be seen as a none-too-happy interlude, when Bergman fulfils a contractual commitment while artistically marking time.

10 Ibid., 80–2.

Gunnar Fischer reappears for the last time as director of photography; the film has his quality look about it, sharp contrasts, intricate framing and all. Bergman does engage in a certain amount of playful theatre-inspired structural bravura, introducing an ironic narrator (Gunnar Björnstrand) and using a film-within-a-film (or is it film-within-a-play-within-a-film?) technique in an overt assault on traditional narrative film credibility and hence on the traditional relationship between movie and audience.

All of this is in keeping with the adventurous spirit of the 1960s and with Bergman's own need to branch out in a new direction. The distanciation, however, may prove too great; and maybe that explains the lack of warmth between Jarl Kulle (who plays Don Juan) and Bibi Andersson (who plays his intended victim). The dialogue sizzles with cynicism in this sulphurous comedy of manners parodying Swedish bourgeois life, religion, and so on while more or less affirming them. By no means bereft of charm and interest, *The Devil's Eye* remains one of Bergman's marginal efforts, though not nearly as disappointing as Bergman's own comments over the years might lead one to believe.

CHAPTER FOUR

THE WANING OF THE LIGHT

Through a Glass Darkly	filming July – September 1960 release October 1961
Winter Light (*The Communicants*)	filming October 1961 – January 1962 release February 1963
The Silence	filming July – September 1962 release September 1963
Now About These Women (*All These Women*)	filming May – July 1963 release June 1964

An artist in search of a cinematic form that would more adequately communicate his soul state: was that Ingmar Bergman 1960? That may seem a rather presumptuous assumption, a notion I seem determined to suggest in a number of ways, and perhaps unjustifiably. After all, Bergman by now was the acknowledged showman of the art cinema, apparently capable of mastering the techniques of just about any school, any method; and, more than that, of integrating everything into an intensely personal, organically coherent, signifying whole. A creative exuberance exploiting to the full the immense resources of film language and glorying in that exercise – that surely was one aspect of Bergman as the decade began. And Hollywoood itself was getting ready to crown *The Virgin Spring* with the Oscar for "Best Foreign Film," thereby adding real possibilities of an international box office breakthrough.

However – as Fellini would soon demonstrate after his 1963 masterpiece, $8\frac{1}{2}$ – an artist can jump onto a merry-go-round whirling in ever-increasing momentum, driven by a compulsion to make each succeeding film more spectacular than its predecessor. Was *The Virgin Spring*, with its Kurosawan explosiveness, pointing in the right direction – for Bergman?

The problem (if problem there is) may lie considerably deeper, touching on the very nature of what Bergman was trying to communicate. Many of us rate the (previous) 1955–60 period as possibly his most magnificent in film achievement. The very texture and structure of the films, the whole range of sights and sounds encompassing so many levels, so many emotional reactions to life, the freshness of the film world he was creating, the unique reflection of culture that was his – all this sang a song to artistic creativity, to culture, and, implicitly, to life, no matter how grim some of the "content." Indeed, what might at times be called a dialectic between content pessimism and formal celebration may well have enriched his cinema of that period with an ambiguity that would resonate meaningfully for a certain western audience itself deeply attuned to that paradox.

For Bergman, however, was that kind of cinematic approach best serving his needs, most truly expressive of what was deepest within him? Desperate affirmation of belief in life is one thing; but could the desolation (if such it was) or the very *mood* of existential anguish be communicated by film techniques, call it a baroque style, far more suited to the celebration of life? At a *conscious* level, the audience – to shift the angle – was understanding the existentialist wasteland. But through the lyrical beauty of the nature/fertility scenes, for example, or the spectacular nightmare expressionism of the dream/horror/death scenes, was it not rather experiencing something else, not really empathizing in the anguish? In other (more abstract) words, the film at its immediate, first level really was the sights, sounds, rhythms – not primarily the anguish proclaimed by the avowed "content."

THROUGH A GLASS DARKLY

All of this smacks of theorizing after the fact, as if in some way I needed to apologize for my enthusiasm for the films just discussed, or for Bergman's evolution. The fact is that an austerity never before seen in Bergman's work permeates *Through a Glass Darkly*. And Bergman himself is fully conscious of what he is up to, announcing that "from now on" his films will be more like "chamber music" or "small chamber plays," trying to explore the deepest levels of the human soul without distraction. Beethoven retreating from the symphony to the string quartet?

Four actors, that's all, and a barren island, scant vegetation, a sunless sky, plenty of darkness, and relative cinematic asceticism – new territory for Bergman, which viewers would come to identify as the "true landscape of Bergmania." Bergman himself tells us that as soon as he discovered his location for the movie, the small island of Fårö (just off the larger island of Gotland), he fell in love with the place; and five years later (1966) he would make it his permanent home.

Bach's "Suite no.2 in D Minor for Cello" renders sacred an opening scene of slightly out-of-focus water – or is it the dissolving mind? – which gradually can be identified as the sea (the Baltic), as four figures emerge, the far-off sound of their voices all but indistinguishable: a straight horizon line divides a slate-grey sea from a slightly brighter slate-grey sky, all of it extending indefinitely beyond the frame. With only "honest" available light and a centrifugal composition, Sven Nykvist is achieving the logical fulfilment of his "purity" approach. We are speaking here of minimalist art in the cinema, with no large apparent effects, certainly with nothing that could be deemed as attempting to overwhelm the audience with spectacle.

A key word in all of this, of course, is the term "apparent," for the very opening scene is extremely rich in "western" cultural connotations: the sacred, with Bach's music and the quotation from St Paul's First Letter to the Corinthians ("For now we see through a glass darkly. But then, face to face. Now I know in part, but then shall I know even as I am known" – chapter 13, verse 12); the origins of humanity, evolving from the sea; the indistinct, impressionistic gropings of the mind; an archetypal image of the fragility of the human condition in a vast, cold, grey universe. Out of that emerge our four protagonists (the young woman, Karin, her mind disintegrating into schizophrenia, her father, David, her husband, Martin, and her adolescent brother, Minus).

Gone "forever" are Bergman's dazzling life-force nature scenes: no sweet birds, no sweet young love, no laughing families with playful children and wise, warm elderly grandparents create clusters of life affirmation. What we have instead is almost barren terrain, the alternating lifeless grey skies with the dark semi-night, dimly lit interiors, rocks, an unfriendly sea, the faint shriek of a night owl or a hawk.

It could be claimed that Bergman has retained only the dark sights and sounds of his 1950s' dialectic, transposed into less expressionistic effects. There are times, to be sure, when he still comes very close to expressionism, especially in those moments when he actually does permit his film to explode in violent suffering. The scene in which Karin seduces her brother in the beached boat, with its extremes of contrasts in black and blotches of light and its tortured, shadowy cross shapes, is reminiscent of Gunnar Fischer in the earlier films. Truth to tell, few are the moments when Bergman has ever previously matched the anguished strugglings of a Karin succumbing to madness.

The overall tone, however, is unquestionably one of immense quietness: depth does triumph over the danger of surface titillation, mystery over the danger of flashy mystification. If existentialism is indeed a mood steeped in anguish and coldness, that mood has found its appropriate cinematic expression: desolation, fear, emptiness, and desperation verging on helplessness have won the day.

And though the film's opening situates us in a context as broad as human existence, Bergman scores no points with any attempt at brilliant portrayal of social mores or history or whatever. He limits his canvas to his four people. The exquisite Bergman psychological probe, however, is at work, this time more piercing than ever in its revealing of suffering, sympathy, and pathetic aspiration, which now take over the role of "positive pole" in the dialectic. Karin (profoundly, stunningly played by Harriet Andersson) is consciously slipping into the definitive phase of schizophrenia, unable to relate sexually or in any other way to her husband, turning that sexuality upon herself and her younger brother. Max von Sydow and Gunnar Björnstrand have exchanged roles up to a point: it is Max who now plays the rationalist husband, Martin, a decent doctor, but a man limited to his own narrow purview and quite incapable of facing the depths – nor to cope, for all his well-meaning gestures, with his wife. David, the father (Gunnar Björnstrand), is a writer convinced of his own failure as artist, father, human being, and especially horrified by his own novelist's fascination with his daughter's progressive deterioration. He also happens to be the clearest incarnation of the Christian existentialist to appear in Bergman's work.

So the great debate is worked through the habitual Bergman themes within the small family unit. The film can be listened to as a desperate succession of cries and whispers, none of them more overwhelming than Bergman's understated scene that captures the father sobbing, alone and unnoticed, as he stands, arms outstretched, clutching the frames of a window through which cold dark light outlines him in a clear crucifixion figuration.

But the father does not despair; and there's the crucial point. Is David a Christ figure? Hardly. Say rather that Bergman is somehow integrating David's suffering into Christ's. Does Bergman realize to what extent he is echoing Karl Jaspers's Christian existentialist shipwreck archetype as he has the father tell Martin (von Sydow) about his life-transforming moment?

> DAVID: I'll tell you something. Down there in Switzerland I decided to kill myself. I'd hired a small car and found a precipice. As I drove out there I was quite calm ... a very lonely road, no traffic. And it was evening; in the valley it was already dark. Empty, without fear, remorse, or expectation, I went straight for the precipice. As I pressed the accelerator down, the engine stalled; the gear stopped me dead. The car slid a few yards on the loose gravel surface, then hung there with its front wheels over the edge. I dragged myself out, trembling all over; I had to sit down under the cliff on the other side of the road. And there I sat, gasping for breath, for several hours.
> MARTIN: What are you telling me this for?
> DAVID: I want to tell you I no longer have any facades to keep up ...
> MARTIN: I don't understand.
> DAVID: Out of my emptiness something was born which I hardly dare touch or give a name to. A love. (*Pause*) For Karin and Minus. And you ... (*for a long time they sit silent, motionless*) ... Maybe I'll tell you one day. I don't dare to now. But if ... I mean if it is as ...[1]

There comes that terrible moment, symbolically on the edge of a cliff (David's story in *Through a Glass Darkly*), or on that narrow ledge, the towering mountain of fear on one side, the bottomless abyss of fire and writhing creatures on the other (the Monk's story in *The Virgin Spring*), when all seems lost. Karl Jaspers's poetic figure is that of "shipwreck": the realization of the

---

1 From Bergman's screenplay in *Three Films by Ingmar Bergman* (*Through a Glass Darkly, Winter Light, The Silence*) (New York: Grove Press, 1970), 47–8.

utter precariousness of existence when the individual is in a state of inner collapse, frustration, isolation, fear. Nothing human can help, no wisdom, no philosophy, none of "the works of man." One's existence lies shattered.[2]

We are back, to repeat what has been stated already several times, to that experience/perception shared by so many Europeans at the end of World War II – and to what made Sartre proclaim that all is indeed absurdity and nothingness. Responding to the same data, the Christian existentialists reach a radically different conclusion, seeing in this realization the catalyst for a final relinquishing of "all illusions, false optimisms, all this-worldly hopes" … and thus becoming free to embrace the Reality behind all these appearances and systems, to "enter freely into the faith which declares: 'It is enough that Being is.'"[3]

A key point: in *Through a Glass Darkly* Bergman succeeds (for a time at least) in exorcizing a vision of God that has haunted him through almost all his films. It is the God imagined by Karin, a horror creation of neurotic humanity, a perversion born of suffering, disease, obsession, fanaticism, and, at least in Karin's case, of sexual frustration. History has proposed many images, many incarnations of this God, in Christianity as well as many other religions, the product of cultural reduction, accretion, fear – very often under the guise of religious fervour. Needless to add that manifestations of that God have appeared many times in the Bergman films we have been studying. So Karin awaits the Coming in her attic: before what look like flickering vigil lights surrounding a tabernacle/female symbol, she enacts her rituals of auto-eroticism. Finally, a helicopter, threatening in its dark shape and mysterious sounds as it flies by the window, becomes the occasion for Karin's imagined final sexual assault by the Spider God.

Thus Bergman identifies that God, a kind of Manichean evil God. But David (Bergman?) the artist has already rid himself, at least for the moment, of all human idols and distortions: on the edge of the cliff he is able to affirm Being and Love, taking the blind leap into an as-yet-unarticulated faith in another understanding of God. By the end of the film, after the horror of Karin's final collapse and the heartbreak of her departure, he is actually able to speak to his son:

---

2 I am indebted to David E. Roberts's *Existentialism and Religious Belief* (New York: Oxford University Press), especially his chapter 5: "Jaspers," 227–75, from which come the quoted bits. The whole question of existentialism's influence on Bergman receives a far-reaching and thorough exploration from a "professional" theological/philosophical point of view (and from a somewhat different perspective from mine) in Charles B. Ketchum's *The Influence of Existentialism on Ingmar Bergman* (Lewiston, NY: Edwin Mellen Press, 1986).

3 Roberts, *Existentialism and Religious Belief*, quoting Jaspers.

MINUS: I can't live with this new thing, Daddy.

DAVID: Yes, you can. But you must have something to hold on to.

MINUS: And what could that be? A God? A Spider God like Karin's? No, it's no good … Give me some proof of God … You can't.

DAVID: Yes, I can. But you must listen carefully to what I'm saying … It's written: God is love.

MINUS: For me that's just words and nonsense …

DAVID: I only want to give an indication of where my own hopes lie.

MINUS: And that's in God's love?

DAVID: In the knowledge that love exists as something real in the world of men.

MINUS: Of course, it's a special sort of love you're referring to.

DAVID: *Every* sort of love, Minus! The highest and the lowest, the poorest and the richest, the most ridiculous and the most sublime. The obsessive and the banal. All sorts of love.

MINUS: (*silent*) Longing for love.

DAVID: Longing and denial. Disbelieving and being consoled.

MINUS: So love is the proof?

DAVID: We can't know whether love proves God's existence or whether love is itself God. After all, it doesn't make very much difference.

MINUS: For you God and love are one and the same thing.

DAVID: I let my emptiness, my dirty hopelessness, rest in that thought, yes.

MINUS: Tell me, Daddy.

DAVID: Suddenly the emptiness turns into wealth, and hopelessness into life. It's like a pardon, Minus. From sentence of death.[4]

Thus Bergman gives us his clearest statement ever of Christian existentialism's affirmation of God. This time there is no partial taking cover behind a medieval reconstituting of a folk ballad (as possibly was the case in *The Virgin Spring*). The time is now, the main character is an internationally famed Swedish writer experiencing both the disintegration of family relationships and a feeling of emptiness about his own art. Could Bergman be more transparent?

Affirmation? Well, it is strong and clear at the *verbal* level. But when we look at the whole filmic context of this scene, what has just happened (Karin's being taken away in the helicopter) combined with Bergman's mise en scène, it may be cold comfort indeed. There is no sound except for that of the two voices,

---

4 From the script of *Through a Glass Darkly*, in *Three Films by Ingmar Bergman* (New York: Grove Press, 1970), 60–1. The printed script is slightly more explicit than the film track in its theological "explicitating."

and both men, in medium shot, are enveloped in semi-darkness: Minus is framed by the window, its wood partitioning creating the usual cross behind him, with the sun in background in its last glimmering, all but disappeared below the horizon. The minimalist aesthetic has won the field, with an austere, cold beauty but no joy, a strange mixture of quiet desperation and quiet serenity.

Herein lies a terrible paradox, one that makes Bergman at the deepest level that much more believable to a contemporary audience as a witness to the ambivalent culture in which we live (i.e., western culture in 1960). He has dared to confront us with the sheer gratuitousness of Grace as proclaimed by Christianity, with its flouting of *reasonableness*, of "adequate motivation" from a rationalistic standpoint. The risk, of course, is enormous: has Bergman gone over the edge, unconsciously (or even consciously) exposing his own dreadful difficulty in making that affirmation, his own other voice trying to scream out, "You see, it *is* absurd"?

WINTER LIGHT

There is no stopping Bergman now. One senses a personal pursuit pushed beyond anything else of the kind that has ever been experienced in the cinema, a pursuit of an understanding of Christ, of Christianity, and of their relevance in terms of his own life, "right now, the way I feel, in this culture, in 1962" (as it were).

"God is love" – is it that simple? *Winter Light* explores that question, and the probing is inexorable, pitiless, as Bergman's new-found aesthetic asceticism evolves well beyond its introductory phase as seen in *Through a Glass Darkly*. There is no music in this film, except for that which is part of the "diegetical context," as when the organ plays the hymn music in the little churches. To be sure, there are beautiful sounds – bells, the rushing waters of a river – and more mundane, heightened by their isolation: a car negotiating winter roads, a train, unlovely singing voices, Gunnar Björnstrand's flu-ridden, throaty raspings, Märta (Ingrid Thulin) snuffling, the shuffling of feet on wooden floors.

Winter Light nonetheless fairly glows with austere beauty; and this may seem paradoxical, given Sven Nykvist's accentuated asceticism of technique. Even the mildly semi-expressionistic dark shapes and hues of the previous film are gone, and with them the last remnants of Gunnar Fischer-isms. Except for a lovely, slow opening and an equally lovely closing montage of countryside shots of a church, Nykvist avoids the pictorial. He works with what seems to be the available Swedish winter light, achieving almost pastel greys that studiously avoid extremes. The winter light streaming through church windows, catching a face, a statue, a floor or pew or other woodwork, creates a cold glow, uniquely resplendent in its subdued way.

Within these severe parameters, Bergman nonetheless permits himself a few moments that do stand out, breaking the austere uniformity: a gradually intensifying lighting of the pastor against a window, until that light fairly scorches him as he is illuminated with a terrible "understanding"; several angled views of tortured crucifixes, reminiscent of those in *The Seventh Seal* and *The Virgin Spring*; and a few stunning tableaux of the pastor or Märta sculpted by streams of gentle light from a sun low on the Swedish horizon — these are the exceptions, and far removed indeed from anything smacking of the baroque.

The usual debate suffers on relentlessly. On the one hand, Blom, the sensualist, cynical, rationalist organist, cognizant of the generalized absurdity (empty churches, empty religion, empty life), mocks Tomas, who used to preach the "God is love" of Bergman's previous film finale (which he quotes verbatim). And he taunts Märta for her useless love for Pastor Tomas and for her wasted sacrifice. Opposed to him is the gentle and crippled sexton, Frövik, the good angel, this one, who understands his own suffering and is graced with insight. He it is who reveals to Pastor Tomas that Tomas's spiritual suffering, his feeling of emptiness, is but the mystical sharing in Christ's dreadful *spiritual* suffering during *His* passion, when He experiences the silence of His Father. "I mean God's silence," Frövik concludes.

This indeed has the ring of an extraordinary affirmation of traditional Christ-centred religious faith — and at the same time of a remarkably apt actualization of Jasper's shipwreck experience, that dreadful moment of the realization of nothingness which clears the way, in the Christian existentialist rhythm, for the intrusion of Grace and a new affirmation, an authentic experience of God.

Bergman goes even further along this path. After Frövik's words with Tomas, Bergman cuts to Märta. Alone, having heard the organist's cynical words, she sits, in close medium shot, at the back of the church, a dimly glowing window framing the usual cross motif in the background. She doggedly goes on loving Tomas, in spite of his rejection of her, and in spite of her atheistic rejection of his calling. Now she is quite overcome, prey to overwhelming emotion. The bells are ringing: she falls to her knees. Cut to a beautiful close-up of her face in profile, etched by the dim light from the window. Her hands are clasped, her bent forehead touching them. In a soft voice she entreats:

MÄRTA: If only we were sure ... so that we dared to show our affection. If only we believed in a truth ... if only we believed ...5

Meanwhile, Bergman intercuts Märta with Tomas, slumped over the desk in the sacristy. As if in answer, he rises. Frövik switches on the church light, and Tomas walks out of the sacristy into the church and over to the altar. He looks up at the crucifix, his back to us. Then, facing us in medium shot, his face inscrutable, he intones the opening words of evensong:

TOMAS: Holy, holy, holy, Holy is the Lord God almighty. Heaven and earth are full of His glory.[6]

Thus ends the film. From the point of view just adopted, here surely is Bergman's strongest affirmation yet of the Lutheran spirituality he grew up with. Or so it might seem ... except that other "readings" are possible. When Bergman was shooting the film in the autumn and winter of 1961–62 (it was released only in February of 1963), he stated in a number of interviews that he was pursuing his exploration of his understanding of God, *Winter Light* extending the development begun with *The Virgin Spring* and pursued in *Through a Glass Darkly*. He was dissatisfied at the time with what he felt was the latter film's forced, "insincere," too comfortable identification of God with love – all kinds of love. The reality was far more complex, more difficult: a more purified, unclear, (ambiguous?) expression was needed. And he felt he had found that, precisely, in *Winter Light*: a more authentic capturing of the reality.

However, in 1963, after *The Silence*, when the script of *Winter Light* was published in Swedish, Bergman seemed already to be revising his thinking. On the title page (as translated in the Evergreen English-language edition of 1970), Bergman writes:

The theme of these three films is a "reduction" – in the metaphysical sense of that word.
Through a Glass Darkly – certainty achieved.
Winter Light – certainty unmasked.
The Silence – God's silence – the negative impression.

The accent already seems more on rejection than affirmation. Later in the decade he would further negate what he had said during the shooting: now he admired *Winter Light* because it further revealed the impossibility of religious belief, and its destructive aspects. Indeed, with hindsight, and especially after

---

5 This is my reconstituting from the finalized film rather than the aforementioned screenplay, which is slightly different.

6 *Three Films*, 104.

seeing the films that he would direct during the 1960s (after *Winter Light*, that is), that reading of *Winter Light* becomes pretty convincing.

But that is through hindsight – Bergman's and our own. When *Winter Light* came out in early 1963, people tended to see it as bathed in ambiguity and ambivalence, an example of a cinema structured on "open signs" (and by that very fact a stunning example of film expressing the fractured modern sensibility, with its roots in Christian belief but with its awareness of other, modernist currents sapping the life blood from that belief). The "affirmative" reading I suggested above neglects what has already been pointed out, the extreme austerity of the overall texture of the film. The systematic rejection of formal celebration goes well beyond even that of *Through a Glass Darkly*, and the unrelieved feeling of the death of the spirit continues through the powerful closing affirmation. How far can one go in reaffirming a desperate faith when nowhere are to be found any signs of confirmation, any signs of life, hope, vitality, joy – nothing but *words*, which themselves ring with ambiguity?

"Holy, holy, holy" indeed. Is this an affirmation of faith, or a final withering irony, a confirmation of empty routine, death, meaninglessness? From the same data, that is, from the same open structuring of open signs, the believer and the non-believer can come to opposite conclusions.

THE SILENCE

Shot in the late summer of 1962, Ingmar Bergman's twenty-fifth feature film, *The Silence*, can be seen as marking the end of a long progression in his career, and, in a real sense, the beginning of another. Looking back at the "long progression" – and this may serve as a kind of review – we have observed Bergman gradually work his way into his overtly "metaphysical" period, which burst upon the world with *The Seventh Seal* in 1956. Up to then his films had been growing in formal mastery and in depth of expression, without yet, however, going all the way in the search for the meaning of life. Even if a solution of sorts tended to emerge through the affirmation of the life force, of nature and of human love, still, more or less hidden, there always lurked the presence of suffering, evil, and death, with the concomitant threat of meaninglessness – and by that very fact presaging a time when a more formal confrontation with the great metaphysical questions would constitute the essential thrust. That came, of course, with *The Seventh Seal*. For Bergman, this meant explicitly joining into the existentialist debate that had, since World War II, been playing so prominent a role in western European intellectual life: were the final words death/absurdity, or were they life/meaningfulness? It is more accurate, as we have seen, to speak about an ongoing dialectic between these opposites, bathed in the Christian sensibility, rich in Lutheran overtones, that was the fruit of Bergman's upbringing. And it is fair to say that, with more or less each suc-ceeding film, the life-affirming pole of this dialectic was finding an expression steadily growing in strength, clarity, and depth, attaining its peak (at least in terms of verbal affirmation) in *The Virgin Spring* and in *Through a Glass Darkly*.

One might even extend that progression into *Winter Light*. But as we have been seeing in this chapter, already by then the overall filmic communication had started darkening perilously, so much so that with *The Silence* one can legitimately question whether there is really any dialectic remaining. Can this film be incorporated into the long series? In any case, Bergman's films often seem to accommodate themselves happily enough to varieties of groupings ripe for intellectual appropriations. If one were to group the last three films (*Through a Glass Darkly*, *Winter Light*, *The Silence*) of the so-called meta-physical series – as, after the fact, they were grouped when they were published together in 1963 – then we do see a "theme of reduction," as Bergman himself put it. *Winter Light* can be seen as "reducing" the affirmation made in *Through a Glass Darkly*; and *The Silence* becomes the final reduction: "God's silence – the negative impression."

In that sense *The Silence* can legitimately be included in the metaphysical, call it even theological, series, because the central thrust is still a desperate search for meaningfulness, however pathetic that search may prove to be, and however overwhelmed the positive pole of the usual dialectic has become. In a very real sense, however, we have come to the end of *something*. With *The Silence*, the external world has crumbled into nightmare. Bergman, as Freud before him, now can no longer commune with the gods. And so, like Freud, he turns to the infernal regions of the mind. As Charles Ketcham puts it so beautifully: "we are in a position best described by Martin Heidegger's philos-ophy. It is 'neither atheism or theism, but a description of the world from which God is absent. It is now the night of the world ... the god has withdrawn himself, and the sun sets below the horizon.'"[7]

The night of the world indeed. Bergman's pursuit of a relatively austere, minimalist cinema would appear to have been short-lived. For in *The Silence*, Sven Nykvist demonstrates that he too can tilt, dolly, and travel with bravura, in a dark, dark world. This darkness and composition, however, are no longer created by spectacular, theatrical lighting effects, and the overall texture is too realistic to qualify as gothic or baroque. This may be nightmare, but it is the

---

7 Ketcham, *The Influence of Existentialism on Ingmar Bergman*, 186, quoting William Barrett's *Irrational Man* (Garden City, NY: 1962), 18. Ketcham in his existentialist placing of Bergman's films is especially rewarding in this particular period of Bergman's film output.

dark and dingy nightmare of the drab, everyday world, where reality itself is its own film noir.

So *The Silence* has its particular kind of austerity, the austerity that breathes death. Bergman limits the speaking characters to three: two sisters holed up with the twelve-year-old son of one of them in a decrepit, formerly grand hotel. The city is Timoka: Bergman has invented it, as he has the language of the inhabitants (which we rarely hear spoken). We seem to be in a kind of nightmare caricature, call it the East European drab of the cold war years. Once in a while the child wanders out of the rooms, through the long hotel corridors, or we are given glimpses of city streets on which grey, more or less faceless citizens shuffle along. A tank rumbles by, making the hotel rooms quake. We are afforded an episode in a vaudeville theatre, another in a restaurant where Anna, the boy's mother, picks up a waiter to satisfy her sexual needs.

The Silence seethes with sexual frustration: Anna (Gunnel Lindblom) is a sullen nymphomaniac, quite possibly the object of lesbian desires in her sister, Ester (Ingrid Thulin). Ester is a spinster, a repressed woman of intellectual dedication whose sexual frustration finds release in masturbation, as she babbles somewhat incoherently about her loathing for all matters sexual, especially male. She is stricken with a terrible lung disease, perhaps near death, as Bergman graphically demonstrates in two harrowing suffocation attacks.

There is a feeling of bitterness and loathing in this picture of two sisters mortally wounding each other, as Bergman returns with a vengeance to his brilliant psychological probing of the female psyche. All the classic oppositions in personality typology might prove relevant here: or are we witnessing two aspects of the same personality?

But there is another character, the boy of about twelve. Time and again the movie gives the impression of being seen through his eyes, with a camera observing from his eye level, guided by his wandering through the rooms and corridors. A troop of Spanish-speaking dwarfs (seven of them, naturally!), in Timoka with their vaudeville act, add a theatre of the absurd touch, vaguely sympathetic to the child, but also – and this extends into the sexual – vaguely threatening. And a tall, spindly, semi-grotesque, elderly *maître d'hôtel* completes the picture – kindly, sympathetic, trying to help the child and Ester, but of course his words sounding like gibberish to them. His formal dark attire reminds us of Bergman's priest figures. And for those who cannot resist the delights of direct, immediate interpretation, he could serve as Bergman's wonderfully ironic symbol of what God the Father and the Christian church are today.

So, there is the horror of the adult world (the two sisters, the dehumanized drabness of Timoka), the inability to communicate humanly, and a somewhat disconnecting other level of vision – whether it be a child's-eye view, or what seems to be Bergman's courting of placelessness, rootlessness, a gratuitousness bordering on the absurd.

But *The Silence* is the kind of film that invites one to indulge in shorthand caricature painting by unduly stressing its dominant dark, grotesque, absurdist texture. The fact is that in keeping with its predecessors it does maintain the dialectic. There *is* another side: Bergman makes us experience a haunting absence. We feel it in the natural beauty of the two actresses playing the sisters, and in the magnitude of their performances. Even the selfish, sensual Anna communicates her distress, her suffering thirst for life. The stricken Ester, austere and intellectual, has heartbreaking moments of wrenching emotional power as she gasps for life. Her love for her little nephew touches us in their shared complicity and in her trying to teach him the very few words (five of them, three of which mean "face," "hand," "spirit") that she has managed to decipher.

There *is* communication, not only between Ester and the boy, but between them and the solicitous *maître d'*. He has Ester listen to the music of Bach, which transcends all the boundaries, bringing harmony and peace – and communion. And he tries to take care of Ester in her suffering.

Even in this harsh and difficult psychological probing of the pysches of two women in what seems to be the most one-sided of Bergman films, the old dialectical battle endures. And especially at the very end. Ester, too weak, has to be left behind in the hotel, in the care of the old man, as the boy and his mother are in a train compartment returning to Sweden. The boy is reading a letter which he jealously guards. It has been given him by Ester, and it contains the few words she has been able to master of that strange language, and which he is trying to mouth.

Earlier on, we have learned what the one word he does say aloud – "*Hadjek*" – means: spirit. Meanwhile, his mother has opened the window. The rain beats down on the racing train, cooling, cleansing her face.

"The end of a long progression"? In *The Silence* Bergman created his most desperate metaphor yet for the human condition. He was now unquestionably to be numbered among the Dark Poets, the Dark Philosophers, who were such powerful voices in the western culture of the 1950s and '60s "It is now the night of the world ... the god has withdrawn himself, and the sun sets below the horizon."[8]

Gone is any talk about God, or any mention, for that matter, of any formalized religious quest. In the context, however, of the manner in which I have situated the films made after 1955, *The Silence* demands some kind of religious or theological/philosophical placing. (And, of course, just about any film

---

8 Ketcham, *The Influence of Existentialism on Ingmar Bergman*.

can be submitted to an analysis run along religious hermeneutical lines.) Well, up to a point, that has been the task of this present chapter: I have approached *The Silence* as an artistic expression of modernism at its most acute state of crisis in the quest for meaning – or, more precisely, as the last gasp of existentialism's dialectical battle between meaningfulness and absurdity.

But one can go further; and at this phase of Bergman's evolution it is most apt to do so precisely at the religious level. On the one hand, *The Silence* reflects the extreme expression of Martin Luther's darkest and most desperate vision of human existence. Whatever may be the definitive, all-encompassing interpretation of Luther's views on justification and on humanity's sinfulness, one thing in his religious writing is inescapable – his deep pessimism about "natural man's" depravity, man's inability to do anything good on his own. Luther's own terrifying experience of inner anguish had convinced him of humanity's desperate state: on their own, humans, reprobate as they are, are destined to hell. So much for human effort unaided, and for worldly achievements, the creations and works of men and women. Thus, Bergman's dark images and angst-ridden faces reflect a long tradition, as does his apparently total lack of interest in human achievement in the social, political, ideological arena.[9]

The other side of Luther (and of Northern European Protestantism as well), however, is also manifested powerfully in the Bergman films we have been dealing with. And that is the irresistibly felt need for salvation, the conviction that God's grace alone can save the human person. One of the ways this need is manifested in story-telling is through a kind of "Christian" archetypal narrative which is structured precisely to accommodate that imperative: the fundamental thrust of the story is directed to "saving" the protagonist. It is when such a conclusion remains unachieved that we have the experience of tragedy (or damnation).

One feels this positive earnestness driving the Bergman stories. Time and again towards the end of plot after plot the Bergman characters, against terrible psychological odds and certainly against all rational probabilities and without convincing cause-and-effect relationships (at least according to the rules of "correct" plot structuring), are given their chance; and many of them make a

---

9 Consult, for example, Martin Luther's *The Freedom of a Christian*, in John Dillenberger's edition of *Martin Luther* (Garden City: Anchor/Doubleday, 1961), 42–86. This dark side of Lutheranism – which is not all Lutheranism, one adds hastily – has continued to influence some North European Protestantism and its offshoots, including major thinkers such as Soren Kierkegaard. For a systematic, much fuller exploration of this question, see Richard Aloysius Blake's *The Lutheran Milieu of the Films of Ingmar Bergman* (Evanston, IL: Arno Press Cinema Program, 1972).

profound, life-restoring breakthrough. (One could add that the Lutheran and the Christian existentialist "rhythms" converge here.) This has been the essential Bergman narrative from the beginning, whether the terms of reference are explicitly religious or not. Thus, in Bergman's first feature filmscript (*Torment*, directed by Alf Sjöberg in 1944), the young man suddenly is freed from his spiritual death: the sun shines, the music swells, he can go on with life. Marie, the ballerina in *Summer Interlude*, at the lowest moment of *her* despair suddenly recaptures the joy of life; and the whole filmic texture, complete with choreographed dance, joins in celebration. The most explicitly religious (and Christian) expressions of this, of course, occur in *The Virgin Spring* and (far more soberly and sombrely) in *Through a Glass Darkly*. Even *Winter Light* and *The Silence* can be seen as following this ritual, though the affirmation is drastically diminishing, even, as we have seen, to the point of quasi-extinction. One might say that Bergman is driven to save his characters because that is the only hope in life: that is what the Lutheran God does (we hope) for us. The very narrative, to put it differently, cannot totally capitulate to absurdity, whatever the evidence from our absurd human existence might seem to indicate.

Those who have criticized Bergman's "imposed hope" endings seem by and large to have missed this point. Bergman was criticized for the "unmotivated" resolving of his protagonists' problems, especially in the overtly religious films. And, of course, for not being "relevant," for not addressing "contemporary" problems in a "modern" way, that is, within the context of the social, political, ideological reality of the day. In other words, Bergman was the victim of a kind of critical ideological closure, which created parameters narrowed to the rationalisms underlying a certain political relevance.

The fact of the matter – and it has been the task of this section to demonstrate this – is that in the larger context of western culture nothing could be further from the truth: Bergman indeed was at the heart of the contemporary cultural maelstrom. This only becomes more evident when one adverts to the fact that even his overtly "God movies" were not so much a statement of his belief in the Christian God as an expression of the effort of contemporary human beings to affirm the existence of such a God in the very face of the doubt: the old wisdom versus the modern awareness and experiencing in a context of existentialist crisis. For a time the affirmation grows; then it diminishes, so that in *The Silence* not only is God silent but also God's prized creation, the human being, is reaching the point of silence.

In the context of this evolution within a broad-based view of European culture, a claim made at the beginning of this exploration may appear more meaningful: it is indeed to Bergman's considerable credit that he is one of the rare film artists who reflected *both* mainline cultural streams after World War II –

his version of the older Christian heritage shared by countless millions, and his version of the modern spirit that rejects that vision. His movies were nothing less than an arena for the agonizing conflict that, consciously or not, besets contemporary men and women, and which centres on the flesh-and-blood, life-and-death issues underlying such questions as "What is life today?" and "How do I live?"

I have deliberately been using the past tense just now as I write about the films ending with *The Silence*. That is because, in the culture of the early 1960s, those questions and concerns were finding radically different formulations. Even the grounding of the cultural debate was changing. True to his (unavowed) prophetic role, Bergman could not fail to respond: he too would reflect that changed emphasis, in a radically altered cinematic creation of his own.

NOW ABOUT THESE WOMEN

Over the years Erland Josephson has played a major role in Bergman's creative life. The two men's friendship and collaborations date back to their university days. In 1963 Ingmar became head of the Royal Dramatic Theatre, Sweden's most prestigious playhouse and theatre company; and when he resigned in late 1966, it was Erland who replaced him. By the 1970s Erland would become Ingmar's main male protagonist. Their collaborations in theatre and television have continued to this day. In the early sixties, the two friends, under the pseudonym "Buntel Eriksson," actually wrote two screenplays together, *The Pleasure Garden* (1961), directed by Alf Kjellin, and *Now About These Women*, directed by Bergman in 1963 and released a year later. Neither ranks among film history's masterpieces.

Perhaps to digress ... the Greeks at the height of their classical theatre period, we are told, would hold religious festivals during which were performed three tragedies, to be followed by a farce. Is this, one wonders, how best to explain the film that would follow the trilogy, Bergman's inconsequential bit of bitter soufflé that fell flat as a pancake? *Now About These Women* features a large, impressive cast – Jarl Kulle and three of Bergman's most gifted and best-known actresses (Eva Dahlbeck, Bibi Andersson, and Harriet Andersson) – working in lavish sets and (a first for Bergman) shot in colour. Alas, however, this is one of those films that loses its way, something totally atypical of Bergman's mature work. *Now About These Women* comes across as a hydra-headed amalgam, seemingly a comic satire, a slapstick sex romp, and a commentary on the *artist* (and hence on Bergman himself?), and, quite likely, incorporating a confusing commentary on all those beautiful actresses with whom Bergman was involved over the years. What emerges, finally and overwhelmingly, is a strident and embarrassing attack on the impotence, pomposity, and inanity of critics, or at least those who had made Bergman's life miserable. There may be a salutary point somewhere in all of this; but the sad truth, most agree, is that *Now About These Women* does not truly connect with anything in any meaningful, let alone delightful, way. Certainly it furnishes neither the type of magical moments referred to earlier on, nor food for rumination about contemporary culture.

One might be tempted to see in *The Silence* and the failed *Now About These Women* signs that Bergman was experiencing some deep personal crisis, or that he was artistically adrift. Biographical detail may prove enlightening: it was about this time, after all, that he was plunging into the million and one duties that went with being head of the Royal Dramatic. Add to that a bout of serious illness that hospitalized him, contributing seriously to a two-year filmmaking hiatus. There were fears that he was suffering burn-out. Time, however, would demonstrate that his powers as an artist were not threatened. A "new Bergman" was soon to astound the film world.

CHAPTER FIVE

INGENTING ... OR ALMOST

Persona	filming July – September 1965 release October 1966
Hour of the Wolf	filming May – September 1966 release February 1968
Shame (*The Shame*)	filming September – November 1967 release September 1968
The Rite (*The Ritual*)	filming May – June 1968 release (TV) March 1969
The Passion of Anna (*A Passion*)	filming September – October 1968 release November 1969

Before *Persona* Bergman was incarnating a cultural struggle very much part of the post–World War II climate, extending it as far as he could in the most personal and yet broadly relevant terms of reference, adhering to an aesthetic adapted to that – an aesthetic that, relatively speaking, remained somewhat traditional, however profoundly he was evolving within those established parameters.

But with *Persona* Bergman bursts out of these parameters, very much in the manner that the 1960s may be said to have exploded with expressions of a new sensibility. That is what we shall be exploring as we follow the evolution of this artist witness to his times.

If, by 1965, Bergman had indeed exhausted his particular line of questioning, and/or if the dialectical polarity structuring the existentialist debate no longer served its purpose – for the simple reason that the desperate need to continue positing an affirmative answer to his quest for meaningfulness no longer corresponded to his own deepest inner reality – we can truthfully speak of a creative impasse.

But one must remember that we are now dealing with the 1960s, when vast areas of the overall culture were experiencing enormous changes. I have been referring to the decades after the war as "modernism at the stage of acute crisis," and I have tried to situate and demonstrate Ingmar Bergman's own particular filmic participation in that cultural phenomenon, in terms precisely of the existentialist debate ravaging the spirit of modernism. Before plunging into the "new" phase, however – and in order, also, not to muddy the issue by imprecise use of labels – it bears repeating that Bergman, in a sense, can never be claimed to have adhered to the tenets of the "positive" side of modernism. Yes, he did share in and feel the modernists' acute awareness of crisis in our culture; but for Bergman that sharing was still from the perspective of the "old verities," from the basically theological point of view. For him the dominant metaphor for the crisis of our times was the abyss: humanity stranded in a world without God, without order, cause and effect, canons of beauty, truth, or goodness upon which to structure our lives.[1] By contrast, most "real" modernists

---

1   See Allan Megill, *Prophets of Extremity* (Berkeley, CA: University of California Press, 1985), xiii. I am much indebted to his descriptive formulations of the world views and cultural movements I am presently discussing.

had replaced the old verities with "modern" systems of belief. At the beginning of the twentieth century these tended increasingly to be centred on Freud, Marx, and Darwin, who elicited the most vital expressions of the still-enduring Enlightenment faith in the ability of "science" to explain the world and human beings and to lead us up to ever-new plateaus of fulfilment. Essentially, a liberal materialistic society was the idea, based on scientific progress, worked out strictly in *this* world's historical time – that evolutionary reality which "emerges when eternal standards collapse and *nothing is left outside the flux of historical time.*"

Bergman, steeped as we have seen in a certain brand of Lutheranism that distrusts secular achievement, could never embrace the rationalist optimism of the Enlightenment, nor could he adhere to the new myths, neither Marxist nor even Freudian, in spite of his amazing intuitiveness in matters psychological and the key role they play in his artistic creations.

"Modernist optimism" is nowadays almost a contradiction in terms: the security furnished by modernism's "positive" affirmations was always considerably less than that afforded by the great metaphysical *ab-aeterno* framework of the traditional view. By the rules of the new game, modernist tenets were always evolving, shifting, one set of icons replacing the next. Hence, a good deal of insecurity was endemic to the new territory, especially since the "new" world was experienced as revolving about anything but a "God of Love." Darwin, Marx, Freud – biological determinism and its survival of the fittest, the inevitable conflict of the classes, and the almost unavowable drives of the subconscious – were not exactly reassuring harbingers. One might indeed see them as the nurturing ground for crisis.

In any case, with the ending of World War II, the very belief in historical progress, with its energizing affirmation that human reason in its most ennobling expression, science, would continue to lead humankind onward and upward, was eroding dramatically. So here was a double-barrelled cultural crisis, however we might describe, define, or explain it. Existentialism was one response, with either an anguished reaffirmation of the need of a God as an answer, or, with the avowal of ultimate universal absurdity, the loss of all faith, religious and/or secular.

It was not all existential anguish, to be sure. Quite possibly, the vast majority of people making up the "western world" were still shaped by a fundamentally theocentric culture, willy-nilly. But for most of the "official" thinkers, the philosophers, the scientists, the artists – those who assume the task of expressing and shaping the culture – the contemporary *Zeitgeist* was shot through with notions growing out of a vastly different understanding and sensibility. God as centre, or even "man" as centre, and time, space, causality – how could these stand up to Einstein's relativity, or Freud's almost irrepressible libido force, hidden in all of us under a rather pathetic conscious ego front?

The undetermined was now an accepted category of knowledge, and perceptual ambiguities became a way of understanding life. Transactional psychology, for example, with its subjective ordering of external stimuli into formal patterns of recognition and value, and information theory, with its demonstration that transgression of the code, in chasing away banality, thereby increases the quantity of information – here were further instances demonstrating that the relative was eroding the bases of stability. Roland Barthes was redefining the parameters of aesthetic pleasure: the glory of the novel and of all art lay in the dizzying interplay of signifiers coupling and uncoupling in fresh configurations, indefinitely expanding and shifting shapes and patterns and possibilities of signification – that is the way he was writing about it in *Le degré zéro de l'écriture*, and so on.

And philosophy? For how many of its practitioners, unable to affirm that our intellectual apparatus is attuned to capturing "external reality" to some substantial degree, was the exercise of philosophical thinking reduced to studying how the mind works, or rather how language functions, since that, and only that, can we lay claim to really appropriating? Linguistics and its Frankenstein offspring, semiotics (the study of signs), were thus triumphant, reducing for many what had once been an (almost) infinitely larger field.

The explosion of "subversive" art forms, inimical to the fixed and stable, was a living, expanding metaphor for it all – serial music, moving sculpture, action painting, theatrical happenings (and, anyway, decades before, had not James Joyce's *Ulysses* and *Finnigans Wake* indicated the path?). Umberto Eco summed it up brilliantly in his 1962 book, *Opera aperta* (*The Open Work*),[2] demonstrating the extent to which the art of that period was consciously and explicitly dedicated to subverting certain "classical" artistic canons – the work of art as complete, perfect, round, blessed with clarity, equilibrium and order – and embracing in their place the informal, the non-structured, the undetermined, "disorder," "chance." Eco found an apt label for this kind of art, dedicated, as he put it, to the creation of "the open work."

The open work and similar notions – when one goes in for broad generalizations, as I have been doing, inevitably much that is essential is overlooked. For example, I am focusing now on the 1960s, while many of these tendencies,

---

2 Bompiani, 1962. The French translation *L'Oeuvre ouverte* (Paris: Editions du Seuil, 1962), proved prodigiously illuminating for me as I struggled to achieve my Sorbonne doctoral work on Jean-Luc Godard's "open cinema." Eco, by the way, less than twenty years later would put what he preached into practice in his immensely well received novel, *The Name of the Rose*.

obviously, had already found expression in one way or another in the '50s or earlier. Moreover, by no means everyone was attuned to, much less understood or felt comfortable with, what was going on. I have not done justice to the proliferation of variations within these movements, and certainly have not alluded to the nuances and contradictions. Finally, I have not even mentioned many of the much-heralded aspects that have come to characterize the '60s: the contestatory political climate, the "return to nature," psychedelia, drugs, hard rock, mod London, the whole "radical" lifestyle.

The essential point, however, is clear enough: "the West," in the 1960s, was undergoing a psycho-social revolution. And that, of course, was affecting movies. Already, as previously mentioned, different manifestations of the cinema had been "discovered" in the '50s and a bit earlier – neo-realism in Italy, the Japanese, the Poles, Bergman himself and the early Fellini, the Angry Young Men in England. And as the '60s were being ushered in, so were the various new political cinemas in Italy, Brazil, Canada, and so on, and the Hungarians, Satyajit Ray, later on the Czechs – on and on it goes during this, the richest ten or fifteen years of film history. The Underground was surfacing, vital as never before in the U.S. Perhaps most tellingly (at least at the level of "quality" feature movies), Antonioni was creating a whole new film aesthetic with *L'Avventura*, *La Notte*, and so on, serving as Eco's specific film examples of "the open work." Pasolini, Bertollucci, and others were set to follow – and Fellini himself with $8^1/2$ (1963) would stun the world with a masterpiece that symbolized that whole era of self-conscious cinema. Finally (to end yet another series of sweeping overviews), France's "Nouvelle Vague" would practically write a manifesto for its own cinema, formally and "officially" dedicated to the creation of new, free, open movie-making. Truffaut would put it into practice in his playful, more subtle manner, Resnais in his monumental and mysterious puzzles; and of course the impudent, tongue-in-cheek, irrepressible, fractured iconoclast, Jean-Luc Godard, would achieve symbol status, his entire cinema a commentary on film and everything else, enunciating the credo that "the adventure of the contemporary cinema is the adventure of *cinematic language*."

Speaking of film language – in the early '60s a new discipline that would revolutionize film studies all over the western world was being developed in Paris by Christian Metz and his disciples: film semiotics (semiology). Henceforth (it was claimed) film was to be appropriated by its study as a functioning text, as a discourse created by the structuring of cinematic signs.

Now is not the time to go into this: suffice it to claim that the implications for the cinema were profound. A new kind of discussion was being shaped, at once filmic and more broadly cultural. Coincidentally (?), during this brief decade or so Hollywoood's world domination was being sorely threatened, and the control of filmmaking was shifting to the film directors, away from the domination of producers and the mammoth studios – and *their* interpretation of "economic realities." For a while.

And, in all of this, what about the Swede whose name was synonymous with artistic cinema? The intuitive artist in Ingmar Bergman could not but respond to the stimuli emanating from this cultural maelstrom. Moreover, as a film lover he could not be unaware of what was happening in cinema. His own dramatic evolution in film language through *Through a Glass Darkly* and *Winter Light* now seemed tame compared to what was happening in western culture. Besides, his own way of structuring and formulating his flesh-and-blood artistic expressions of life's problematic seemed to have reached a point of impasse, to have been superseded even in his own mind.

Bergman's response would be *Persona*.

PERSONA

Persona is a remarkable incarnation of one of the darkest, most desperate aspects of the 1960s culture. The very nature of art as communication is subverted. And one might extend that to the concept of existence itself. *Persona* is a bewildering succession of mesmerizing images begging for interpretation. And that precisely is what Bergman will deny us the satisfaction of achieving – a fact which in itself may be highly revelatory.

On first viewing, *Persona* is indeed bewildering. For those for whom interpretation of story and character is the beginning, middle and end of film "analysis," it proves to be a most frustrating experience. If, however, one concentrates on the sights and sounds, on how they are put together, and above all on how they are structured into some kind of "functioning text," one may begin to understand what is "really going on"; and the film then becomes a creative viewing experience, open to a plethora of connotations.

A good way to start is to unearth the different levels of the "narrative" – if plot, narrativity, story can be affirmed as having any kind of validity at all in this artistic construct. *Persona* in this sense becomes a set of Chinese boxes or Russian dolls, each box or doll containing, and in turn being contained by, another box or doll – even if this analogy is repeatedly done violence to in one way or another. From a slightly different but parallel point of view, one might speak of a series of levels of "being," or rather of "being perceived."

Say that the "main" box, the one that moviegoers habitually give themselves to, is the diegetical context: the story, the characters, the world contained by the movie. Thus, in a Stockholm hospital, Nurse Alma (Bibi Andersson) is attending Elisabet (Liv Ullmann), a famous actress who has lost the ability, or at least the desire, to speak. The doctor, explaining to Elisabet (and to us) her reading of the case, sends patient and nurse to a comfortable, isolated house by the sea on the island of Fårö, in the hope that the relaxed and intimate new surroundings will exercise their therapeutic magic. The story follows the evolution of their relationship.

Within this box, however, is (literally) another tiny box, a television set – which, seen from another perspective, is really a larger, outside box, of course, revealing a far bigger world, the mediated "world reality outside." *Persona* was made in 1965 and released in 1966, remember; what the TV reflects is the Vietnam war: specifically, what has become an icon of suffering of our mid-century, the self-immolation of a Buddhist monk, witnessed repeatedly by Elisabet in horrified fascination in her hospital room. Later on, on Fårö, she gazes in anguish and guilt at a photograph also stamped on our collective psyche: a little Jewish boy being rounded up in the ghetto by the Nazis.

So call these the first two boxes of (more or less) the diegetical "reality." Elisabet may be contemplating contemporary mediated reality. But *someone* is controlling Elisabet and her story: this is box 3, a very discreet one – the voice-over of narrator Ingmar Bergman (himself) informing us at the appropriate moment (and thereby covering a sizable hiatus in the narrative) that Elisabet and Nurse Alma have indeed gone to Fårö. And at the end of the film, he and cinematographer Sven Nykvist are seen shooting a film (?) with Elisabet, though this is none too clear: Elisabet, the doctor had told us early in the film, stopped talking during a *theatre* performance of *Electra* … and here she is, in what seems like her Electra makeup, being *filmed* in the same role?

Bergman, however, is far from through with his structuring game. Box 4: Before he gets into any of this, we see what seems to be an unfocused face in huge close-up, no, *two* faces which Bergman dissolves back and forth into each other, and which we eventually recognize – at least in hindsight – as those of Bibi Andersson and Liv Ullmann, or Alma and Elisabet. This segment is repeated very briefly at the end of the film, when the Alma/Elisabet story is "completed."

But all of this is contained by yet another "reality," call it box 5. Those faces are being experienced by yet someone else, who is, well … We see, as part of some kind of introduction, cold grey shots of what seem to be hospital grounds, and then of an adolescent boy lying on a cot, covered with a white sheet and reading a book. In a hospital emergency ward, a morgue, on those grounds? He is surrounded by other, presumably dead, bodies. An old woman's eyes pop open, though, at the sound of loud, prolonged telephone rings. This is the same boy Bergman aficionados have seen in *The Silence*; and, myopically, through his glasses, he peers at us in the audience, or is it at the camera?

Then he looks at what seems to be a movie screen, reaching out gropingly with his hand: we see what he sees, the unfocused face(s) just referred to.

Box 5 is not the final "container." Before we see the boy and the hospital grounds, the screen, backgrounded by threatening, dramatic "concrete" music, explodes in box 6's montage of images from well-known Bergman themes – a crucified hand, a spider, and so on – and from other films, some of them recognizable – the slicing of a sheep's eye (referring back to Bunuel's *Un Chien Andalou*), and slapstick silent-era cartoon bits (including a death figure) used in Bergman's early feature, *Prison*. Parts of that montage flash by again during the credits and around the middle of the film.

With box 7 Bergman goes about as far as he can go. *Persona* actually begins with a close-up of the carbon arcs of a movie projector being ignited, followed up by a closeup of film stock flickering through the projector's aperture. We see that aperture bit again, along with some film stock actually melting, some-where near the middle of the film; and the "final *finale*" of the movie reverses the opening figuration, ending with the extinguishing of the carbon arcs. That's it: the film is terminated, from darkness back to darkness.

The boxes-within-boxes metaphor may prove helpful in grasping Bergman's overall structuring of *Persona*, at least in the sense of establishing the different levels of what the spectator is seeing and hearing. But this is something beyond the grasp of anyone, I believe, during a first experiencing of the film. Rather, it is the fruit of repeated "laboratory controlled" analytical viewings. And it hard-ly leads to any "full" understanding of what has been going on.

Bergman very obviously is subverting any such possibility. For example, he brutally invades the "main," diegetical box (no. 2?) with elements from the other boxes, wrenching our viewer consciousness out of the story flow. Moreover, the story is further done violence to through a variety of means. Elisabet actually photographs us – the audience/film camera – a few times; both characters take turns in looking at each other – but also at the camera/audience – straight in the eye. Strange things happen within the story: Elisabet's blind husband (Gunnar Björnstrand) appears: mistakenly (it seems) he makes love to Alma, with the connivance of Elisabet, standing, film-direc-tor-like, close behind them. There is an eerie sleep-walking (?) scene when Elisabet seems to join Alma – surely (?) this is all dream, imagination, thought projection, or the unconscious? Sometimes the dialogue is repeated "without reason." Or, "outside the story," the film stock breaks; or two halves, one from each actress's face, are joined in a composite close-up. And so on.

Where is traditional filmmaking in all of this? If the '60s at their most heady were a time of art's disintegrating and reintegrating in novel juxtapositionings, then (to put it mildly) *Persona* passes the test. At forty-seven years of age, the master of film form is now truly "attuned to the times," dedicated to the subverting of classical filmmaking, a poet of the self-conscious open form. And precisely because of that mastery of film form, he is in *Persona* probably pushing the process further, at the time, than any other renowned feature filmmaker.

What I have just written might seem to indicate that *Persona*'s fascination is exerted pretty strictly at the intellectual level, a kind of super-sophisticated jigsaw puzzle, brilliant in any number of ways but fabricated essentially to titillate the mind – not to touch the heart. But that is not so. *Persona* is a movie richly laden with what I described earlier on as "Bergman moments" – and hence that includes power, magic, and emotion. Time and again the spectator is mesmerized by visions of beauty, or mystery, or suffering, drawn in irresistibly by the enchanter's art.

The temptation here would be to celebrate any number of these scenes and to go in depth into at least one of them, as I did when dealing with *The Seventh Seal*. Has Bergman, for example, ever matched that night scene in the Fårö house: Alma is asleep in a bedroom bathed in impressionistic non-definition, as the Swedish summer light filters through like a haunting mist; and we hear the stillness beautifully punctated by the muffled sound of a muted foghorn. A spectral apparition floats into our perception: Elisabet comes silently to Alma's bed. Alma, it seems, awakens, and unprotestingly is helped out of bed. The two women, Elisabet's arm around Alma's shoulders, move to a mirror, captured almost in close-up as their faces all but meld. What exactly happens we cannot tell, but one feels the audience suspended in a breathless state, bewitched. Gnawing at the edges of our consciousness, fleeting connotations suggest … what? tenderness? love? lesbian overtones? a metaphor of the subconscious or unconscious? is this an impressionistic vampire film, one personality consuming the other? the fusing of two personalities into one? the different sides of the same personality fleetingly merging? It is all so ethereal, so beautiful, so deeply, vaguely menacing, so mysterious … an open sign if ever there was, recalled in part near the end of the film by Alma as she looks into the mirror. And of course Bergman does not seek to explain anything by any of the rationalistic "motivating" habitually serving this purpose in your usual "well-made" movie.

Each of the many memorable moments enjoys its own uniqueness, its own special brand of magic power. This is the old Bergman pulling out the stops, but with a new ambiguity. On another summer evening, for example, we see the two women sitting in a room. In another *tour de force* Bergman has Alma doing all the talking in the film (except for two brief moments, previously alluded to, with the doctor and with Elisabet's husband), while Elisabet "only" listens and looks and reacts (mostly inwardly). Alma, feeling the liberating effects of the wine she is sipping, relates a sexual episode from the past when she and another young woman seduced two teenage boys on a deserted beach. Bibi Andersson, in what may be the role of her career, goes through the moods, leading us from what could be a prurient, voyeuristic experience into a deep and compassionate personal involvement, sharing, to an extent, Alma's fascination, her vulnerability, her anguish and guilt, her cry for absolution and for a sense of meaningfulness in life. And Liv Ullmann, nothing short of astonishing in her first Bergman movie, looks on, beautiful, inscrutable. Compassionate or cold? Judging or liberating? God or vampire? The artist exploiting, betraying the trust of a confidante who so wants to be her friend but who is being reduced to mere grist for the artist's mill?

Sven Nykvist revels in what is a cameraman's feast as he captures his two beautiful actresses in endless compositional and lighting variations. And not all of it is ethereal and impressionistic, as time after time the grain of the image grows coarse and the background harsh and jagged, for example, on some rock-strewn Fårö beach. Nykvist may be true to his aesthetic of simple effects, but rarely has a film so excelled in image celebration.

There are other, searing moments, created to a great extent by technical legerdemain. Bergman dares the "impossible" in another terrifying outburst of cinematic audacity: he begins with each face in close-up, perfectly divided by light and dark in complementary fashion; then he joins both lit halves, forming a new, "third" physiognomy. A metaphor for personality merging, of course: and it is seen as something unendurable, its force heightened by the cruel concrete music in the background. This is cinematic violence at the artistic level, truly upsetting and totally achieved by artificial cinematic means, the product of Bergman the prestidigitator at his most exuberant and yet most deliberate.

It is this power to enthral and this communicating of moments so rich in human resonance that force the spectator to fall into spontaneous habits of interpreting, to explain the personal relevance of the experience – in spite of the countless distancing devices described earlier. We simply want to know "what it means"; and that generally is translated into centring the meaning on the two protagonists. "What in heaven's name is this film all about?" tends, in other words, to mean focusing on the diegetical context, and especially on the story as it pertains to Elisabet and to Alma.

At least – and this is not at all surprising – that seems to have been the path followed by most interpreters. It would prove highly interesting to review the interpretations arrived at by any number of critics or film analysts: each one comes with his or her point of view, system of hermeneutics, mind-set, personal experiences, whatever. And much of this can prove highly enriching, contributing to this or that aspect of the movie. What one might categorize as primarily psychological theories tend to dominate; I have already referred to a number of them – such as the two women being two facets of the same person, or one personality being absorbed by another, or the problematic interrelationship between the rational and the irrational, the conscious and the subconscious, the id and the superego. For some, the whole story takes place only in Alma's mind.

It is not all psychological interpreting, of course, even though many of these interpretations tend to criss-cross or briefly become one. Others, pursuing Bergman's God thematic, see Elisabet as a benign God figure, respecting Alma's freedom, helping her tear away her false rationalizations and superficiality. Or she may be a version of the cruel Spider God, toying with his/her creature. Vampirism of one kind or another is another possibility. That, of course, comes close to Bergman's guilt feelings about how artists exploit people. Or is it art freeing the bourgeois from her illusions of doing good and leading a well-ordered life? One could pursue these and other paths … One conclusion seems unavoidable: the very nature of the cinematic signs used by Bergman, that is, his choice of materials (including "narrative" and "themes") and the way he presents them, seems to encourage all manner of understandings and, yes, interpretations.

The flip side of that particular conclusion could be that *no* definitive interpretation is possible, at least in the sense of adequately explaining the "total" film. And that is what makes the last word voiced in the film, the only word uttered by Elisabet, so bitter and tragic: *ingenting* … nothing.

We do not really know how the film ends: what does happen to Alma and to Elisabet? Has either been helped in any way by the experience? Far more upsetting (at least in terms of habitual expectations) is a rather more fundamental question: has either character "really" existed? Or are they mere figments of the imagination of the boy of box 5, as he reaches out to those two screen images dissolving back and forth – the adolescent reaching out for woman, the abandoned son for Elisabet? Is it Bergman the child/artist, reaching out to his own mother (so distant, as he has told us), or exploring his confusion about "all his women," even about the very important real-life women, one who has shared, the other who is beginning to share, his life, Bibi Andersson and Liv Ullmann?[3]

3 *Persona* marks the beginning of Bergman's personal involvement with Liv Ullmann, as well as of their professional collaboration. Bibi Andersson enjoyed that status earlier on, as well as remaining, off and on, an important friend and artistic collaborator in film and theatre. Indeed, Sven Nykvist was smiling as he described for me everyone's (including his own) special, bewitching, confused mind space during the shooting of the film on Fårö.

One must have multiple approaches, it is safe to assert, when dealing with *Persona*. But here too there are pitfalls: whatever approach one may take, downright contradictions tend to emerge; or, at least, no interpretation seems capable of including "everything" and is reduced to skipping what cannot be truly accommodated to whatever specific theory is actually in play. Bergman throws in plenty of monkey wrenches.

And that may be the point, or at least one of the fundamental points of this movie.

Bergman claims that he wanted to name the film *Cinematografet* (Swedish for cinematography) but that he was dissuaded (perhaps wisely) by Svensk Filmindustri, the production house. That title may point the way to a concept vast and indefinite enough to encompass what he is up to. For here is a movie, it seems to me, whose very subject matter is filmmaking, its process, the technology, the play of light, the interplay of screen and subjectivity for both filmmaker and audience, film consciousness and reflexivity, the complex and indeterminate sources of inspiration, the themes, subjects, narrativity, the role of art and of the artist, the truth/lie that is cinema, its power on others and yet its emptiness – and beyond that, the ability/inability to communicate and to relate to anything, and perhaps even the ultimate avowal of nothingness.

Not that Bergman has never touched upon these questions before: on the contrary, they have been at least implicit in just about all his movie work. His overt theatricality and the very precision and bravura of his craftsmanship have frequently served as delightful, self-conscious acts of complicity with his audience. And how often have his films centred on artists or writers, their struggles, their guilt feelings, or other themes in this general area?

But never before have film process and film consciousness been the very essence of the movie, its own subject, its overt structuring. *Persona*, in that respect, is Bergman's $8^{1}/_{2}$. And while not reflecting Fellini's sensibility and lightness of touch, it nonetheless shares not only that film's creative bravura but also its profound pessimism and its symbolic status signalling a new approach, a change in outlook – an entering into the postmodern world.

So there it is: the material base of the movie experience, carbon arcs bringing light and shadow onto a dark screen (box 7). And what are these figurations bursting through the play of light and shadow on the screen if not projections of the artist's mind, the "themes," universe, images, movies we recognize as his own – and of the culture that shapes him (box 6)? Out of all this, both artist and audience must nonetheless focus on something particular, something obsessing the artist at this point in his life, whether at the conscious or the subconscious level (box 5). So there are the conditions which were the catalyst or occasion for making this particular movie: where he was, his memories, whatever.4 The filmmaker is always there, of course, overseeing, manipulating, telling the story that is emerging (box 3). And there is the story itself, with the world it creates (box 2), which in its turn reflects aspects of the "real world outside" (box 1).

What is essential to this film, then, is *not* the exploration of the themes that we have grown familiar with – however intense and mesmerizing they may be – but the fact that Bergman *treats them explicitly as such*, as part of the material used in this artificial manufacturing of an object of communication (or of art). It is also essential that what is on the screen is consciously *not* reality, *not* truth, but a fabrication by the artist. And so, Bergman's deliberate strategies: the use of "open signs," the derailing of the story by appeals to our consciousness of the process, the contradictions and the avoiding of the kind of explanations that usually create a semblance of credibility. Finally, the very enterprise of "interpreting" the diegetical context into some kind of meaningfulness is exposed for what (Bergman feels) it is: an exercise in giving meaning to a filmmaker's fabrication which probably has no real meaning, since (as he implicitly more or less claims) he himself does not understand anything anyway. It is an exercise in futility, signifying nothing.

Nowhere is film's manipulative falseness more cruelly evident than in Bergman's demonstration of his ability, in spite of all the self-consciousness-creating tactics, to mesmerize us when he chooses to, to pull us back into the story with his moments of magic and power, and then to break us off. A dialectic is at work here, but it is not the old dialectic between God/non-God, meaningfulness/absurdity, love/alienation, life/death. Now it is between film as signifying, as reflection of reality, and film as sheer factitiousness and duplicity, the artist's game.

Bergman has gone a long way, then, in *Persona*, a film that indeed exemplifies that Godard dictum that "the adventure of the contemporary cinema is the adventure of film language," while adding its own pessimistic philosophical undertones. More than an example, really, it is a demonstration of this dictum in action. To put it another way (coming, as it were, from the opposite direction), it is an exercise in the *deconstruction* of cinema, the deconstruction

4 In his autobiographical *The Magic Lantern* (London: Hamish Hamilton, 1988), 202–7, Bergman is very specific about this. He speaks of his experiences at the Sophiahemmet (hospital) in Stockholm, when as a ten-year-old boy he was locked into its mortuary with a number of corpses, and much later, just before *Persona*, when he was ill, suffering dizzy spells and so on, in a room overlooking the grounds. This obviously bears amazingly on box 5. And so it does, too, on box 4, as he relates how fascinated he was at the time by the resemblance between Bibi Andersson and Liv Ullmann.

of the myth of Bergman's movies, and of Bergman himself as artist.

And with its snake-swallowing-its-own-tail structure, the whole film rings out that terrible knell: *ingenting*. Art, communication, human relationships, relating to reality, reality itself? Nothingness seems to be the conclusion.

But beware. As always – and this seems to be a constant when dealing with genuine works of art – things are not nearly as clear and definitive as all that. I am overstating the case, in the quest for brevity and clarity. Can one accept *ingenting* literally, when one experiences the film's creative brilliance and complexity, which in themselves are living affirmations of a vitality that is, consciously or not, the strongest built-in refutation of what seems to be a stated nihilistic reduction?

Many issues indeed are surfacing in these last few pages, things which have the ring of *postmodernism* about them. As this study progresses to its conclusion, we shall be returning to this notion. In a way, however, *Persona* may well illustrate most of the "new things" with an explicitness and clarity beyond what would be achieved in this direction by any Bergman film that would follow – with the possible exception of his last movie, *Fanny and Alexander*.

Persona is a quintessentially mid 1960s phenomenon. Bergman worked on its creation in 1965, and the movie was finally released in the fall of 1966. *Persona* serves as a fine example of Roland Barthes's "vertiginous interplay of signs and significations." There is more to it than that, of course, nothing less than a philosophical premise holding that "real" signification, the ability of the (cinematic) signs to connect with "reality out there," is impossible to achieve (at least with certainty). A more cheerful perspective from which to view the phenomenon might permit one to say that Bergman had finally freed himself from both the need to reaffirm traditional "signification," and from the concomitant need to adhere to certain filmmaking strategies appropriated to that need.

Let's return to what has been briefly alluded to in the preface and elsewhere: the mid 1960s was the time when movements still dominant today in criticism – postmodernism, for one – were beginning to be formulated. Louis Althusser, remember, was bringing his Marxist insights to bear on the notion of the artist as a controlling, free subject or creator: the social order, ultimately determined by the economic, itself determines and shapes language; thus the artist becomes a mere channel or conduit for that language, a factor in an already determined equation. Jacques Lacan, like Althusser, attacked the same "bourgeois" notion of "creative artist," but on the basis of Freudian insights: language becomes the tool of the subconscious and of the social context's suppression of that subconscious, much along the same lines that mark the child's process of development into adulthood.

Where, then, is the controlling, conscious *subject*? What happens to notions such as those of filmic auteurism (which, to a large extent, informs this particular study on Bergman)? In the Lacanian and Althusserian systems, all the myths, themes, figurations, cultural understandings, etc. tend to be seen as constructs, to be revealed as such (that is, without "real scientific" foundation in "reality") through methods growing out of the only "valid scientific" approaches, the Marxist or the Freudian, or a combination of both. Now is clearly not the time to join into a discussion that still produces an immense amount of writing, teaching, and polemics. Suffice it to say that the concomitant act of faith in either the Freudian or the Marxist view thus necessitated is breathtaking.

Any other "reality," so the theory goes, is revealed as illusory, the product of bourgeois manipulation or vague mysticism or poetic impressionism. And above all, to repeat, the bourgeois notion of the free, controlling artist/creator/subject is proscribed. Literary and filmic schools of analysis and criticism continue to ride this unlikely tandem of transliterated Marxism and Freudianism, regardless of what might be called the logical consequences. How, for example, is social action possible for such decentred subjects? And is there really no such thing as artistic creation?[5]

Jacques Derrida carries the process through to its inevitable conclusion. Just as Althusser, say, and Lacan furnished the tools to deconstruct everything else, so Derrida turns on *them*: what justifies the exemption accorded to these two privileged approaches? *All* the myths must be exposed, *deconstructed*. Deconstruction becomes the name of the game, and Derrida gleefully gives himself to it with energy and immense cleverness. The "bourgeois myths" having been exposed, displaced by the Marxist and the Freudian, now deconstruction must direct its enterprise to all of language and its forms and creations. Derrida even "deconstructs" himself, insisting that both he and whatever he says should not be believed.

We can see how beautifully this fits into a certain understanding of postmodernism. Since language is but a structuring of cultural signs referring back not to any underlying ontological foundation but merely to other signs agreed upon by a culture, which signs themselves refer back to other (yet previous) cultural signs and so on, how can one possibly look for any "objective truth," or, for that matter, for a "reality"? Many might experience this kind of impasse

5   I cannot begin to do justice to the intricacies of this discourse. It is not only opponents of these orientations who object: many of the disciples of these systems have attempted to correct the most excessive expressions of what I have been referring to, while working within the very systems. See, for example, Paul Smith's *The Discerning Subject* (Minneapolis: University of Minnesota Press, 1988).

as rather tragic. But Derrida refuses to be depressed. *Au contraire*: since that's the way it is, why not dance and enjoy it and join in the game of language and of "functioning texts" and their dizzying formations of figurations and signs?

Seen from this perspective, *Persona* becomes astonishingly prophetic, a movie incarnation of movements that would soon become enshrined at least among substantial areas of the academic and intellectual life. True, it would be absurd to claim that Bergman was joining in the "Derrida-da dance" described above, that exuberant and playful aspect of postmodernism almost before that phenomenon began to be recognized as such. Impudent, impish Godard down in Paris, maybe; but hardly Bergman up in post-Lutheran Sweden. But if by postmodernism we mean the deconstruction of myths that had previously nourished his culture's understanding of life, without being able to replace them with any compensating beliefs, then *Persona* serves as a powerful indicator that Bergman was indeed significantly attuned to at least some grim aspects of the postmodern sensibility.

How, indeed, could *he* join in the dance? After years of anguished effort to embrace the Christian-affirmation side of the existentialism dialectic, Bergman was burned out: the Sartrian side apparently had won. But Sartre and Camus, at least during significant periods of their evolution, had not abandoned the secular city. Unlike Bergman, they still – in spite of the "evidence" – could commit themselves to social action. Not so Bergman, given his particular religious heritage with its profound distrust of "the works of man." And as for that heritage's God, well, that too gave every sign of being extinct. The '60s, of course, had its own "God is dead" theological movement. But that tended to be different, at least for those proponents of the movement who affirmed that, once present culture's false and devitalized representations of God were finally "put to death," a new grounding for a truer, purer manifestation of the divine could be hoped for.[6]

Yet that was hardly Bergman's point of view: none of his movies from 1965 to 1970 can be experienced in any way as God-centred. It seems clear that the God question that had fuelled Bergman's creative élan was now deflated. In its stead one experiences bitterness and desolation, a harsh and tragic quasi-despair over the impossibility of communication. Jon Tuska quotes a stunning few lines from Nietzsche that bring light to one's reading of *Persona* and the ensuing films, especially given Bergman's previous belief system: "Belief in the

---

6 This is the view some theologians seem to cling to in their interpretation of Bergman's post-*Persona* films. I admire their point, admitting that it touches on the possibility of ambiguity, but ... See, for example, Arthur Gibson's *The Silence of God* (New York: Harper & Row, New York, 1969).

absolute immorality of Nature, in lack of purpose, and in meaninglessness, is the *affect* psychologically necessary once belief in God and an essentially moral order is no longer supportable."[7]

More than ever before, Bergman will turn inward, into the "infernal regions." *Persona* launches a grim movement, extending Bergman's work of deconstruction into his very protagonist(s). The implacable portrayal of personality disintegration is now the obsession, with no longer a need to "save" the central character. Tuska, once again quoting Nietzsche, might well have been referring to the ending of *Persona*. In this paralyzing situation, finally acknowledging the evil of the human situation, "invariably man would rather will nothingness than not will."[8] And so: *ingenting*.

THE HOUR OF THE WOLF

Persona has the look of a calculated, controlled experiment in creating an open cinema. No ensuing Bergman feature will go as far in that direction, though many will push further into this or that aspect of what we might call the postmodern sensibility. The succeeding films represent an ebb and a flow in this tendency, part of a new dialectic, one might claim, set up between a more traditional manner of filmmaking (Bergman in the past) and the "open" option. At this stage of Bergman's career, however, the new openness tends to signify an opening out onto a meaningless void, in what probably constitutes the darkest and most bitter series of films he has ever made.

The Hour of the Wolf fits into this kind of dialectical context quite neatly. It can be understood as a psychological gothic horror film, part of a genre long honoured in the cinema. *Persona* had done its job, say, in freeing Bergman from some of his own previous aesthetic and philosophical dictates. No need to do that all over again. Why not follow the heavy, "important" creation with a semi-spoof, much as he had done for *The Seventh Seal* and *Wild Strawberries* with *The Magician*? So, *Hour of the Wolf* does not labour under the obligation of systematically dismantling a conventional plot and just about everything else. Johan (Max von Sydow) is a painter who is prey to hallucinations, or, more literally, to personal demons. He and his wife, Alma (Liv Ullmann), live on an island owned by a baron who lives in a neighbouring castle. They are invited to an evening dinner with other guests, very strange ones indeed, who at times turn into evil creatures (Johan's demons?). Johan is driven to his death, called by his

---

7 Jon Tuska, *Dark Cinema* (Westport, CI, and London: Greenwood Press, 1984), xix, quoting (and translating) Friedrich Nietzsche, *Werke in Drei Banden*.

8 Ibid., xvii, footnote 6.

voices to disappear into a gothic marsh. So far, so good: *The Hour of the Wolf* tells its story in relatively "normal" horror film fashion – most of the time.

Bergman, however, sets up his story in an obviously subjective, self-conscious framework. It is *Alma*'s story, you see: she is telling it to us, addressing the audience directly at the beginning and especially at the end of the film. It is as if Bergman were distancing himself from the artist Johan and putting quotation marks around the horror-genre experiences that constitute the heart of the film. At times, no doubt, the film smacks of tongue-in-cheek.

But there is also a dialectical game going on. We feel far from "protected," still less comfortable: the jaws are clenched too tight for that. *The Hour of the Wolf* assaults the audience with an almost unrelieved battering of horrors: it strikes painfully into our collective psyche. Johan's near-maniacal and only fitfully suppressed violence, his attempts at killing Alma, the hallucination of killing a boy (complete with homosexual overtones), the various graphic sexual humiliations, an old woman removing one of her eyes, then peeling off her face to reveal a death skull – the stuff of nightmares, these hardly constitute laughing matter.

Terrifying, horrifying – but Bergman bounces us back and forth, playing with our sensibilities. The monsters tease us now and again into a smile of recognition; and most of the audience are at least vaguely conscious of the references to classic Hollywood gothic horror – Bela Lugosi's *Dracula*, and maybe Boris Karloff's *Frankenstein*, and *Freaks*, or even Hitchcock's more contemporary *Psycho* and *The Birds*. Modernism's anguish at the disintegration of the artist's psyche is never quite made fun of; but Bergman's postmodernist playing with signs surely affords some measure of sardonic relief.

The filmic text, experienced in this fashion, becomes a fascinating game of shifting from one level of the audience's experiencing to the other and back. But within limitations: the introspection rings so intense and so tragic, so deep and true, that even the Hollywood recalls are not untroubling. Whatever our cultural consciousness, they still exercise mysterious cinematic power as dark projections of a barely controlled subconscious.

This, I believe, is tied in with Johan's corrosive contempt for his own art and for the role of contemporary art in general. At one point he states: "I realize the supreme unimportance of art in the affairs of men ... I go on creating simply out of compulsion." This has a familiar ring, an articulation of a longstanding Bergman theme. The pessimistic aspect, however, seems to be reaching all-consuming proportions, reflecting the mood informing his acceptance speech for the Erasmus Prize which he shared with Charles Chaplin about the same time (in 1965): "The artist stands before a *must*, a continual torment, a toothache ... There's just sickness there, a perversion, a five-legged calf ... Art is the dead skin of a snake. It *seems* to have life, but only because of the millions of insects swarming within the skin and devouring it. We the artists are those insects."

Point zero seems to have been reached, as Bergman expresses his loathing over the futility of his own art and of contemporary art in general. And yet ... as one has grown to expect in Bergman ... in this same very dark film there is a most evocative and beautiful scene, as mysterious and haunting as anything he has ever attempted.

The elegant guests (part-time demons?) are assembled in the baron's castle. After the dinner the baron has them seated about a tiny puppet stage, in a kind of impromptu theatre gathering, for a special performance of perhaps the most sublime section of Mozart's *The Magic Flute*. One of the guests, Lindhorst, acts as impresario/commentator/puppeteer. His face expressionistically lit, his eyes glinting malevolently, he is a bird man, striking in his resemblance to Lugosi's *Dracula* as he towers behind the little stage, manipulating, directing, explaining the spectacle. The guests sit transfixed as the glorious music pours forth, doing its job of enshrining for the ages humanity's desperate seeking, yearning for the meaning of life, time, eternity, destiny. Tamino, in darkness and ignorance, is asking the unseen powers, "When will my eye find the light?" And in a mysterious serenity, the answer comes from the invisible choral voices: "Soon, or never." As we watch, the puppets become minuscule, moving, "real" human beings singing in the theatre. Nykvist's camera captures the radiant troubled faces of the guests in a magical counterpoint to the scene.

A Bergman moment this surely is, transcending the categories, connotation rich at so many levels: the artist as vampire/trickster/controller, yet revealer; art as artifice and yet as communication of truth, as exquisite beauty and yet as menace. Mystery, depth, soul sound their echoes in all of us – and the light in the immensity, the darkness.

Bergman briefly extends the magic as Johan and Alma leave the castle, the camera capturing them against the light of the Swedish night, still intoxicated by the experience, above all by the brief moment of enchanting at-oneness and respite – for them and for us.

No question here about Bergman's complete control: in a film of overwhelming darkness, he has managed to return to an articulation of the great dialectic of earlier years, but with a difference. This time the positive affirmation, while by no means less powerful in its brief expression, is contained within formal quotation marks: a classic operatic moment in one of the greatest artistic creations of our culture, staged in a weird and ambivalent context, in a most self-conscious, theatricalized manner. Bergman has managed to do the postmodernist thing, distancing himself and protecting himself from making that statement his own, while still presenting the possibilities that art can create. But of course that distancing, as we have seen, operates equally through the far more dominant, horrific part of the film. Can there be any affirmation of meaningfulness at all in this self-conscious semi-parodying of film genre?

Another force is at work in *The Hour of the Wolf*: call it the exploration of another aspect of the human psyche and of human experience. At times it takes over the Bergman text. I have not gone into it in this study, because I do not feel that it is a dominant, something around which Bergman structures his films. More and more, however, I am convinced that I understate its importance, for it is there, in certain moments, in certain characters, scattered all through his movies, even from the beginning, revealing the breadth of Bergman's awareness and sensitivity – and certainly of his eclecticism.

In some of the movies it is especially evident, movies such as *The Hour of the Wolf*. I am referring to what might be termed the cult of suffering, a flirting with sadism or masochism, when the film unquestionably reveals an obsessional fascination with, almost a connivance in, the portrayal of suffering self-destruction. Indeed, this has been the basis for perhaps the most widely held reservations of many who "do not like" Bergman. While I believe that Bergman never elevates this force into the status of a fundamental principle around which to orchestrate one's life – in the manner, say, of a de Sade or the more contemporary Mishima – at times he nonetheless manifests, as I have said, an amazing awareness and sensitivity, particularly during this *ingenting* period.9 Bergman can go pretty far, some of the films cultivating an almost ritualized enactment of this, in a kind of black-mass celebration. A Foucault, for example, might bring a great deal to the understanding of this, shall we call it, dimension. Deep waters, indeed. I leave them to others to navigate.

SHAME

Previous films gave us brief glimpses of Bergman's awareness of and consternation about war. *Persona* had its Vietnam and Nazi holocaust images, *Winter Light* an ominous military train, *The Silence* its rumbling tanks, and as far back as *Three Strange Loves* a train journey revealed sights of a war-ravaged Germany. The subject of war, however, was simply not part of Bergmania. Some critics might add, how could it, given Bergman's non-involvement in the

9 Perhaps apropos: Bergman's direction of Yukio Mishima's *Madame de Sade* at the Royal Dramatic Theatre has been acclaimed as masterful, not only in Stockholm but wherever else around the world it has been performed.

political-ideological-social reality?

Shame is not one of the Great War Movies, and there is no connivance with the usual war genre myths. There is certainly no propagandistic aspect, one will not be surprised to note: no good guys versus bad guys, totalitarians versus democrats, communists versus fascists. Indeed, one really has no idea whom the warring factions represent, nor even what they are about. And there is none of the operatic intensity and breadth of an *Apocalypse Now*. In no way, finally, can it be seen as an action thriller complete with typical exciting effects and feats of derring-do.

Shame simply continues Bergman's contemplation of human disintegration, this time extending it to a broader social dimension in the life of one small community. Liv Ullmann (Eva) continues to represent some fragile incarnation of humanity, but basically the overall fresco describes the horror of human behaviour. That is not surprising, war being what it really is. The Vietnam war had long been stamping images of dreadful suffering on our collective psyche, as indeed had a whole catalogue of well-known icons from World War II, the death camps, and so on, thanks to the modern media. *Shame* is nurtured on this and on the vision of war as sheer folly, stupidity, evil – in distinct contrast to the obscene rationalization, sanitization, and ultimate glorification of war to which the western world would be subjected two decades later in the coverage of the Persian Gulf conflict.

Bergman does give us a sense of some of the physical realities as Sven Nykvist's camera tracks over the farmland of Fårö, over hedges and into courtyards, with gunfire and explosions, fire and smoke, and bodies of victims strewn about. We feel the sense of communal confusion and terror, as victims, refugees, are pushed about or huddle in frightened little groups, wanting to get away, not knowing where to go.

Bergman's war, however, is much more the extension, on a broader scale, of the personal disintegration already explored in previous films. The Bibi Andersson character experienced that disintegration on the secluded island of *Persona*; the Max von Sydow character turns inward, to be devoured by the demons of his own tortured, gothic-horror psyche (*Hour of the Wolf*); and now the mad rituals of war reveal the same basic equation, the same basic process as war rips off the thin veneer of "humanity," with Max von Sydow once again playing the central exemplar in this process.

Shame, paradoxically enough, is formally a more sedate and traditional film than its two predecessors. There is no postmodern deconstruction of film language, no assault on the traditional formal filmmaking ways. The human beings, too, have a more normal, rounded humanity. Bergman actually touches on what makes life beautiful, what he yearns could be the way we live. But these moments are few, and they are ruthlessly snuffed out: there is no real dialectic, except in the sense of an implicit yearning that things be not as they are. In these years, the succession of films relentlessly serves one end, it would seem: to manifest, precisely, what it means to be in a world of *ingenting*.

THE RITE

Personality disintegration continues on its decidedly unmerry way in Bergman's next effort, a sardonic, cruel comedy about three actors, accused of lewd behaviour, on trial before a judge. All four fare extremely badly in this succession of humiliating unmaskings and self-revelations, complete with ambiguous religious rites. Indeed, in one part of the movie, Bergman actually films what seems to be (literally, this time) a black mass (echoes of *The Hour of the Wolf?*).

The Rite represents a whole series of choices by Bergman with the apparent purpose of demeaning the characters and rendering them rather despicable. As such, it takes its place with a few other films (say, *Now About These Women* earlier on and *From the Life of the Marionettes* later) that in their various ways manifest a very dark and cynical side of the Bergman persona, a side seemingly denuded of hope or aspiration of any sort.

It is difficult, strictly speaking, to call *The Rite* a movie at all: in reality it is a play written for television, made up of nine scenes, staged on one set, with four actors, and lasting seventy-four minutes. It is, in fact, as television that it was presented initially in Sweden on 25 March 1969, although (with Bergman's consent) it was later released internationally as a feature film.

Its very starkness in terms of the use of film language probably adds to its corrosive character. It is fair, it would seem, to conclude that the anger and bitterness in Bergman's work are nearing the point of nihilism. And one may be tempted to see, in his opting for a very limited and obvious use of theatrical language adapted to the rhythms of the stage and to the physical limitations of the television box, a further revelation that the (film) artist can no longer be comfortable with the magical properties of what used to be his own use of (film) language – at least at this precise moment in his evolution, and that of his culture (1968–69). Admittedly, that may be reaching a bit.

THE PASSION OF ANNA

It is a cold, grey day. Sven Nykvist's camera captures the sparse landscape, its colours muted, somewhat faded. Andreas Winkelman (Max von Sydow) is observed in long shot, stumbling, half-walking, half-running erratically up and down a roadway near the seashore. Slowly, ever so slowly, Nykvist's camera zooms in, ruthlessly, relentlessly. And through a combination of various technical procedures – focal apertures, laboratory developing, and so on – a strange, terrible thing happens. As Andreas and his surroundings are slowly pulled closer to us, the image becomes progressively grainier, and the colour and shapes progressively lose their definition, until Andreas literally disintegrates before our eyes in a canvas that has become an impressionistic, pointillist miasma of soft, rough-grained melded colours. And Bergman's voice-over tells us: "And this time his name was Andreas Winkelman."

The film ends – and Bergman has pushed personality disintegration one step further, into the very disintegration of the film image. *Ingenting*.

The Passion of Anna is an amazing movie, in some ways pursuing the quest for a new, open film form beyond even the experimentations of *Persona*. The hard-edged, precise brilliance of the former gives way to a loose, freewheeling, almost haphazardly structured film text breathing the indeterminate and the elusive, in a world still dominated by the experience of nothingness.

This is a typical Bergman world, limited to four main characters, plus an old peasant marked as chief victim to a never defined force of sadistic evil that infests the island (Fårö once again). There are unmistakable echoes of *Shame*'s world, where indeed the evil was defined, at least at one level. The social fabric is being threatened and injustice abounds, so that the poor victim is hounded into suicide. In rather horrific outbursts of sadism, animals are slaughtered or tortured. And, of course, personality disintegration is very much the prime concern as Bergman continues to explore the interpersonal relatings between the Max von Sydow character (this time a failed writer) and the Liv Ullmann character (Anna), through the many rhythms, nuances, contradictions, understandings and misunderstandings – and, one must add, in the eventual collapse. This time the pathology is not reserved for the male half of the pairing. And in any case, another couple, played by Erland Josephson (Elis) and Bibi Andersson (Eva), are essential to this study of intertwined quadripartite relationships.

Though the dominant tone in *The Passion of Anna* is unquestionably one of suffering, loss of direction, and illusion unmasked in spiritual defeat, the film is allowed to breathe, the sterility of its predecessors making way to an extent for signs of life. Bergman permits himself some of his "positive moments": near the beginning, a warm, witty, and delightful meal shared by the four friends; Andreas's exquisite tenderness after rescuing a puppy from hanging; a mesmerizing scene, shot in soft-red filter, when Eva comes to Andreas's cottage and to the strains of a romantic, soft and lush swing record more or less seduces him, irresistible in her vulnerability. And there are numerous intimate moments in the shared life of Andreas and Anna as they work or shop or play together.

Thus, in a sense, we are back to one of the older, well-recognized Bergman "dialectics": moments of life-nurturing tenderness or beauty, struggling to survive in a world of loss, confusion, evil. This is accentuated by Bergman's capturing of the small, "non-significant" moments in daily life, endowing them with refreshing beauty and interest and thereby capturing the elusive life rhythm that Jean Renoir's cinema was so dedicated to.

We feel the presence of a master at work, with apparent effortlessness, able to communicate so much and to enthral his audience with a minimum of means. The fact that Bergman is using colour for the first time "seriously" (*Now About These Women* was his only previous effort) probably accounts for much, because, combined with Nykvist's unaggressive, "natural" use of light, framing and movement, a new verisimilitude emerges, less dramatic and schematic than the previous black and white.

This accounts for Bergman's seeming to be much more personally in this film, especially at the level of sympathy and involvement with his characters. But one must tread softly here: for *The Passion of Anna* is one of Bergman's most decidedly "modern" and "open" of texts, with all the self-consciousness and distanciation that such notions imply. He brings this about through a variety of artistic strategies. For one thing, in voice-over, Bergman himself is integrated into the film as narrator (as he was in the end of the film as just described). It all happens in normal, leisurely fashion, without fanfare or apparent striving for effect. For example: great gobs of plot information are given us by Bergman, such as "the months have passed, Anna is now living with Andreas," and so on. Thus Bergman seems perfectly comfortable in slipping over some of the "important" (from a narrative or dramatic point of view) moments, precisely in favour of lingering on the in-between, everyday little things of life. Plot exercises anything but tyrannical control in this movie. Moreover, so many things are never explained. The island's strange, perverse goings-on remain a total mystery, as does the eventual fate of the main characters.

I have mentioned that the use of colour adds to the natural look of the film. But colour is used in another way as well, with artificial contrasts, or by draining the intensity out of the colour, or by using filters, and so on. Add to that the image disintegration of the finale. Just how are we to react in the presence of such obvious devices? Is this all part of Andreas's mind state? And certain events that *we* witness: are there really three suns in the sky at the beginning? Finally, time and again Bergman fills the screen, Godard-like, with a huge close-up of a sentence being typed, warning us of Anna's neurotic tendencies. In other words, nothing in this film is quite what it seems, nothing is finally resolved. The very structuring of the film pushes us out of the story, forcing us into a highly conscious mode.

Bergman is hardly subtle in this regard. In what appear to be four individual entr'actes, each of the four main actors literally steps out of character. The shot is announced by the clapperboard with the name of the actor on it, and in answer to Bergman's voiced question, he or she, addressing us directly in a warm and becoming close-up, tells us something about what he or she thinks the character is, how the actor is trying to play it, what will happen eventually to that character, and so on. The viewer may initially be bewildered, but there is nothing aggressive or shocking in the way Bergman does this. All flows "naturally." And we go along with it, undisturbed, even delighted. (Well, not everyone, especially if we do not know our Godard. Many, it appears, are merely confused.)

Bergman, in other words, is sharing the "text-in-process-of-becoming" with us. The actors seem to be sharing in creating the plot and the character: there are possibilities, probabilities; this could happen or that. Here is a kind of cinema of virtualities, showing us various potentialities, and in that, reflecting the filmmaking process. Alain Resnais was doing something of the sort in a number of his films (especially *Providence* later on), but with an *aggressive* and overt brilliance. In *The Passion of Anna* we have a leisurely and "open text," deliberately "imperfect," "unfinished," much as Eco was suggesting in *The Open Work*. Without the showy super-intellectualism and super-craftsmanship that exploded in *Persona*, Bergman has found a way of directly addressing his audience, as it were, sharing with us the awareness of what the nature of film, this film, really is. The final image may be of the actual visual disintegration of the central character, commented on by "author" Bergman; but we are very much aware that we are witnessing an artificial act of artistic legerdemain. Bergman makes us feel the nothingness, but also he makes us distance ourselves from it with the consciousness that it is an art object we are contemplating, and a highly complex one. Perhaps, because of the visible structuring of the film, we are prevented from taking the ending literally, at face value. For there are, after all, *four* factors in the equation, each with his or her possibilities. And so for life: we are watching Bergman work out some of the feasibilities. The context may still be grim, and nothing is clear; but here are four types of people reacting, each with his or her virtualities.

The Seventh Seal presented different kinds of fates for different individuals. But there one felt Bergman personally involved, working his way to some kind of affirmation and imposition of order. This would be pursued with growing clarity, as we have seen, in succeeding films. But with *The Passion of Anna* Bergman no longer feels the compulsion to be the prophet seeking *the* answer. For better or for worse, having faced the unbearable anguish of *ingenting*, he is now able to step back, seeing all options represented by the characters as data or possibilities (or maybe not!). Maybe *ingenting* itself is just that, one of the possibilities; and maybe, braced by that conviction, one can survive, can get on with one's life.

Perhaps.

CHAPTER SIX

JUST DOING MY JOB

The Fårö Document	filming March – July 1969 release (TV) January 1970
The Touch	filming September – November 1970 release August 1971
Cries and Whispers	filming autumn 1971 release (U.S.) December 1972
Scenes from a Marriage	filming summer/fall 1972 release (TV) April – May 1973
The Magic Flute	filming spring 1974 release (TV) January 1975
Face to Face	filming April – July 1975 release (TV) April – May 1976
The Serpent's Egg	filming autumn 1976 release October 1977
Autumn Sonata	filming September – October 1977 release October 1978

The following are excerpts from my interview with Ingmar Bergman that took place in 1970 a few weeks before the actual shooting of *The Touch*. The fifty-three-year-old Bergman was fairly bouncing with vitality and good cheer, and speaking very positively about life and about movie-making. So of course I objected:

Q.: And yet your most recent films seem, if anything, more pessimistic than ever. In *The Passion of Anna*, for example, what can be more hopeless than Andreas Winkelman's despair and humiliation (even to the point of the disintegration of the image at the end)?

BERGMAN: In a way that's true. I think the human condition is not a very happy one – or at least the conditions we human beings live by. But you have to reach out. There are so many things, so many relations with human beings …

Yes, take *The Passion of Anna*. Winkelman is not the whole film. There are four characters, four voices within me, if you wish. It's the totality you must see. Remember the part played by Bibi Andersson. Bibi steps out of the part and tells us that the character she plays will probably attempt suicide, out of despair. But she will live, come back to life again. She'll get out of herself and start to work for others.

And that's the only important thing, I think. To forget, if you can forget yourself.

Q.: And that's why you have that Bibi Andersson sequence end flooded in white light?

BERGMAN: Yes.

In Ingmar Bergman's own mind, at any rate, *ingenting* was no longer the word to use to describe either his psychological or his philosophical space. We were perhaps heading into a "new Period," distinct from the Bergman 1950s but also from the Bergman 1960s.

Q.: But the extraordinary things you wrote … you know, the beautiful cathedral business, and later, the horrible dead skin of a snake … do you still have such feelings about art?

BERGMAN: Oh, that was very romantic. No, now I have the feeling that each of us tries to do his job, tries to be honest. I do my job as well as I possibly can, like a craftsman who makes a table or a chair. It's just a table, a chair, a cup, or spoon, to be used today, now. It has nothing to do with eternity, or tomorrow, or yesterday. It's for people, made for people.

Because the only importance – if we can talk of any importance in all of this – is in coming in contact with other human beings. People ask us to give them something. And if we don't, we can all go to hell.

Q: So art is no longer the dead skin of a snake, and you're no longer the insect, as you claimed in accepting the Erasmus prize?
BERGMAN: That was long ago, six years ago!

You know, at first you have romantic notions. First you see yourself building the great cathedral to faith and humanity, in the light of eternity. Then you grow disillusioned, you turn very pessimistic – you're still being romantic! – and you see yourself inside a snake. But finally you're just alive, you do your work – and that is enough, that's marvellous. As long as you're allowed to do your work, to go on doing your work – I think that is marvellous. And to get paid well for doing it! (*laughter*) To do our job, to go on working, that is what matters.

Just doing his job, no causes, no great belief systems, no more trying to figure out what life is all about, but only trying to touch people, to be of use – this does indeed sound like a "new" Bergman. Up to a point, it has to be admitted, the twelve or so films (depending on how many you include as movies) he was to make from 1969 on bear this out. But "new" does not necessarily mean better.

By and large, the passion is greatly diminished. And certainly Bergman seems more detached from his work. Forever the eclectic, he now does not seem to be developing any particular style, approach, or thematic exploration that would permit one to speak of a consistent, identifiable "period" in his work. If there is one constant, it is, not surprisingly, the continued communication of what has almost always been his main preoccupation, the psychological examination of human beings in their mostly suffering inter-relationships. In that sense the shadow of Strindberg is never far.

There are a few extraordinary works, to be sure; but overall this final period of work is not his most distinguished, and certainly not his most popular – with the TV exception of *Scenes from a Marriage*.

Of course it was not only Bergman: the whole world film scene changed radically after the collapse of the "revolution" of 1968. Many of the great of the previous fifteen years were either dead or well past their prime. Even those who might have been expected to produce some of their finest work (a Fellini, say, or a Godard) seemed in a state of creative exhaustion. Some of the grand old names might reappear on occasion, or new names might show promise, but by and large the golden age had ended.

The *film auteurs* lost both their inspiration and their control over filmmaking. Once again it was the producers and the studios who were in command; and ever increasingly, Hollywood was reasserting its overwhelming movie-industry supremacy. But that was not all: even film theory and research had turned against the *auteurs*. As we have seen, the very notion of art was now suspect, replaced by concerns and by a methodology growing out of psychoanalysis and political science: the ideological was *in*, with a vengeance. And, of course, the whole postmodernist spirit, with its fascination with signs and images and fads, was eating away at the very possibility of films based on belief and conviction, films trying to come to grips with a "reality" beyond the "sign."

In this to be sure the cinema was merely reflecting the huge overall cultural shift. And that shift was part of a larger movement totally dominated by business, commerce, technology, computerization, materialism in its various manifestations.

Now is not the time to go into the new developments, nor into the other side of the equation, i.e., how these developments were offering extraordinary opportunities to create a better world, universal peace, solutions to all kinds of problems. In any case, few were the films informed by a passion for these kinds of preoccupations, even if a good number of the movies were tending to reflect a basically decent desire for justice, and a desire, too, to "touch others," to be useful – and to lead a comfortable life. But that, more or less, was as far as it went then, and as far as it goes today.

When human vision is contained within such parameters, great and profound art may be difficult to come by.

THE FÅRÖ DOCUMENT

Perhaps the *ingenting* period really was coming to an end, for after *The Passion of Anna* Bergman turned his hand to directing his first documentary, *The Fårö Document*, destined for Swedish television. He had long been accused, mostly by ideologically motivated critics, of not being socially responsible; and after *Shame*, that accusation was renewed with vigour. *The Fårö Document* may well have been his response. Totally unpretentious, decidedly "non-arty," shot in 16mm by Sven Nykvist, *The Fårö Document* reveals ordinary citizen Bergman filming with curiosity and sympathy the ordinary people, most of whose world is that small island. Concentrating mostly on the faces of some of Fårö's less-than-a-thousand inhabitants, Bergman's film listens to them, trying to bring their way of life and their views to the attention of the Swedish people.

Miles removed from Bergman's artistic endeavours, *The Fårö Document* may indeed be a political act in that it tries to help the citizens of his island to protect their way of life. There may not be a great deal of hope, since so many of the young people express their disenchantment and their desire to leave. But Bergman is indeed trying to be of use, to touch people whose insular life, up to a point, he shares. Film here is experienced not as an art but as a medium of communication destined to a practical end. That is his job: that is "reaching beyond himself," it would seem, in a manner radically different from that of his brooding, overwhelming artistic creations.

THE TOUCH

Now in the 1970s, in the film world there was more than passing interest in what had to be seen as a new development for Ingmar Bergman. Aware of the "new realities" governing filmmaking in countries like Sweden – what with rising production costs, the consequent need for serious involvement in the international markets, the ever-increasing cultural domination of the English language worldwide – Bergman was, at least up to a point, testing the international waters: his own company, Cinematografet, in conjunction with the American ABC Pictures Corporation, was producing *The Touch*. ABC would pay Bergman one million dollars on completion. English was to be the main language of the film. And, most excitingly, Elliott Gould (considered a major American star at the time) would join Bibi Andersson and Max von Sydow as leads.

Shot by Sven Nykvist in Eastmancolour, mostly in Visby, the capital of Gotland (the relatively large Swedish island that dominates Fårö), *The Touch* is not typical "Bergman": the colours tend to be naturally bright, and an everyday, ordinary look makes Visby much more recognizably a typical modern European town than one expects in Bergmania. Bibi and Max are your average comfortable and successful middle-class couple, with two typical western-world teenagers, living in a comfy bourgeois home. The conversations and routines are indeed everyday, with a good number of shots given over to watching Bibi Andersson keeping house, shopping, and getting into and out of the family car. Obviously, this is not the world of Bergmanian depths and intensities, the world dogged by the Big Questions.

It does appear that the old Bergman world is being demythologized at every level – but that is overstating things. Bergman, for example, cannot hide his fascination for a medieval statue of the Virgin entombed within a wall. A mysterious something beyond the mundane is being communicated, especially since the statue, once freed, is revealed as being eaten away by an unknown kind of seemingly indestructible insect. Bergman, in other words, cannot resist evoking echoes of we know not what and suggesting vaguely threatening, maybe symbolic, forces at work.

Also central to Bergman and central to the film, the Elliott Gould character progressively reveals his self-destructive neurosis, tied, it would seem, to his Jewish holocaust background. And that factor is very much part of the fundamental equation: the power and destructiveness of the force of attraction between himself and Karin (Bibi Andersson). Bergman, in typical fashion, relentlessly reveals its hopeless, irrational nature as it ravages the woman's safe, bourgeois Swedish world.

Something, however, seems terribly missing in *The Touch*. The literal, prosaic approach to its filming may explain why the mutual lacerating of the illicit lovers is vaguely unaffecting. Perhaps that is because there is no dimension of vision or depth served by any of the cinematic power that has made the many other similar Bergman moments so mesmerizing. Mystery has been pretty well exorcized from this cinematic text, and what we are left with is relatively banal, not to say boring. A typical example: Bergman's literal (and rather unflattering) undressing, to an unusual extent, of Bibi Andersson – all in the name of that literal, demystifying approach – works against the movie, purging it of the magic, poetry, mystery.

Bergman's reducing of his cinema, then, proves an unhappy experiment. His American tryst, far from his usual heightened movie-making, seems headed toward the rather unexalted terrain so triumphantly occupied by soap opera. Fortunately, it would prove to be a one-shot affair.

CRIES AND WHISPERS

By 1972, had Ingmar Bergman joined the category of those artists who have nothing left to say, but go on saying it? For many, the signs were alarming. It had been quite a while since he had made a film eliciting a broad spectrum of critical acclaim, as far back as *Persona* – and *Persona* itself was not everyone's cup of tea. Were all the introspection, the loss of belief, the ruminating about the (almost) uselessness of film and of just about everything else pointing to a case of burn-out? In other words, was Bergman still capable of creating a great filmic work of art?

Cries and Whispers would answer that question in spectacular fashion. Here is a movie of formal perfection, a masterpiece of the modern cinema, strictly itself, a rounded creation similar to no other film made and yet typically Bergman, recognizably informed by his sensibility, his experience and understanding.

The action takes place in nineteenth-century Sweden. Two women (Karin, played by Ingrid Thulin, and Maria, played by Liv Ullmann), aristocrats, have returned to the family country manor to be at the side of their dying sister, Agnes (played by Harriet Andersson in another overwhelming performance). A fourth woman, a servant of the family, is ever by the death bed. Four men flit in and out, but they are on the periphery. The heart of the film is these four women, "the four faces of my mother," as Bergman has stated. The "four faces of woman-as-seen-by-Bergman" might serve as well.

The film centres on the two realities which Bergman has communicated better than any other film director in history: women and death. Terrifying and tender by turns, *Cries and Whispers* mesmerizes its audience in the finest Bergman manner, and as is usually the case, it is relentless in its probing of human mystery and ambiguity, digging deep into the women's psyches with matchless insight.

Rarely has film form been so supple and free. Effortlessly Bergman mixes reality, memory, and thought projection. As a friend of mine put it, the dead and the past seem more alive than the living. The film may place us in that nineteenth-century manor, but the space, all rich, velvety, intense reds and blacks and dazzling whites, cannot be pinned down so literally: a strange place that may be mind and memory, or the womb (as Bergman has said).

A story, sort of. But a more apt description might be a musical composition for four instruments. Or a symphony of reds and blacks and whites and verdant greens. Or a poem made up of cries and whispers.

Cries and Whispers can also be understood as a movement of reconciliation – at a number of levels. The relative austerity of the Bergman 1960s is gone. Gone too is the feeling of futility and emptiness, in spite of the intense suffering and the ambivalence. We watch a thing of beauty, and we follow the artist as once again he strives to find a meaning for life.

Ultimately, there is no rational answer to the suffering and death; and, for Bergman, there may be no meaning at all for existence, at least not in the formulations of great western patterns of thinking. In an extremely moving passage of the film, the local pastor makes one of the most beautiful prayers uttered in the history of the modern cinema. He is standing at the head of the coffin containing the body of Agnes. Dressed in his Lutheran pastor's gown, back-lit in misty, shimmering light and framed against the windows in a style reminiscent of that of Carl Dreyer's *Ordet*, he puts aside his book of prescribed ritual. From the depths of his own doubt, he struggles to find the answer to the girl's agony and death in terms of his own Christian belief, confessing his own inadequacy and torment in a kind of continuation of Pastor Tomas's struggle in *Winter Light*. The very intensity and beauty of the scene make one feel that

Bergman is making his peace with his own struggle, his own conscience and bitterness, and with his own dead father, a Lutheran pastor. It may no longer be Bergman's personal belief, and yet there is holiness here, and respect, and a longing. (And speaking of reconciliation, one need but compare this portrayal of a cleric with that of the hate-filled monk fifteen years before in *The Seventh Seal*, played by the same actor, Anders Ek.)

The "real answer" for Bergman himself? All the suffering, and deception, ambivalence, and even death itself, are worth it, if we can touch each other at certain moments. Life in these moments of love and tenderness is its own *raison d'être*. The film ends as these thoughts are being read from the dead sister's diary by Anna (Kari Silwan), the young peasant servant woman who alone has showered total love upon the suffering victim:

> I closed my eyes and felt the breeze and the sun on my face. All my aches and pains were gone. The people I'm most fond of in the world were with me. I could hear them chatting round about me, I felt the presence of their bodies, the warmth of their hands. I closed my eyes tightly, trying to cling to the moment and thinking: come what may, this is happiness. I can't wish for anything better. Now for a few minutes, I can experience perfection. And I feel a great gratitude to my life, which gives me so much.[1]

As the terribly non-demanding and fragile words are uttered in Agnes's voice, the screen lights up, flooded with nature's innumerable summer greens, recalling a scene from earlier in the film. Agnes, attended by her two sisters and by Kari, their flowing white gowns adding to the enchantment, is slowly strolling through the grass; finally, they all sit together on a swing. It is a moment of incomparable serenity and at-oneness, sufficient unto itself, needing no explanation.

Bergman's return to cinematic greatness is both heartening and intriguing; and the temptation to explain this phenomenon proves irresistible. It is as if he had been through it all: the progressive perfecting of filmic mastery according to the aesthetic canons he grew up with, the deepening of the artistic thrust into a quest for meaning in life, the struggle toward an affirmation reflecting both his religious background and his modern doubt, the gradual rejection of all of this, both at the philosophical and the aesthetic levels, the consequent feeling of bitterness and sterile meaninglessness that reflect to an amazing extent the

---

1 From *Four Stories by Ingmar Bergman* (Garden City, NY: Anchor/Doubleday, 1977), 94, the very end of the story, written by Bergman as basis for the film script

various contemporary communication theories dismantling language.

But life must go on. In *Cries and Whispers* Ingmar Bergman seems to come to terms with himself (I am still resolutely in the "it is as if" mode!): "All right, all right, I am who I am: now let's get on with it. No more denying my artistic gifts, no more apologizing for creating things of beauty, no more clarifying exactly what I do believe and what I no longer believe, my emotional relationships to everything, my 'usual themes.' These things are all part of me."

Magically, he finds the form that reflects these new attitudes. A free-flowing structure embodies a plot while removing its chronology and the usual other demands and obliterating the lines between "reality" and imagination, past and present. Now Bergman can spend more time, for example, looking at and listening to clocks rather than explaining story, time and again breaking the diegetical context with totally, consciously artificial invasions into inner psyche and time disruptions, and so on. The artistic distancing achieved is real: the audience is forced to see the myths as myths, even as these myths are being reaffirmed. For example, the pastor's prayer is beautiful; but Bergman makes it clear that it is the *pastor*'s prayer, and not necessarily Bergman's.

Here is an art work obviously referring back to Bergman's own life (e.g., his relationship to his mother, in the person of the mother figure – also played by Liv Ullmann – in a memory moment harkening back to Bergman's childhood); but what really is personal reference and what is not? So, of course, there is ambiguity, here and all through the film. Here, too, is the triumph of film poetry, which, like all great poetry, cannot be totally appropriated by the intellect.

Better perhaps than any other Bergman film yet, *Cries and Whispers* is the demonstration that film comes closest to *dream*, as he has so often claimed. In dream nothing is definitively signifying, at least not in a rational sense. Dream and emotion, remembered sounds and sights, whispers and cries – the cinema.

SCENES FROM A MARRIAGE

1973: As the Cannes Film Festival began, I so well remember, the big news was that Ingmar Bergman, after all these years, would be in Cannes *in person*. The occasion was the prestige showing of *Cries and Whispers*, already a smash hit in New York. But a good number of Swedish critics with whom I had been jousting over the years (about Bergman) were far more enthusiastic about something else: a Bergman television series then being shown in Scandinavia that was causing a sensation. For the first time Bergman was a *popular* success in his own native Sweden, to a degree never experienced in the television medium there.

It was not only a matter of wild television ratings. As a friend of mine, long a severe critic of Bergman's work, confided, "I never thought he had it in him – all those heavy, metaphysical things – and now look, addressing us where we live, really in today's world, our real problems, the way we feel. It's extraordinary!" He went on to relate how he and his wife, in the throes of ending their marriage, would sit week after week, glued to the television set, reliving their own experience, bringing new understanding to it.

Scenes from a Marriage represents yet another radical departure for Bergman. The original TV version is made up of six episodes ("scenes"), each lasting fifty minutes. A vastly reduced, but still lengthy, 168-minute version was re-edited for international film distribution. It too was successful, though not nearly as satisfying, I feel, as the TV series. But any way you look at it, *Scenes* stands as a prodigious *tour de force*. Bergman wrote the first draft in a month, the shooting schedule was forty-five days, the crew numbered five people, the budget was $240,000, and Sven Nykvist shot it in 16mm.

In a way, Bergman is still very much in the familiar Strindberg territory of a couple's agonized inter-relationship. But the rhythm and style of *Scenes* has an immensely different feel. If Bergman showed signs of focusing on the everyday bourgeois way of Swedish life a few years earlier in *The Touch*, this work pushes that option much further. There is, first and foremost, a radical simplification of setting, framing, lighting. Camera movement is strictly functional, though unerringly effective in serving Bergman's clarity of purpose: following a movement, showing what is to be shown, picking up the telling detail, catching the look in the eye, unobtrusively zooming in at the right moment. Nothing extraordinary in this, but we are dealing here with professional skills given over to creating a style that is self-effacing in order to highlight something else. What counts are the actors and the words – and the spirit animating them.

And that determines every aspect of the filmmaking process. Bergman's writing is brilliant in the way it captures the mundane, the rhythms of conversation, the games being played. There is a deliberate literalness in all of this, an ordinariness. The behaviour is observed, and successive layers of mood or subterfuge are peeled away, exposing the feelings, the strivings, the concerns, and, of course, the malaise. Bergman avoids anything resembling melodrama, thereby also avoiding a soap-opera flavour, something this kind of drama tends to be prone to (and which undermined *The Touch*).

This is minimalization of a sort vastly different from the highly stylized austerity of the early 1960s. Call this television naturalness – an everyday verisimilitude in lighting and framing and movement – that shuns effect, "depth," lyrical comment, in favour of surface authenticity, "normal" colours, locations, and so on. Liv Ullmann and Erland Josephson face the monumental challenge brilliantly, bearing the acting weight of the enterprise. Bibi Andersson, Jan Malmsjö, Gunnel Lindblom and a few others move in and out, but essentially it is Liv and Erland, at home, at work, on the street, in the country house. Bergman captures the sophisticated, comfortable Swedish middle class, its rituals, its way of talking – and its relative emptiness. This is powerful stuff, a study of the relationship of a man and a woman through marriage and divorce and the aftermath, seen exclusively from their point of view and their limited vision. As such, it is tellingly recognizable not only to Swedes but to all western peoples who have achieved a certain standard of living in today's materialistic society.

There are many ways to situate what has happened. It is probably quite accurate to surmise, as Peter Cowie does, that Bergman was being fiscally responsible. Strictly Swedish film financing had become too difficult and risky an undertaking. Not wanting to go the American route as he did with *The Touch*, he felt compelled to turn to television and, thanks to vastly cheaper filmmaking techniques, thereby vastly to reduce the costs.

And why not? In his new freedom, and with it the lack of compulsion to do certain kinds of things in certain kinds of ways according to certain grandiose ambitions, was he not free to turn to the simple, fundamental, pared-down language of television? Here was an opportunity for Bergman the *writer* to be served by Bergman the director, giving his all to the words and the actors instead of to the immensely complex and signifying medium of film language as a whole. Having gone through the period of positive rejection, and with the mystique of aesthetic beauty no longer binding, he could now do whatever he felt like doing. This kind of television enterprise was offering a new challenge.

Was *Scenes* his implicit judgment on television drama: drama brought down to the size of the TV box, mundane, despiritualized, small, everyday – and far, far removed from the world of his movies with all the *deep* mystery, the *heightened* anguish, the *isolated* islands, the *ravishing* countryside, the voices from *another* level of existence, the *existential* probing, the searching for the deep *meaning* of life?

I am overstating the case, but one might be excused for feeling that the fundamental reason for *Scenes from a Marriage*'s success in Scandinavia was precisely because it ruthlessly limits itself to surface-behaviour observation, eschewing the poetry, the metaphysical soul journey. In other words, most Swedes, living their lives in a decidedly secular culture, would watch themselves with fascination portrayed in *Scenes* with a reduced cinematography that itself reflects the drastically reduced horizons. Especially for those who could not accept Bergman's metaphysical probing, *Scenes from a Marriage* was signalling his acceptance of a world view they were comfortable with. Or so it might seem.

THE MAGIC FLUTE

Ingmar Bergman, as we have by now often repeated, had been through his period of agonizing loss of faith in the ability of film language – and therefore of his own artistic activity – to reach reality and communicate it. But having destroyed (for a while, anyway) his own mythology and accepted his role of "humble artisan" incapable of dealing with the great issues, he was free to exercize his craft. Just as he gloried in bringing all manner of dramas to life in the theatre with brilliant eclecticism, solving this craft problem and that, trying this variation or innovation and that, so now his movie films and his television films were following that same kind of agenda. And in all this, as also we have seen, he was reflecting some of the mainline preoccupations and attitudes of western culture.

Inevitably, then, he would be exploring television, a medium related to but not identical with film. Earlier on, in 1969, *The Rite* had really been a minimalist theatre play transposed to television. In the same year, *The Fårö Document* was film documentary with many talking heads using television to reach a large audience. And, of course, a superb though aesthetically modest "televisual" experience, crafted expressly for the medium, followed in 1973 with *Scenes from a Marriage*.

The artist in Bergman, however, could not be long contained within the narrow parameters even of these markedly different kinds of television presentations. Inevitably there would be more experimenting, more unleashing of the gorgeous possibilities growing out of his renewed creative exuberance. Since television is not cinema, since it is another medium, this meant a different approach, a different feeling and texture, from those experienced in his movies.

The Magic Flute is a marvellous case in point. Bergman's next television venture, it proved an immensely intelligent and delightful one. It reveals a Bergman totally conscious of the artistic, "not real" character of film creation, and of the sheer joy of artistic spectacle whereby indeed the artist "touches" other human beings in a kind of communal celebration. This he achieves by filming what seems to be an actual stage opera performance before a live family audience.

The Magic Flute was shown on New Year's Day, 1975, Sveriges Radió's (and Bergman's) holiday gift to the nation. Unlike *Scenes*, it was a production of great technical (and financial) ambition – symphonic orchestra, huge cast, a reconstructed Drottningholms stage in the studios of the Swedish Film Institute, the first stereo soundtrack for a Swedish TV production, and a special high quality 16mm film stock that was then blown up to 35mm for theatrical release, with amazing success.

Hordes of Swedes, it seems, worked to ensure the highest quality. And that they succeeded in doing.

Bergman's *The Magic Flute* is not really *The Magic Flute*. Perhaps it should be called *The Magic Flute: A Joyful Theatre Event* ... or some such thing. I described earlier on the bewitching power of the Pa-mi-na scene from that opera re-created in 1968 by Bergman in *Hour of the Wolf*, and I was expecting something similar, and even more fulfilling, since Bergman was now filming the entire opera. No way, as they say! Bergman's *The Magic Flute* is the very antithesis of what I had seen – for a number of reasons.

Replacing the solemnity, mystery, might, and profundity is a spirit of sparkling joy, fairy-tale wonder, and exuberant youthfulness. Bergman has cut out certain of the more grim or menacing sections. In restoring the Drottningholm Palace stage, he goes back to Mozart's late eighteenth-century period, complete with the tiny stage space, props, and sets of that time. The whole look of the opera is one of childlike wonder, magic, fantasy, with bright colours and tongue-in-cheek backdrops. There is a total rejection of realistic verisimilitude: all is patently, delightfully theatrical make-believe. In perfect keeping with the dominant tone, Bergman's cast is obviously chosen for their youthful good looks; and cute youngsters act as angels, floating down in a balloon-powered basket.

It is not that Bergman throws away the profound and serious moments of beauty and mystery of Mozart's sublime work. They are still affecting, but they are also very self-consciously "sublime": sacred artifacts of our culture with whatever meaning or resonances we attach to them. (In that, they do share a common quality with the *Hour of the Wolf* segment.) Above all, they in no way determine the overall rhythm and tonality.

This applies to the opera as captured and structured by Bergman, and still much more to the *film as a whole*. For, as suggested above, this movie is not only a transmitting of Mozart's opera to film and television. Bergman's camera is omnipresent: Nykvist captures the stage bits from the audience, from the wings, and from different stage perspectives. But he also captures the stage hands, the singers in their hustle and bustle before, during, and after the performance, and, most importantly, the theatre audience itself. *The Magic Flute* is made up of all these elements, mixing all three levels in one creation, one communal celebration of beauty and joy involving everyone there, on or off the stage. No wonder the victory of joy, love, and life in the story is assured: Bergman's repeated cuts to beautiful, glowing close-ups of children (including his own) and of other members of the audience (many of them his friends or colleagues) communicate an excitement, a benign and glorious connivance that is irresistible.

Bergman exposes the stage medium for what it is and the experience of the stage audience for what *it* is; but by that very fact, the *film*-viewing audience is made aware as well of its own role in the process in a further conscious act of affectionate connivance. If demystification, deconstruction, and self-consciousness are all part of the postmodern experience, Bergman in his amazingly sophisticated direction of *The Magic Flute* has demonstrated that joy and fun can be part of that experience as well.

And another point: perhaps Bergman shares the feeling that the medium of television is at its best and most unique in capturing *events* (hence the immense popularity of televized sports), and in sharing their relative totality with the audience. In that respect *The Magic Flute* is a complex hybrid – part event, part stage performance, part movie.

FACE TO FACE

Ingmar Bergman's performance as a film artist from 1969 through the 1970s is a phenomenon fascinating to watch for anyone attuned to the evolution of an art form, and, really, of a whole culture. The range covered, as we have seen, is extremely broad. And it is brilliant in its creations, at least if we think of those films between 1969 and 1975 – *Cries and Whispers, Scenes from a Marriage,* and *The Magic Flute.*

Alas, most people agree, Bergman's next effort, *Face to Face,* appearing on Swedish television in the spring of 1976, cannot match these three predecessors. The four-part TV series was edited down to a two-hour-and-a-quarter movie; that is the version I saw, although I did read the screenplay for the entire series.

In many of the criticisms one senses a hesitancy about being severe, probably because the film has a tone of high seriousness, a desire to grapple with real and relevant human experiences – and probably too because of the feeling that the film is terribly personal, reflecting Bergman's still unresolved fears (no matter his occasional claims that he was finally freed from these), the tortured aspect of his psyche, the danger of his living on the edge of neurosis and nightmare. In other words, those destructive forces that seemed (at least partially) to take over his film work during what I have been calling the *ingenting* years could never wholly be purged.

Just why *Face to Face* does not come together satisfyingly as a work of art is difficult to pin down. At one in-depth level, it may well be as Frank Gado brilliantly asserts:

> If *Face to Face* does not quicken because Bergman could not create sufficient distance between his persona and himself, the deeper reason for its

artistic failure is a function of his despair: Art and magic have always been inextricably bound in Bergman's mind; after he had firmly rejected the possibility that, through art, he could discover – or conjure – a credible escape from the terrors of his personal prison, his fictions, drained of their vitalizing purpose, steadily lose coherence. Instead of seeking the magic key to pass through the walls of the self into a daylit world, he turns inward to describe the darkness of his cell and its instruments of torture.[2]

Gado attempts nothing less than a psychoanalysis of Bergman through his films and, as I have remarked, one may experience reservations along the way. This particular insight, however, is immensely enriching when applied to most of Bergman's films from *Persona* through to the end, though not to the four or five among them that rate among his best. Moreover, Bergman's "despair" about art's ability to reveal to him an escape route from his personal terrors – paralleling what I have been alluding to as the inability to reach and communicate reality – is not as simple as all that, being only part of a never completely extinguished broader dialectic (as we have seen in its various guises).

Be that as it may, the fact remains that *Face to Face* is not terribly affecting, and it does not break new ground. True, Bergman does reflect the shattered syntax of the "new cinema" by having his protagonist Jenny (Liv Ullmann) and, really, the whole film, do all kinds of "unprepared things," defying logic, reason, causality, structure. The problem: it is as if Bergman, the total master, were pressing different keys of the (pre-programmed) creative computer. This thing or that happens, this or that artistic effect is produced, but does he really care about it, does he feel it? Is he involved? Liv Ullmann's technically spectacular performance seems to undergo the same fate. All is there, and yet … we are curiously uninvolved. The contrast with the obvious parallel situations in earlier films makes this eminently clear. In those films the screen fairly sizzled, Bergman was discovering and sharing and trying to work things out with us, and we were mesmerized. The Bergman "magic moments"? *That* is what is missing in *Face to Face*.

And this relatively uninspired tone permeates the conversations. There is something pedestrian and literal, too spelled out and controlled, as Bergman psychoanalyses and explains Jenny. The dreams and horrors are there on the screen but scarcely resonate within us; and certainly the TV-esque long dialogues and modest film language do not make these moments cinematically fresh and exciting. Even the title of the film is revelatory. Remember *Through a Glass Darkly*, taken from Paul's First Letter to the Corinthians, chapter 13,

2 See Frank Gado, *The Passion of Ingmar Bergman* (Durham: Duke University Press, 1986), 448.

verse 12: "For now we see through a glass darkly. But then, face to face." In the earlier film one felt Bergman's very life on the line, its anguished need for meaningfulness and the suffering that entailed. "Face to face" is Paul's answer: in the future life we will experience God as He really is (and with that, meaningfulness and fulfilment). Does Jenny's finally *facing* things really convince us, does this breakthrough experience resonate in any way – even though Bergman trains his camera on light coming through a stained-glass window after comforting words about love's outlasting of death?

The old Bergman cycle that ended most of his films in a reaffirmation of the life force rings rather hollow in *Face to Face*. If one truly shares the postmodernist credo, it can prove extremely difficult at times (I mean, without mockery, irony, and so on) to summon the creative energies capable of being vital and convincing in the reaffirmation of "myths" one can no longer embrace.

THE SERPENT'S EGG

Face to Face was to be the last feature movie Ingmar Bergman would make in Sweden until *Fanny and Alexander*. The infamous "tax scandal" was the reason, a tragicomic series of events begun at a rehearsal in the Royal Dramatic Theatre at the end of January 1976 and terminated only in 1979, with Bergman's triumphal return to Sweden. There were major consequences, obviously for Bergman and those close to him, but also for Swedish culture as a whole, and, almost surely, for Swedish political life.

Accused of not fully paying his taxes, Bergman was treated with reprehensible lack of respect by the government and the police, being forced thereby to experience in public life the humiliation that haunts his films and the explosion of those nebulous forces always threatening his protagonists. He collapsed, spent time in hospital, and in April left Sweden, vowing to remain in voluntary exile, "unable to work in a country run by such a heavy-handed bureaucracy." Paris, Los Angeles, New York, Berlin, Copenhagen, Oslo – such was the odyssey of Bergman and his wife before they finally settled in Munich, eventually to establish home base there at the Residenztheater.

Meanwhile back in Sweden Bergman's lawyers were winning one court battle after another, Bergman eventually being completely exonerated. Too late, however, for the ruling Social Democrats, who had been in power uninterruptedly for over forty years: in the fall 1976 elections they were pushed out of office, Bergman's boorish treatment, most feel, proving to be the *coup de grace*.

Bergman's fall into exile, however, was sagely provided with a safety net: unofficially, he often returned to Fårö, increasingly so with the passage of time, until the final official homecoming. But that is another story.

The Serpent's Egg is his first feature made outside Sweden, and it is tempting to see it as resulting from this exile, and as some kind of metaphor growing out of his tax hounding. In point of fact *The Serpent's Egg* was already scheduled before that event by producer Dino de Laurentiis and Bergman, and it is the making of that film that in the first place brought Bergman and his wife to Munich in the summer of 1976 as planned, along with his major collaborators, Sven Nykvist and Liv Ullmann.

As a child of this century Bergman was marked, of course, by the Nazi nightmare. In his writings and interviews he has often spoken about his political non-involvement, his own and Swedish guilt feelings, even his boyhood enthusiasm for Adolf Hitler and the Nazi Youth Movement after he visited cousins in Germany. For a while it became commonplace for him to confess that he and his father were among those Swedes who sympathized with what was going on in pre–World War II Germany, even including some of its anti-Semitic measures. "Not true," scoffs Erland Josephson. Referring back to their university-days production of Shakespeare's *The Merchant of Venice*, in which the Jewish Erland himself played Shylock, he points out that young director Bergman slanted the play into a clear condemnation of Nazi anti-Semitism and that they had press conferences where they made that clear. Bergman was part of the university anti-Nazi protestations; his father, Pastor Erik Bergman, actually sheltered in his home off and on for a number of years a young Jewish refugee from Nazi persecution. "Ingmar, I think, at times feels the need of dramatizing this kind of anti-Semitic persona both for himself and for his father. Good old Swedish guilt? It becomes a kind of novelist's truth for him – but it does not correspond to reality!" Erland smiles.[3]

One can make of all this whatever one wants, up to a point; but the dehumanized madness so long tolerated and then enshrined, consciously or not, by the German people had its profound effect on Bergman's sensibility. And it certainly nourished his consciousness of the rampant human potential for absurdity and evil. That he should make a film on that phenomenon, then, should not prove terribly surprising.

By and large *The Serpent's Egg* fared well neither at the box office nor at the hands of the critics. The movie brings us back to 1923, re-creating cabaret life in a Berlin staggering under inflation reaching surrealistic proportions. For those looking for insightful analysis, a rich historical placing, or a profound and new symbol of Germany on the brink of Nazism, *The Serpent's Egg* may prove disappointing. As for portraying Bergmanian personality disintegration –

3 From my transcribing of that informal conversation already alluded to that Mikael Timm and I had over brunch with Erland Josephson in June 1992.

in this instance as experienced by the circus and cabaret artistes Manuela (Liv Ullmann) and her brother-in-law Abel Rosenberg (David Carradine) – well, the *ingenting* period had already produced far deeper and more nuanced incarnations.

I remember my first viewing of the film: what on earth was Bergman up to? In my disappointment I turned to his own words: how right he had been over the years when he insisted that his films had to be made in Sweden, for that really was all he knew and lived, the very grounding of his imagination and memories.

Possibly I was missing the point. One of the cruel *bons mots* aimed at Bergman in his early films was that he was the "best German director in Sweden." That, of course, referred to his obvious and sometimes heavy reliance on much of the atmosphere, figurations, themes, and even philosophic gloom of the German films of the 1920s – which we tend to label, somewhat inaccurately, as German expressionism. Bergman, to be sure, was far from alone in this: everyone was influenced by that German period, even the Soviets. That includes especially France's poetic realism, Alfred Hitchcock, and the whole film noir tradition in Hollywood and elsewhere.

Years later, near the end of a course I was giving on the so-called "German expressionist cinema," I decided to take a chance and show another incarnation of this filmic approach, call it "Swedish film *auteur* Bergman returning to the period and place that gave birth to this kind of cinema" – expecting, of course, to have to come to grips with why the film in question (*The Serpent's Egg*) did not work.

The effect on my class – and on myself – was electrifying. Most of the students (typically in their early twenties) had little contact with Bergman's film work, but they were astounded at his ability not only to capture with such brilliance and intensity the spirit, types, mood, and settings of the German films we had been seeing, but also, in hindsight (of course), formally to translate all of this into an explicit metaphor of the nascent rising Nazi phenomenon.

In other words, within the particular context of that class we were bringing a specialist's kind of filmic awareness to the viewing of the film. An essential part of our appreciation grew out of our ability to experience Bergman's re-creating of the *filmic signs* of that era, relating them back to the German period, and seeing what Bergman himself was bringing to them. As for those who had significant contact with Bergman's own work, we were going through the same exercise with his own familiar concerns and figurations – his signs, as he came to grips with this genre.

This is very much (I believe) an essential part of the contemporary sensibility and awareness, that part of it that we call postmodernist. In this context, as we have seen, the main thrust centres on that game of signs referring back and forth, *that* being the main "meaningfulness," the major motivator for the expenditure of creative energy. Which is fine, as far as it goes. But those seeking "reality," "truth," "understanding," "depth," "commitment," "action" may well be demanding a vastly different film experience.

Experienced in the postmodernist way, *The Serpent's Egg* sees and reveals things through a *screen* ... consciously. Those Berlin expressionistic streets (created in a Munich studio), that livid colour and lighting, those garish cabaret scenes (grotesque, obscene, sardonic), the circus ambience, the mad scientist, the sterile labs; those labyrinthine passageways and winding stairwells, the general humiliation and degradation, the faceless zombie crowds in rhythmic queue – on and on it goes – we've vaguely seen it all before, say, in Fritz Lang's *Metropolis* and the various *Dr Mabuse* films, in *Variety*, in *The Cabinet of Dr Caligari*, even in *The Blue Angel*, as well as in how many subsequent films recapturing this or that aspect of the era.

Mix it in with a dash of Nazi Brown Shirts and some dreadful street beatings with Jews as the primary target, and you have a world through which Manuela and Abel wander listlessly, almost helplessly, already burdened as they are with their Bergmanian human condition. *They*, however, are not the main concern, as they would have been in typical Bergman films. Now it is the external world within which they are entrapped that counts. I say world, but what I should say is the external metaphor of what history has revealed to us as a horror period leading to the most murderous war yet created by humanity in its collective folly.

So we are dealing here with highly complex responses, whereby we are pulled in yet pushed away almost simultaneously. Bergman's main energy unquestionably is given to re-creating a *filmic* world, which itself (historically) was reflecting something it did not understand, something about which it had, at best, vague premonitions and perhaps more than a touch of voyeuristic connivance. Bergman does not "believe in it" literally, and neither do we. But when viewed with postmodern awareness, *The Serpent's Egg* becomes a fascinating, if none too reassuring, experience.

AUTUMN SONATA

If *Cries and Whispers* can be referred to as a "musical composition for four instruments," then *Autumn Sonata* can indeed be called a sonata, a duet (for cello and violin?). And what two artists, one is tempted to add, and what a maestro! Ingmar Bergman is in splendid form, privileged to be working with two great actresses. This was to be his last film with Liv Ullmann, the actress who dominated the second half of his career. And as for *Ingrid* – with Garbo, Sweden's most luminous gift to international super-stardom – the film world was awaiting with immense expectations the first collaboration between the two legendary Bergmans. So much so, as it turned out, that before shooting began, the film was already sold across the world.

A note about a film drenched in personal overtones: still refusing to work in Sweden, Bergman does the next best thing, shooting the film in Norway, Liv Ullmann's native land. Their daughter, Linn Ullmann, plays the Liv character (Eva) as a little girl. The romantic Bergman/Ullmann saga, of course, has long since ceased. In 1971 Bergman married the Countess Ingrid von Rosen: their marriage would last until her death in 1995. However, Bergman continued to work in friendly professional collaboration with Liv Ullmann through a whole series of films. This may not all be germane to *Autumn Sonata*, but it may help account for a certain tone of reconciliation that I allude to later.

Norway: I was intrigued, more than a little hoping that that country's glorious landscape might reactivate Bergman's old enthusiasm for the natural paradise (because I like that sort of thing). But that use of nature had long been discarded: Bergman all but ignores the mountains, fjords, green pastures, and blue skies. Except for a modest incidental background at the beginning and at the end (especially when Eva – Liv Ullmann – visits her dead child in the graveyard), *Autumn Sonata* resolutely stays indoors: this is indeed a chamber music film, an intimist drama that recalls *Through a Glass Darkly*, *Winter Light*, and *Cries and Whispers*, going even beyond them in the minute and painstaking observation of the relationship between a mother and daughter.

However, there is no reduced-for-TV paring down of film language à la *Scenes from a Marriage*. *Autumn Sonata* fairly glows with beauty, the modest interior of the vicarage home of Eva and her pastor husband captured with loveliness by Sven Nykvist. All is suggestion, presences, the past, cries and whispers. We are back in the Bergman inner world, softened this time by the play of light on wood textures, and by the muted, burnished tones of the house.

All that we know about Ingmar Bergman points to the intense personal nature of this story about a world-famous artist and the daughter who feels unloved. We sense that it is both Bergman's relationship with his mother and his relationship with (at least some of) his own children that we are experiencing. The movie explodes with intensity in scene after scene as Bergman excels in what he does so matchlessly, revealing the almost limitless complexity of the women's interrelating. Confession, accusation, hatred, love, longing, discouragement – it's all there, played with unerring precision and intelligence by Liv Ullmann, and with awesome, invisible artistry by Ingrid Bergman in this, her greatest filmic display of acting.

And the film has its dazzling moments. One cannot write about *Autumn Sonata* without waxing rhapsodic over the Chopin A Minor Prelude scene. We are mesmerized by the music and by the faces of the two women registering endlessly complex, ambiguous emotions, defining the relationship to a devastating degree, as first Eva, then Charlotte, give their rendition of the Prelude – the mother all but annihilating her daughter in the process, as she brilliantly analyses the piece. This as well is Maestro Bergman celebrating art and his love for music. (On a personal note again, it is a Bergman ex-wife, the professional pianist Käbi Laretei, who does the actual playing.)

Everything I have written above would seem to indicate that *Autumn Sonata* signals Bergman's return to his earlier, pre-deconstruction cinema. That, however, is not the case: deconstruction consciousness has left its mark on the very structure of the film – and, of course, on the way we experience it. We are now, in a manner of speaking, being addressed directly, and not just through the story, by Bergman.

For example, near the beginning of the movie, after speaking with her daughter and Pastor Viktor (Halvar Björk), Charlotte putters about her bedroom, alone and chattering away. Speaking to herself, however, she is not, for eventually she looks directly at the camera (and so at us). All along she has been confiding in each one of us spectators, as in a personal friend. In reality, of course, the question arises as to *which* Bergman is addressing us directly. In any case, we are made aware of our existence as partakers in this experience of film watching. And Bergman uses other strategies, at the level of plot and time, to achieve the same distanciation from the diegetical context (which I shall not go into here).

But there is more. Bergman frames his story with Pastor Viktor, a very minor character in terms of the characters and plot within the world created by the film. Viktor is a pleasant, intelligent, unaggressive, kindly, and also slightly ineffectual, unimposing person: the quiet, patient husband of Eva, with problems of his own. However, *he* is the narrator of the story, speaking directly to each one of us, eye to eye, occupying the "downstage" foreground area of the screen to one side, with Eva "upstage" in the background – and this both at the beginning and at the end of the film. Viktor tells us all about Eva and her mother, expresses his hopes and so on, confiding in us, he the storyteller, we the listener-spectators. Occasionally he jumps back into the diegetical dimension of the movie, where he plays a much more humble role.

This gives us a certain distance. We concentrate more on the presence of the story-teller/film director; and he establishes a tone of serenity and kindliness, containing and controlling the histrionics of the two protagonists. It is as if Bergman were telling us that he has achieved a certain emotional distance from all of this. Both of his own parents are now dead, and the past is remembered with a relatively benign and forgiving attitude. It is not by accident that Viktor happens to be a Lutheran pastor, and that Ingrid Bergman plays a world-famous artist! While brilliantly communicating the passions, beliefs, hopes, anguish, selfishness – whatever – of each of his characters, he makes us see that it is *they*, and not Ingmar Bergman, who are going through the experience. There is a spirit of reconciliation here, and good will, a kind of unexalted hope. But the intense "content" is never diluted: the implacable close-ups of Ingrid Bergman, no longer the enchanting young beauty but a mature woman already struggling with the cancer that would end her life, ensure this. So there also is the presence of aging and the premonition of death – as there is, too, in Bergman's use of his old friend Gunnar Björnstrand (he too not far removed from death) in the silent role of Charlotte's confidant.

Autumn Sonata, then, is a beautiful, mature, and benign "contemporary" Bergman film text. It reveals yet another aspect, this one noble and serious, of postmodern art, the re-constructing of the Bergman text that has survived the ravages of deconstruction and the loss of the mythic struggle for meaningfulness but is now endowed with a benign consciousness revealed as part of the formal structure.

CHAPTER SEVEN

THE LITTLE WORLD?

The Fårö Document (II)	filming fall 1977 – fall 1979
From the Life of the Marionettes	filming October – December 1979 release July 1980
Fanny and Alexander	filming November 1981 – June 1982 release Christmas 1982
After the Rehearsal	filming 1983 release May 1984

THE FÅRÖ DOCUMENT (II)

After *Autumn Sonata* Ingmar Bergman's activity as a film director, one is tempted to say, peters out anti-climactically – with of course the prodigious exception of *Fanny and Alexander*. Bergman was spending more and more time "unofficially" in Sweden, and that permitted him, in leisurely fashion, to make his second *Fårö Document*. The theatrical activity was continuing back in Munich; there he directed his strange and anti-cinematic movie, *From the Life of the Marionettes*, hardly a Bergman "film," even though he himself rates it as such. Then came his "official" finale, *Fanny and Alexander*. That was to be followed by a number of filmed television subjects, notably *After the Rehearsal*, which was actually released in most countries as a feature film, in spite of Bergman's strenuous – and justified, I feel – objections that it was not meant for film screens.

To what extent Bergman's self-imposed semi-exile significantly changed or even abbreviated his career as a film director is impossible to determine, naturally enough. My own hunch is that after the *ingenting* years the film-directing game was played out, in spite of some rather dazzling exceptions.

It was pretty well inevitable that he would settle back into Sweden, especially after being totally cleared of the tax evasion charges. All along he had been returning to Fårö, especially in the summers, and in the spirit of a growing serenity and sense of belonging, he decided to follow up on his 1969 *The Fårö Document*. For almost two years, beginning in late 1977, he had Arne Carlsson shooting in 16mm just about anything and everything on the island; the TV film was released by Sveriges Radió on Christmas Eve, 1979.

Fårö Document (II) has really nothing to do with Bergman's artistic output as a feature film director. It testifies rather to his abiding dedication to the people of the island that had become his true home. It reveals an aware, socially conscious human being trying to capture the spirit of a certain people, a certain way of life, in an effort to serve both in their struggle for survival. As such – and like its predecessor – it is a tribute to Bergman as a human being, to that "other side" not so clearly evident in most of the films that have enshrined him as one of the major artists of our century. It serves too to reveal his growing detachment from the problems of film language, its manipulation, its relationship to reality, its attempts at creating "art."

FROM THE LIFE OF THE MARIONETTES

It seems necessary to tarry a few moments on the two film/television efforts that immediately precede and follow *Fanny and Alexander*. Both *From the Life of the Marionettes* and *After the Rehearsal* serve as strong reminders that the playfulness and good humour sparkling through *Fanny and Alexander* are far from a total picture of the "final" Bergman, who still is informed by a sensibility haunted by a dark, harsh spirit verging at times on the nihilistic – one side of the recurring dialectic that is the very essence of Bergman's work, the wellspring of his creativity.

From the Life of the Marionettes, which Bergman shot in the last three months of 1979, closes off the filmmaking ventures in Munich (even though he would direct a number of theatre plays there before returning definitively, full-time, to Sweden). *Marionettes* plunges us back into the *ingenting* period. It is an example of what is left after one has "disarticulated" film language and removed all the layers of make-believe, Bergman reducing his film text as never before.

He uses colour at the beginning and the end, and he shifts locations a few times, but what dominates are long, seemingly interminable monologues or dialogues succeeding one another lifelessly. Often the actors talk straight on camera; and always there is a deliberately cultivated feeling of artificiality. The setting shifts from the sleazy – the protagonist murders, then sodomizes, a prostitute in a Munich strip club – to the clinical grey of psychiatric offices and prison cells. People are walking zombies, but completely deprived of cinematic gothic layerings and above all of mythical overtones. Bergman, it seems clear, meant the production to be seen consciously as a *movie*; and perhaps his point is to remove all hidden artifice from filmmaking, by theatrical distanciation and denuding beyond the point of return.

As usual he relentlessly peels away the psychological layers; but now the operation reveals ... *ingenting*. Even the psychoanalyst is revealed as one more symbol of futility as he pursues psychological "understanding," one more unlovely victim in a world of meaninglessness. So the signs are just that, empty surfaces: we are light years removed from the use of sign in, say, our strawberries and milk scene of *The Seventh Seal*. The nature of film to entertain, charm, or enlighten is denied in its very texture. And as for the alienated audience, Bergman may well have succumbed to what seems to be (as my friend Nils Petter Sundgren likes to put it) the sacred duty of the German cinema to produce boredom.

AFTER THE REHEARSAL

First projected as a movie at the Cannes Film Festival in May 1984, *After the Rehearsal*, Bergman insists, is anything but cinema: it is meant as a seventy-two-minute television play, an austere exercise for three actors on a deserted stage (except for two brief flashbacks on that same stage, centred on a boy and on a girl). As such, it constitutes an example of the immense creative activity outside of *film* direction that Bergman has pursued since *Fanny and Alexander*.

In a way this is a Bergman we know well, in his traditional role of eliciting superb acting performances from his gifted team. Erland Josephson does the honours as the self-introspective director (with strong Bergman resonances, need one add), and Ingrid Thulin makes a welcome return as an actress and mistress from the past. There is something touching in seeing the fine performance of Lena Olin as the young and manipulative actress, some thirty-eight years after Bergman's first feature film, *Crisis*, in which her father, Stig Olin, figured prominently (as he did in a number of Bergman's other earliest features).

After the Rehearsal is yet another exercise in the scalpel-and-incision method of psychological revealing so familiar to Bergman film fans. Little relief here, little joy, hope, vitality – except that there is some recognizable humanity, some groping towards something, some manifestation, yes, of the human heart. There is a striving to come to terms with one's character; this is imbued with pathos by the awareness of the onset of old age. These characters, indeed, are far from zombie-like in their incarnations; they are served by a strong, clever dialogue that does not forsake the joy of inventive repartee, however sombre and pessimistic the mood may be.

Theatrical austerity is the key note – a denuded stage, a few props, long dialogue encounters, and controlled lighting on a black background. But Sven Nykvist is there, ever the master of the human face, permitted to render movement, light, and framing into aesthetically fulfilling patterns.

And that seems to be that, two minor exercises in anti-cinema, though of special interest for those fascinated by Bergman's dialectical progressions. What we are encountering here is a sort of negative manifestation of the postmodern sensibility, i.e., a distrust of cinematic signs, belief systems, visions of what reality is or could be – and the ensuing anguish, or bitterness, or sense of quasi-despair. These two bleak texts express the withering of the human soul. Of course the "total" Bergman of this period is so much more, and that explains why he chose to leave the film-directing scene in a far more spectacular and affirmative manner, as the world well knows. *Fanny and Alexander* was to be his official adieu.

FANNY AND ALEXANDER

The expectations surrounding Ingmar Bergman's farewell feature film were immense. Here was his first *Swedish* feature fiction film since 1976, the most expensive Swedish movie ever made. Besides, when Bergman publicly insists that "this is my last," well ...

Fanny and Alexander has met those expectations, both as a three-hour-plus feature movie and even more as a five-hour television series. Joyous, playful, a loving celebration of filmmaking and of life, breathing fun and the spirit of reconciliation, it brings the film-directing career to a triumphant close. From the particular vantage point of the concerns of this book, *Fanny and Alexander* completes the circle: more than any other film Bergman has made, it becomes a kind of incarnation of one aspect of what has been playing a dominant role in our contemporary culture. The prophet may not be using the jargon of the western intellectual/cultural elite, but he is profoundly attuned to the phenomenon it is attempting to describe and explain. I am referring, as already stated in this part of the essay, to postmodernism, to a tendency in Bergman, begun in earnest with *Persona* and informing to a greater or lesser extent most of his subsequent film work. But whereas *Persona* and the other *"ingenting"* films, along with *The Serpent's Egg* and *From the Life of the Marionettes*, were anguished expressions of postmodernism's dark side, *Fanny and Alexander* incarnates its celebratory, tongue-in-cheek, playful spirit.

In my first viewing of the film I watched as the children's father, Oscar Ekdahl, lay dying, the whole family gathered round his bed. In a tight medium shot the camera isolates him and his actress wife, Emilie, sitting close beside him. Bergman eventually shoots them in individual facial close-up, in a reverse angle series, as the dying actor utters his last words. He laughs ironically: "I could play the Ghost now, really well." And he looks at his wife, murmuring *"Ingenting ... "* I remember groaning interiorly. Oh no, thought I, is this Bergman's final (and definitive) statement about his art, his life, everything? Are we back to the nothing that was *Persona*'s final word?

But then, wonder of wonders, Oscar continues: "Nothing ... nothing separates me from you. Not now and not later. I know that. (*He shuts his eyes.*) I see it quite clearly. I'll be closer to you now than when I lived."[1]

Bergman had pulled the rug from under my feet, tricked me, played with my expectations. For here is the radical antithesis of the ending of *Persona*. The *ingenting* of that film has been turned inside out, into an affirmation of

---

1   Taken from the soundtrack of the film. Not in the final cut, but in the published text, Bergman has Oscar add: "I'll soon be dead. Will you hold my hand? (*Emilie nods*) Eternity, Emilie! (*Pause*) Eternity!" See *Fanny and Alexander* (London: Penguin, 1982).

love and of life. To put it another way, the Bergman of the later film has reduced the *Persona* moment to its value as mere sign, a Bergman-imposed sign. And by that very fact he has exposed Oscar's ringing affirmation equally as a Bergman-imposed sign. I am unquestionably touched by the solemnity and the gentleness of this moment, but I also chuckle at Bergman's sly tactics.

Here is a film that exults in this game, appealing to that postmodern awareness which sees all as a game of signs interrelating. My response is a delightfully divided one, for there is no denying the beauty and power of the moment – of those "sacred" moments in real life that it represents. And there is no denying the pathos, right after, engendered by Alexander's fear as he is called to the bedside, his hand forcibly clasped by his father's, and then by his fleeing that unbearable grasp – oh yes, have we not often seen Bergman's revulsion at human suffering, evil, death? And then Bergman pursues his complex game. Oscar's mother enacts the reverential ritual of folding the dead man's arms over his breast, sacralizing the moment. Bergman then abruptly cuts to two illuminated shots from one of Alexander's lantern slides, depicting an angel hovering over Jesus, Mary, and Joseph – thereby revealing that the signs he is showing of the faith the Ekdahls have been born into are just that, Bergman's chosen signs from the culture, from memory, from whatever. Lest we relax with that somewhat intellectual awareness, he cuts to the two children in bed, awakened by their mother's cries. They tiptoe to the sliding doors of the room in which their father's body lies at rest. The doors are just sufficiently open to permit them to see the body, with their mother, clad in her nightgown, walking back and forth, rending the silence with primal screams of bereavement. No laughing matter this, no intellectual game.

Finally, Bergman tops it all off with a cut to the grand funeral march, Emilie accompanied by the elegant bishop who will try to replace their father – and Alexander, forced into the procession, muttering all the four-letter obscenities he can muster to give vent to his blasphemous rage.

Where is Bergman in all of this, what personal belief, precisely, is he trying to communicate to us? This one example testifies to a very complex aesthetic strategy, and to an attitude about film and its ability to capture reality. There was a time, as we have seen, when the artist would have made us resonate to the experience, literally, as a communication of his belief, or at least of his desire to believe. In spite of doubt, irony, culture awareness, and the rest, there was some kind of sharing of meaningful aspiration to revelation or meaningfulness. But now it is the fabricated spectacle, or rather, the self-conscious awareness that it is an artistic fabrication inspired by familiar Bergman thematic concerns of the past, that strikes us. And yet, it *is* powerful and beautiful and moving at the same time.

Conclusion? *Fanny and Alexander* spills over with gorgeous, self-conscious re-creations played out before us, immensely moving in themselves for what they represent, yet subverted by the cultivated awareness of their artificiality as signs. The opening Christmas family celebration, the return to the soul-warming nature/paradise scenes of the past, the vision of the flagellants, the angst-ridden couple, the sexual romping, the tortured crucifix, the God puppet hiding in the wall, the masks and prestidigitation, the sexual ambivalence and death-camp overtones in Uncle Isak's hidden cellar – on it goes, almost every moment a referring back to this or that Bergman film, this or that cultural icon, adding to and transforming the viewing experience. There is brilliance and beauty here – and the simultaneous avowal that nothing here is the "objective truth," the "objectively real."

The fact that the film cultivates so many radically differing styles, jumping from the warm, "real" world of the Ekdahls to the ravishingly re-created Dutch lighting and composition of the bishop's cold and austere palace, to the frightening, haunted, gothic/baroque/infernal world of Uncle Isak's hiding place only intensifies the awareness of *spectacle*. Bergman goes even further in creating the conscious make-believe quality: we see ghosts, moving statues, thought projections, even flagrant plot contradictions (e.g., the children's rescuing from the bishop), speeches, plays within the movie, slide projections.

A new dialectic has now emerged with clarity, representing the contemporary (1982) Bergman way of relating to life and to art. Bergman is not denying that for him these problems or visions or things were rooted in "reality," perhaps even *are* "real." Their objective reality is neither affirmed nor denied. For who can know? Is this reality, or is this fabrication? Who, indeed, can know? *Fanny and Alexander*, in its overall structure and in so many of its moments, has a built-in "Derrida-da-istic" deconstructionist flavour invalidating all systematic answers. *Ou presque.*

Bergman has come to terms with all his data, his myths, his concerns, his past creations of the imagination. Smilingly, he confesses that he no longer can define his life or his art in terms of whatever beliefs or world views underlie all of these. And that signifies a major change from the Bergman of previous decades, paralleling, in his own fashion, some of the great cultural evolutions of the last half-century. So what is left? Let us listen to Oscar's brother, Gustav Adolf, near the end of Bergman's last feature film:

> We Ekdahls have not come into the world to see through it, never think that. We are not equipped for such excursions. We might just as well ignore the big things. We must live in the little, the little world. We shall be content with that and cultivate it and make the best of it. Suddenly, death

strikes, suddenly the abyss opens, suddenly the storm howls and disaster is upon us – all that we *know*. But let us not think of all that unpleasantness.

We love what we can understand. We Ekdahls like our subterfuges … Dear, splendid actors and actresses, we *need* you all the same. It is you who are to give us our supernatural shudders and still more our mundane amusements.

The world is a den of thieves and night is falling. Soon, it will be the hour for robbers and murderers. Evil is breaking its chains and goes through the world like a mad dog. The poisoning affects us all, without exception, us Ekdahls and everyone else. No one escapes, not even Helena Victoria, or little Aurora over there in Amanda's lap. (*Weeps*) So it shall be. Therefore, let us be happy while we're happy, let's be kind, generous, affectionate, and good. Therefore it is necessary, and not in the least shameful, to take pleasure in *the little world*, good food, gentle smiles, fruit trees in bloom, waltzes. And now, my dearest friends, my dearest brothers and sisters, I'm done talking and you can take it for what you like – the effusions of an uncouth restaurant-owner or the pitiful babbling of an old man. It doesn't matter to me, I don't care one way or the other. I am holding a little empress in my arms. It is tangible yet immeasurable. One day she will prove me wrong, one day she will rule over not only the *little* world but over – everything! Everything![2]

Maybe Bergman has not changed that much: the simple, loving world and the nature paradise of the earlier films have not disappeared after all. They still furnish the only answer, however fragile, to the terrible realities of the *big* world. And Bergman still affirms (at least here) a kind of belief in the life force: she (the baby/life force) will rule everything. Everything!

On this rather sublime, quasi-religious note, Bergman ends. Well, not quite, nor has this essay quite ended. And on that note, let us proceed to what had been intended as the "conclusion."

2 From *Fanny and Alexander*, 207–8.

CHAPTER EIGHT

FADE INTO A DREAM:
A CONCLUSION?

Almost thirty years ago, late August, 1970: We are at Svensk Filmindustri's Råsunda Studios, which will soon close its doors, thereby ending a long and distinguished chapter in the history of Swedish filmmaking. We are enjoying one of the regularly recurring hiatuses forced upon us by the changing of the 16mm film reels every ten minutes as we interview Ingmar Bergman. My chair is close to his; with a rueful smile, he reaches over and grabs my arm. "I'm sorry to be talking this way. You mustn't be enjoying what you're hearing!"

I remember protesting, with something like "No, no, please go on. We really do want to know where you stand on these things right now ..." Something to that effect, with a game smile, of course.

In a way Bergman was reading the situation perfectly. In those days he had not given in-depth television interviews in anything but the Swedish language, despite endless requests from all over the place. But he was making an exception for me (for Canada's national English-speaking television network, the CBC, for a program called *Man Alive*), thanks to Nils Petter Sundgren's setting it up and promising to keep the interview flowing smoothly, should Bergman's English falter. (As it turned out, Bergman's English was just fine.) But why me? Well, I am pretty certain that Bergman's knowing that I am a Jesuit priest played a role in his agreeing to do the thing. In spite of his publicly stated reservations about so many aspects of Swedish Lutheran Christian practice, there still was, in this son of a Lutheran pastor, a reservoir of complicity and good will and who knows, even trust, for "men of the cloth." Besides, on more than one occasion Bergman has expressed his relative admiration for a number of things Catholic. And he was fully aware of the immense enthusiasm generated in Catholic intellectual circles by *The Seventh Seal* and what followed during the "metaphysical period." Humorously (I presume!), he refers to that mixed blessing: "I've been plagued with Catholic interpretations ever since."[1]

Well, some years had passed. Here it was, 1970, at the end of what I have been referring to as the *ingenting* years; and here I was, one of those "Bergman priests" sprung up here and there all over the western world.[2]

I have already alluded to this interview in chapter 6. Bergman had just been speaking about the evolution in his thinking on the role of the artist and on the existence of God:

> As I see it now, there has been a development in my relating to God, a development from an existing question to a non-existing question. It's of no importance, that question, to me any longer. Because, you see, my feeling that God doesn't exist is not a terrifying feeling; on the contrary, it is a feeling of security. We are here, there is a wholeness, and that wholeness is *inside* us. This sort of God-within-us is a creation of generations … generations of hope, fear, desire, creative minds, prayers. And *that* still exists. I'm very happy to have it, it's one of the best parts inside me. But that some sort of God *outside* may exist … I can no longer believe in something like that. I've left it, it's ridiculous.

Break, signalling the end of the ten-minute reel – and hence Bergman's spontaneous gesture of sympathy concerning what he gauged must be my reaction.

He was right: this was *not* what I would most have liked to hear. I have already revealed what Bergman's movies meant to me when I first encountered in them that moment of self-fulfilling insight. Ah yes, the strawberries and milk experience of synthesis … And as Bergman kept probing the metaphysical questions, I was experiencing the poetic communication of so much that was so meaningful to me. Sometimes there are those privileged encounters when an artist's work is expressing a sensibility and a vision and a set of priorities so akin to one's own that one wants the whole world (well, at least a good number of people one cares about) to share in that experience.

With the dawning of the *ingenting* period, however, Bergman's experience and his way of communicating it, though still capturing my imagination and eliciting my admiration, began diverging substantially, if not totally, from "where I am." And the subsequent Bergman, the one I have characterized as sharing in the spirit of postmodernism, is not the Bergman I find most enriching, however masterful an artist he undoubtedly remains.

Inevitably this brings us back to the critic's options, his or her set of preferences. Behind each act of critical analysis or of cultural placing, I am quite

---

1   *Bergman on Bergman*, interviews with Ingmar Bergman by Stig Björkman, Torsten Manns, and Jonas Sima (London: Secker & Warburg, 1973), 146 (translated from the Swedish [1970] by Paul Britten Austin).

2   I even had written my *theology* thesis in 1964 on "Ingmar Bergman and the Experience of God."

convinced, lies an ideal film that the critic/writer implicitly would like to create, or at least to experience. This becomes obvious in my case as I do a final situating of Bergman's *cinematic* last will and testament, *Fanny and Alexander* – I say "final," knowing full well that he has *not* stopped thinking (and evolving!) since then. As stated before, his artistic activity *after* the film's completion in 1983, and *outside* the strictly defined area of film directing, has continued to be impressive.

To clarify my thinking, I find myself with what I suppose are slight misgivings setting up a comparison between Bergman's film-directing finale and the final film of another giant of recent film history, the Russian Andrei Tarkovsky. *The Sacrifice*, as the fates would have it, was made in Sweden in 1986, shortly before Tarkovsky's death (of cancer); it witnesses to the heroism of his struggle right to the end: he refuses to give up his infinite quest, still trying to find that impossible, total statement affirming the ambivalence and yet the meaningfulness and purpose in his life and in all of existence. Assuming all the contradictions, the doubts, the ambiguities besetting space/time/perception/consciousness, the beauty and limitations of culture, the absurdities of the human condition, the fears, the hopes, the knowing and the not knowing, *The Sacrifice* soars to a final, mystical, dynamic hymn to the infinite, to the profound belief that has become the artist's very life in its last moments of creative vitality. Intelligibility ... love ... life ... Tarkovsky finds the final word: and for him, that word is just that, the WORD.[3]

Bergman cannot in honesty make that kind of affirmation – precisely the kind he struggled so mightily to achieve through so many of his films at an earlier time in his evolution. *Fanny and Alexander* is charming, heartwarming, and full of life; but what it concludes on is the avowal of not knowing, in the sense of a kind of impotence, a retreat (as we have seen) to the relatively safe womb of the theatre as temporary shelter from the horrors of the terrifying big world *outside*. There is a new semi-serenity and gentleness here, something quite marvellous in its own right, built on the knowledge that we are what we are, with our limitations and foibles and inconsistencies: so let us at least love one another and be grateful to life for a little while. One is reminded of Guido, Fellini's alter ego in *8½* (1963), as he comes back to life from despair, paralysis, and imaginary suicide to join in the dance of the circle of life:

> What is this sudden joy? Why do I feel strengthened and renewed? Forgive me, sweet creatures, I understand. I didn't know. I do accept you ... I do love you ... How simple it is!

3 From the beginning of John's Gospel: "In the beginning was the Word ..."

Life is a holiday. Let us live it together. Accept me as I am … only then will we discover one another.4

But that is not quite the end. No, by no means: gradually the "real" and imaginary figures of the past and of the present, of Fellini's life and of his fiction, disappear, leaving little Guido (Fellini) alone in the circle, alone in the spotlight, playing the flute, gradually leaving the circle and disappearing into total darkness.

Gustav Adolf's speech near the end of *Fanny and Alexander*, completing, to an extent, his brother Oscar's speech near the beginning, is not that different from Fellini's. It too is surrounded by ritual, the circle of the family celebrating birth and unity about the dining-room table. "We don't pretend to have the answers, but we Ekdahls [we artists] try to make life bearable." No rousing cry here to conscience and consciousness; there are no *causes*, no struggles in the name of humanity, no urge to change the world, no calls to reform society or to create a new world. And certainly no artistic presentation of a world, which, through struggle, sacrifice, and a profound wisdom, breathes *ultimate* serenity, intelligibility, eternal hope à la John Ford or Kenji Mizoguchi. Finally, no further attempt at *understanding*.

It is not to *Fanny and Alexander* that we turn for such visions. Bergman is aware that his spirit of affectionate self-mockery, and our awareness of that, are essential to the film and its power to delight. We watch as he parades the figures, the figurations, the symbols, the themes, the gropings for meaning of the past. All of these, complete with his past desperate attempts at affirmation and his anguished proclamations of futility, have become part of a self-referential progression of familiar signs from his movies "referring back to further familiar signs referring to yet further signs" in what may well be a closed system – and with it an avowal of the inability to go beyond into true meaningfulness and, still less, into "reality."

This in itself has its profound resonances, nothing less than the partial expression of the tragic dimension of a postmodernist world view which strands humanity on the edge of the abyss of directionlessness and ultimate futility. Then again … here I feel terribly conscious that I am structuring the Bergman film experience from *my* vantage point, my convictions and understandings. And I feel bound to reveal that to the reader: may I not be guilty of rather gross oversimplification in the quest of a certain clarity? The "Bergman text" even of *Fanny and Alexander* is surely far more complex and ambivalent. Time and again (as we have seen in the previous chapter) there can be felt a straying

4 English approximation from the sound track of 8½.

away from the playful tone. One feels Bergman's involvement at the deepest personal level, a semi-hidden avowal, perhaps, that those very signs he treats half-mockingly may indeed be touching on reality, may even be bearers of ultimate meaning, some kind of answer to humanity's unrelenting exigencies for what is beyond the mundane.

Well, be that as it may. Perhaps Bergman's oft-quoted statements about film being akin to the dream state may ultimately say it better, making more sense, coming closer to the complex intangibles that constitute his reality. And maybe Strindberg, his avowedly greatest influence, should indeed be given the final words, coming closest to expressing Bergman's world.

Words, statements, cultural placings – Bergman soars beyond the inevitable reducing of experience, he makes us *feel* the personal intensity, the complexity, and the mystery; and he ravishes us with the beauty. At the end of *Fanny and Alexander*, Alexander, in his nightshirt, is wandering about his grandmother's apartment, munching on a piece of leftover cake. Suddenly, punctuated by one note on the harp, the black-clad figure of the (dead) bishop looms up behind him. We feel the weight of his hand pressing down on Alexander's shoulder, pushing him to the ground. The camera catches the bishop's pectoral cross in a series of reverse angle shots between the towering cleric and the boy on the ground. Just before leaving, he says to Alexander: "You can't escape me." Cut to close-up of Alexander's troubled, frightened, pondering face – and to pertinent Freudian interpretations and Bergman personal biographical details.

Then Bergman cuts to Alexander's mother and grandmother, affectionately chatting. Both women protest but eventually give in to each other as they share plans for the future. Granny tells Emilie that she, Emilie, will now head the theatre. And Mummy hands Granny a copy of Strindberg's A *Dream Play*, insisting that she act in it: "That misogynist? No thank you!" But, yes, Granny will come back to the stage. The two women having taken over a universe, the "little world," now become more tender and loving.

They rise and Mummy leaves; and Granny, alone and smiling, walks to her favourite chair, Strindberg's play in hand. She sits, begins to doze – and silently Alexander comes to her, curling up, his head on her lap. With one arm around her grandson, smiling contentedly, she picks up Strindberg and reads:

Anything can happen. Anything is possible. Time and space do not exist. On a flimsy ground of reality, imagination spins out and weaves new patterns ...5

5 Quoted in Bergman's scenario of *Fanny and Alexander*.

Maybe it is not only film that is dream. Is "the real" itself but a dream we project from a "flimsy ground of reality" beyond our reach? Look at the irresistible image of humanity of that last shot. Alexander is cradled in his grandmother's lap, in fetal position, secure for the moment as she reads ... just as Peer Gynt is curled up at last at rest in the blind Solveig's lap in Bergman's remarkable theatre production of *Peer Gynt* some eight years later.

Poetic archetypal images lead in many directions and along many levels, and sometimes interpretations of them may be eminently justifiable. In the days when Bergman's films demanded a God-centred interpretation, some might have read this one as the soul's need to return to God, its only true destiny – and in (what has now become) a politically correct maternal incarnation of God at that. But of course it is the psychological terms of reference that come to mind with greatest immediacy and spontaneity, capturing the basic insecurity springing from our having to leave the mother's womb, source of nourishment, security, comfort, and being forced to inhabit a threatening, difficult outside world (beginning with the father), forever burdened with a desire for the initial (and safe) identity. It is as if Bergman's insatiable demand for personal honesty in his movies can lead him no further: the beauty of and need for love and life, the struggling and evil and fear and death – the complexity of it all, the impossibility of making sense of it all – can permit him no affirmation more dynamic and heroic than that. There is exhaustion here, a quiet and humble resignation. And unutterable pathos and love in this human vulnerability – and beauty.

One can judge this attitude severely as a refusal of adult responsibility and even of self-possession, a regression to the fetal state of non-responsibility and non-consciousness: "In the developing consciousness of the individual the hero figure is the symbolic [signifying] means by which the emerging ego overcomes the inertia from the unconscious mind, and liberates the mature man from a regressive longing to return to the blissful state of infancy in a world dominated by his mother."[6]

All of the above may indeed be relevant as far as it goes, a fair situating, in terms of various currents of our culture, of Bergman's cinema: what it is and what it is not. And that is fine, that is how culture expands and evolves, how human consciousness broadens and deepens, is it not? Yet it would be manifestly ridiculous to end on such a note, to claim that the pointing out of what an artist "is lacking" serves as some kind of "final summation" – always, it needs repeating, from a particular point of view.

6 Joseph L. Henderson chapter in *Man and His Symbols*, edited by Carl Jung et al. (New York: Bantam Doubleday Dell, 1968), 111.

As has been (laboriously) pointed out in this study, powerful currents within contemporary professional culture simply dismiss the kind of significance many of us attribute to Bergman's films: film as art, art itself, the very notion of artist are reduced to the function of manipulated conduits limited to operating within certain more or less fixed pre-determined positions.

But human freedom and creativity, however mitigated and diminished in certain contexts, are facts of life – at least most of us still feel that way. Artists do play a privileged role, exploring, reflecting, extending our awareness and our experience. We may agree or disagree with their insights and visions, but if they are artists the odds are that we will be genuinely moved, challenged, deepened. Art can indeed propel us, at least momentarily, into living at a more intensely aware and responsible level.

Ingmar Bergman, as I hope I have demonstrated, is remarkable in this regard. In his artistic evolution since World War II he has pursued the truth about himself, his culture, life. It is difficult to find an artist who even comes close to him in recording this pursuit so faithfully in terms of the evolving context of his culture and his times, and in so doing who has exposed himself with such depth and such feeling. With him no solution seems ever to have sufficed, to have permitted his spirit to rest. The dialectical possibilities keep returning in the guises and formulations of the contemporary moment or of the larger and more complex tradition. And perhaps it is by that very fact that Bergman opens doors for us, helping us to see deep within ourselves and to understand our relationship to the culture. And maybe even to life.

It is precisely because he has been able to serve this relentless search and this ruthless sincerity with such poetic intuition and matchless technical mastery that he has mattered to us, indeed, that he has been able to nourish the inner life, the expanding possibilities. That, ultimately, is his greatest contribution. In that sense Ingmar Bergman truly has been a prophet of our times. And those of us whom he has succeeded in reaching are all the richer for it.

Or could it be that older, maybe wiser strands of our tradition have understood the richness of the gift more simply, more profoundly, and certainly more soaringly? It was Plotinus who some 1,750 years ago, said: "The soul that beholds beauty becomes beautiful."

THE IMAGES

Forever lurking ... German expressionism

Torment, 1940. Director: Alf Sjöberg; First Screenplay: Ingmar Bergman (Svensk Filmindustri)
Alf Kjellin, Stig Järrel

Shadow of Carné

Crisis, 1946 (Svensk Filmindustri)
Inga Landgré

And then there was neo-realism

Port of Call, 1948 (Svensk Filmindustri)
Nine-Christine Jönsson, Bent Eklund

Art, mirrors, shadows, life: remove the paint

Summer Interlude, 1951 (Svensk Filmindustri)
Maj-Britt Nilsson, Alf Kjellin, and Stig Olin

Theatre, dance, music ... and cinema

Summer Interlude, 1951 (Svensk Filmindustri)

Bring in the clowns – angst

Sawdust and Tinsel, 1953 (Sandrews)
Anders Ek, Åke Grönberg

A sunlit forest, man, woman

A Lesson in Love, 1954 (Svensk Filmindustri)
Gunnar Björnstrand, Eva Dahlbeck

Bring in the clowns — and the life force

Smiles of a Summer Night, 1955 (Svensk Filmindustri)
Eva Dahlbeck, Gunnar Björnstrand

Midsummernight's dream

Smiles of a Summer Night, 1955 (Svensk Filmindustri)
Harriet Andersson, Åke Fridell

Summer witchcraft

Smiles of a Summer Night, 1955 (Svensk Filmindustri)
Naima Wifstrand

And the stakes are life and death

The Seventh Seal, 1957 (Svensk Filmindustri)
Bengt Ekerot, Max von Sydow

A move towards life — at least for now

The Seventh Seal, 1957 (Svensk Filmindustri)
Max von Sydow, Bibi Andersson

Examination: Dr Borg's turn now

Wild Strawberries, 1957 (Svensk Filmindustri)
Victor Sjöström

Premonitions of mortality/immortality

Wild Strawberries, 1957 (Svensk Filmindustri)
Victor Sjöström

Icon of innocence, nature at peace

The Virgin Spring, 1960 (Svensk Filmindustri)
Birgitta Pettersson

Must Töre join Macbeth?

The Virgin Spring, 1960 (Svensk Filmindustri)
Birgitta Valberg, Max von Sydow

The cycle of violence

The Virgin Spring, 1960 (Svensk Filmindustri)
Max von Sydow

Angst, disintegration, shipwreck

Through a Glass Darkly, 1961 (Svensk Filmindustri)
Harriet Andersson, Lars Passgård

Humanity's ascent from a cold sea

Through a Glass Darkly, 1961 (Svensk Filmindustri)

Gunnar Björnstrand, Harriet Andersson, Lars Passgård, and Max von Sydow

And some must dance the dance of death

The Seventh Seal, 1957 (Svensk Filmindustri)

My God, my God, why hast thou forsaken me?

Winter Light, 1963 (Svensk Filmindustri)
Gunnar Björnstrand

Where is the light, where is the love?

Winter Light, 1963 (Svensk Filmindustri)
Gunnar Björnstrand, Ingrid Thulin

Will he too hear only God's silence?

The Silence, 1963 (Svensk Filmindustri)
Gunnel Lindblom, Jurgen Lindström, and Ingrid Thulin

Eyes, faces, entanglement

Persona, 1966 (Svensk Filmindustri)
Bibi Andersson, Gunner Björnstrand, and Liv Ullmann

Artifice

Persona, 1966 (Svensk Filmindustri)
Bibi Andersson, Liv Ullmann

Breaking the context

Persona, 1966 (Svensk Filmindustri)
Liv Ullmann

The actress

Persona, 1966 (Svensk Filmindustri)
Liv Ullmann

Persona team

Bibi, Liv, Sven, Ingmar, 1966 (Svensk Filmindustri)

A genuine postmodern Bergman vampire

The Hour of the Wolf, 1968 (Svensk Filmindustri)
Ingrid Thulin

Personality disintegration

Shame, 1968 (Svensk Filmindustri)
Max von Sydow, Gunnar Björnstrand, and Liv Ullmann

Winter interlude

The Passion of Anna, 1969 (Svensk Filmindustri)
Max von Sydow, Bibi Andersson

A Bergman Pietà

Cries and Whispers, 1972 (Svensk Filmindustri)
Kari Sylwan, Harriet Andersson

Middle class, secular, successful: a Swedish couple

Scenes from a Marriage, 1973 (Svensk Filmindustri)
Liv Ullmann, Erland Josephson

A redeemimg moment

Cries and Whispers, 1972 (Svensk Filmindustri)
Kari Sylwan, Liv Ullmann, Harriet Andersson, and Ingrid Thulin

Celebrating *The Magic Flute*

The Magic Flute, 1975 (Sveriges Radió)

Preview of the Third Reich, looking back

The Serpent's Egg, 1977 (Rialto Film)
David Carradine

Germany in the 1920s

The Serpent's Egg, 1977 (Rialto Film)

The artist

Autumn Sonata, 1977 (Munich ICA)
Ingrid Bergman

Artist and daughter

Autumn Sonata, 1978 (ITC)
Liv Ullmann, Ingrid Bergman

A director dreams

Fanny and Alexander, 1982 (Sandrews)
Bertil Guve

Luther,
Bergman,
Dutch masters

Fanny and Alexander, 1982
(Sandrews)
Jan Malmsjö, Ewa Fröling

Christmas at the Ekdahls'

Fanny and Alexander, 1982 (Sandrews)
Börje Ahlstedt, Christina Schollin, and Jarl Kulle

Uncle Isak's magical world

Fanny and Alexander, 1982 (Sandrews)
Pernilla Allwin, Bertil Guve, Mats Bergman, and Erland Josephson

A safer, warmer little world

Fanny and Alexander, 1982 (Sandrews)
Ewa Fröling, Gunn Wållgren

Alexander/Ingmar and colleagues

Fanny and Alexander, 1982 (Sandrews)
Pernilla Allwin, Bertil Guve

FACES

INGMAR AT WORK AND AT HOME

An icon of suffering

Cries and Whispers, 1972 (Svensk Filmindustri)
Harriet Andersson

Woman, high comedy, the life force

Smiles of a Summer Night, 1955 (Svensk Filmindustri)
Eva Dahlbeck

Ingenting

The Passion of Anna, 1969 (Svensk Filmindustri)
Max von Sydow

Bergman man

Shame, 1968 (Svensk Filmindustri)
Gunnar Björnstrand

Ingrid Thulin: the rose period

Brink of Life, 1958 (Svensk Filmindustri)

Liv and Bibi

Scenes from a Marriage, 1973 (Svensk Filmindustri)

Ingmar and daughter Linn, 1977

(Bo-Erik Gyberg)

Erland Josephson – working with Ingmar
since university days

Scenes from a Marriage, 1973 (Svensk Filmindustri)

Persona – changes

Fårö, 1965 (Svensk Filmindustri)
Bibi Andersson, Liv Ullmann, and Ingmar Bergman

Ingmar and Sven:
still the magic

Ingmar, Fanny, and Alexander

Fanny and Alexander, 1982 (Sandrews)
Ingmar Bergman, Pernilla Allwin, and Bertil Guve

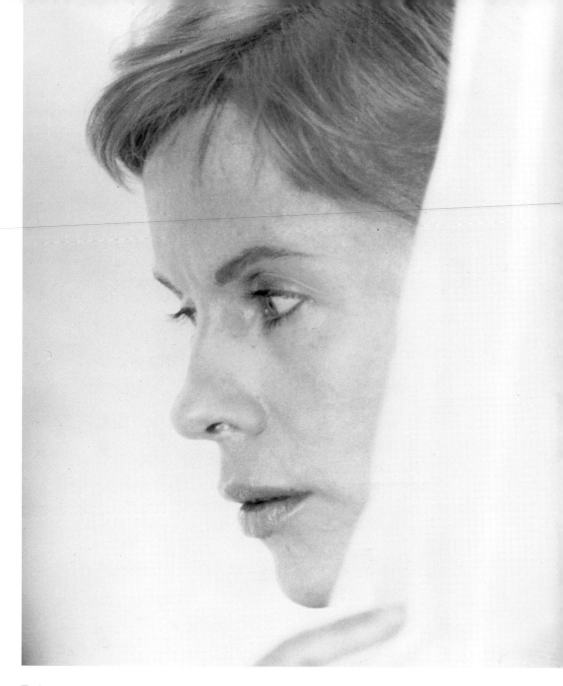

Bibi

(Bo-Erik Gyberg)

Symbol

Golgberg Variations by George Tabori (Bengt Wanselius)

A new team

Private Confessions, 1997 (Bengt Wanselius)
Sven Nykvist, director of photography, Ingmar Bergman, writer, Liv Ullmann, director
Following page: (Bengt Wanselius)

MAGICIAN OF THE CINEMA

PREAMBLE TO THE PRIVILEGED MOMENT

It's strawberries and milk time again. Finally I set about doing what I admitted in the preface that I would have liked to do much earlier on in the book. Yes, *truly* to describe in depth a privileged moment, seriously "to get at the data" and, proceeding specifically from this base, to demonstrate how "meaningfulness" emerges, i.e., how from one's own particular appropriation of aspects of our culture, one brings meaning, in terms of that culture, to Bergman's artistic communication. To an extent, of course, I have been fulfilling the "bring meaning" part of that mandate, but as I have confessed throughout, the description/analysis part has not been sufficiently demonstrated.

When analysing film, as also I stated earlier, writers generally give imprecise, often inaccurate mini-descriptions of the film language, if indeed they give it any attention at all. The very grounds apt for giving legitimation to their assertions are simply ignored, or at best taken for granted, as if it were not precisely here that the effects are produced, and most often where the deepest "intentions," conscious or not, are revealed. That is why I include this complementary "special section" in this study, a sampler that attempts to demonstrate to the reader that film art is a most complex and subtle process, the fruit of prodigious effort, and that to do it justice, the usually superficial affirmation that "the movie is the way it is is because I say so" is hardly an adequate approach.

Inevitably, it would seem, when we see a movie we seek some kind of understanding, some kind of interpretation. That is all part of being a human being. But to do justice to the film, one should be able to demonstrate just why one has come to one's conclusions – *and this from the movie itself*. In other words, the exercise should be grounded on *filmic evidence and analysis*. At this point, therefore, I am trying to show in practice that I first worked at the nuts and bolts of Bergman's use of film language, that, precisely, I really studied the sights and sounds of his movies and the way that they are put together in order to arrive at conclusions based on some sort of serious objective observation.

How indeed does Bergman achieve his particular brand of film magic?

Finding out *at this level*, that is, by a thorough "return to the filmic text," not only helps explain highly personal experiencing (such as the berries and milk episode in Lidingö), but, I hope, adds serious credibility to the long section of the book already completed, i.e., the elucidating of Bergman's role as a prophet of his times and the situating of his considerable contribution to the contemporary culture.

There is a problem, however. "Returning to the text" has a nice simple ring to it, but the truth is that such an exercise demands a tiring, at times repetitive and alienating kind of technical work. And there is definitely (at least in part) a quixotic aspect to the enterprise: the task must be undertaken in the realization that it must fall short of complete scientific accuracy and anything approaching totality.

I shall not go into a lengthy, abstract, and highly theoretical exposition here on the problems of methodology involved. Instead, the following tiny practical example seen so often in the history of the cinema may be sufficient in suggesting the immensity of the hidden part of the methodology iceberg.

Take an ordinary shot of a horse galloping across a plain, captured by a threefold camera movement: travelling, panning, zooming. You are aiming at objective precision. But how can the describer measure the real movement of the horse being filmed, the distance travelled by the camera, the constantly changing angle of its pan, the changing lens aperture demanded by the zoom? And how fast, or how slow, is each one of these movements at various moments of the shot? Or what are the changing degrees of light and shadow, and the camera's shifting direction in relation to the sunlight? How could one *accurately* measure and then describe these kinds of things, all of which, to be sure, shape perception and the concomitant emotion and understanding? Add the degree of graininess of the film stock, the type of focus, the limitless details of composition, the intensities of the colouring, the varying intensities of sound (noise, dialogue, music). And all of this can be modified by the editing and the lab work. And so on – I have not even mentioned the myriad of less "specifically cinematographic" but equally essential elements, such as what is actually photographed, the landscape and sets and actors and costumes and makeup, and of course the narrative and various thematic considerations, all of which in their own way can be considered as functioning elements of the overall filmic text.

So it is for one simple little shot, out of how many hundreds (probably) in one single movie. Achieving "scientific" accuracy (if that is what one sets out to do) is an illusion. But that is only the beginning: the shot is only part of a sequence, its character, tonality, and meaning perhaps transformed by the interplay with other shots making up that sequence. And of course the sequence itself is usually merely a small part of the entire movie. If a movie is indeed a work of art, its various moments and elements are constantly relating backward and forward in time to other elements of the film – threads in a tapestry, echoes in a musical composition, multiple shifting meanings. To attempt a thoroughly scientific encompassing of a movie, one should break it down into all its cinematic data, describing, analysing its components, while respecting the essentially dynamic nature of the work, as if it were breathing a life of its own, its patterns forming and reforming (à la Barthes) for the viewer, its meanings shifting and expanding.

In that sense, and to some small extent, movies can be seen as approaching the complexity of life. And as with life, so the art object is beyond total intellectual appropriation.[1] However, this most decidedly is not meant to imply that total neglect of cinematic data-gathering of this kind is justifiable when one truly is coming to grips with a *film*. It all comes down, really, to common sense and a judicious narrowing down, in a spirit of respecting the film and of coming to terms with what is actually there, while at the same time being perfectly aware that the data under consideration has been chosen because of one's preferences, one's purpose, one's approach – and of course one's conditioning.

But even then, description of the *entire* film generally proves out of reach. One is obliged to limit the description/analysis to especially pertinent moments, a symptomatic segment, perhaps, well suited to revealing how, overall, the director chooses, organizes, gets the results – if the job is to be done with any degree of thoroughness in a context of attempting what is manageable.

Years of university film teaching have convinced me that, even within these very real limitations, immensely enriching material can be unearthed that can lead to insight into how the *artistic* is created, and how the artist arrives at creating meaning – as well as what that meaning can be for each one of us. Once you really get into the artist's choices, the nature of the work is revealed in rich, not so obvious ways. Time and again, in hundreds of viewings of Bergman's movies, and in many courses I have given on these films, I have concentrated on such moments, having the advantage, of course, of benefiting from the "laboratory" viewing conditions that permit the demonstration to emerge from

---

1 I attempted as thorough a "scientific" accuracy as I could achieve in order to legitimate my conclusions (re: the "quest of the *open form*") for my doctoral thesis (Sorbonne, 1977). The lab specimen was Jean-Luc Godard's *Bande à part* (*Band of Outsiders*); and the data (description/analysis) went beyond the equivalent of one thousand pages. But even in such "privileged" circumstances I could not escape the realization not only of how incomplete my data-gathering was (mine and that of two teams of seminar students), but also of the impossibility, precisely, of "total scientific appropriation" in this area.

the movie itself as we go over the privileged moments unravelling before our eyes and ears. What also inevitably happens is that one's understanding of the film, one's set of priorities or interpretations, tend to be seriously modified.

And so for *our* moment, already highlighted in other contexts of this book. For obvious reasons (length of the book, for one), what follows is only that, one moment. And, yes, by itself it hardly can claim to do justice to the whole movie, much less to *all* of Bergman's film work, but it does help to demonstrate my method in the quest for understanding Bergman's creativity. The hope, of course, is that the reader will remember many of the other moments already sketched out in preceding portions of this book, and may thus be able to give the writer the benefit of the doubt, trusting that these other moments also have been subjected to a careful and conscientious scrutiny. And a loving one, to be sure.

In conclusion, it may be worth adding that this is how I arrive at my own resolution of the subjective/objective dialectic. My privileged, chosen moments are mine, and the reader might well choose others. But what is there, I hope, really does come from the movie, and really does bring light to the understanding of an essential aspect – and all of this in a very serious attempt at respecting the text.

Thus the life of the movie(s) expands, the culture too undergoing its modifications for better or for worse … and the final word is never said.

The second part ("Into the Trenches") of this section follows immediately: it does the groundwork, unearthing the filmic elements of that one sequence.[2] But even here interpretation peeps through at a primary, obvious level.

The third part ("The Bergman Magic") is far more free-wheeling – and a lot more fun, at least in the writing. It is indefinitely expandable, in a real sense the "turning and returning" to the text in full flight. Using the previous part's findings, it demonstrates how Bergman imbues a movie with enormous cultural potential, creating signs that impel the viewer into encountering self and culture in many ways. Intellectual, if you wish: but it is intellect at play, affording aesthetic delight, and that particular adult sense of Bergman movie richness.

2 Tiny 16mm frames from each shot within this sequence had been intended to supply bits of the visual aspect, however imperfectly. This proved impossible, as Svensk Filmindustri, the owner of the film rights, refused permission. However, a far better alternative is available for the reader: use the video or laser-disk versions (readily obtainable) and experience the sequence as Bergman intended – as a moving picture – pausing at the moments indicated in the text.

CHAPTER NINE

INTO THE TRENCHES

The "Strawberries and Milk" segment is the middle sequence of *The Seventh Seal*, the eighth sequence out of a total of fifteen. It is made up of forty-one shots, lasting just over nine minutes and forty-seven seconds.[1] The setting is a forest meadow by the sea, one end sloping gently down to the water, the other running up a slight incline, leading to an uneven horizon line broken here and there by small trees and shrubs.

The tone and general atmosphere breathe peace and serenity, with the stillness of nature only heightened by soft bird sounds, a baby's gurglings, the quiet conversation of human voices, and, in the latter part, music.

The sequence makes up a perfectly balanced, self-enclosed unit, starting with the solitary Knight, reclining as he muses over his chessboard; he joins Mia and her infant a little way up the glade; they in turn are joined by her husband, Jof, and then by the Knight's Squire and the mute young woman; and then the scene ends with the Knight returning to his chessboard to continue his match with Death, who is waiting for him (and who, all along perhaps, has been lurking there unseen).

The sequence lends itself admirably to being divided into five major movements (or steps, stages, moods, thematic progressions). This facilitates what follows: a description/analysis of some of Bergman's operative choices, that is, what he chooses to put into the scene and how he puts it all together. This implicitly includes his conceptualizing of it as well as his actual putting of it in place – the mise en scène.

Although there is a laudable attempt at achieving objectively based results in all of this, it must be understood that my description/analysis, while trying

---

1 The lengths of the sequence and of each of its shots are given in seconds, a figure arrived at by dividing the number of film frames – obtained by using a frame counter – by twenty-four (the number of frames per second in a sound film). To avoid the cumbersome I shall not in the regular text include fractions of seconds for each shot, since these appear in their column on the diagram pages.

to remain anchored in the sights and the sounds and the structuring that are "really there," is nonetheless somewhat subjective even in the choices it is obliged to make. It cannot include every single element of every single frame, and still less can it claim the scientifically precise measuring of size or duration or intensity of every element. Even in dealing with what is less than a ten-minute segment of film, such a task would prove overwhelming.

Rather, the attempt is to give an objective description of the main elements (i.e., my choice, after repeated viewings, of what constitutes the main elements) from a cinematographic point of view. As this can prove rather unexciting for the normal healthy reader, I try to avoid needless repetitions. Also, a certain amount of *interpreting* (always more exciting stuff) beyond strict description/analysis is in evidence, even at this first stage. But this is an elementary, first-level, obvious-to-any-informed-viewer kind of interpreting, of things that would come to mind to anyone sharing our general culture.

Once this part of the work has been completed, both writer and reader will, in chapter 10, be allowed to gambol in the larger and more intoxicating fields of Bergman interpretation, using the accumulated data to arrive at less obvious and more largely human conclusions about what Bergman is up to, and maybe at a better understanding of just what goes into creating the "Bergman magic."

And so, dear readers, into the trenches of first-level digging.

PRELUDE

The previous sequence (no. 7) has taken place in a tavern, a nasty, smoke-filled place dominated by a flaming hearth roasting a pig as it slowly revolves on a spit. Coarse folk well into their drinking, and squealing, grunting pigs running about as they await their turn, no doubt, add their cacophonous notes. The scene turns cruel when Raval, the detestable defrocked seminarian we have met earlier on, leads the mob in a torture game: they force Jof, the strolling player and father of the little family, to dance like a bear over burning logs. The cruel sport is cut short as Jöns, the Knight's Squire, enters the tavern, and, sizing up the situation, strides up to Raval. True to what he previously threatened he would do, he slashes Raval's face with his knife. Jof steals away from the scene, but not before availing himself of a bracelet (part of Raval's plundered goods). Raval, moaning and clutching his face, stretches out on the tavern floor. On this, Bergman dissolves into Movement A of our sequence.

Dissolve
(Raval)
to
Shot 1:   9 8/24"

Introduction: The Knight's existential anguish encounters Mia's life force.

MOVEMENT A

Movement A is made up of thirteen shots lasting one minute, fifty-four seconds.

Shot 1. A quick dissolve from the last shot of sequence 7 reveals the Knight: he is lying in a position similar to Raval's, and though he is further removed from the camera, he is in the same part of the frame. But what a contrast: the flames, smoke, filth, and noise have given way to an open glade bathed in muted sunlight and classically composed in depth. The Knight, in medium long shot, is reclining on the grass, absorbed in studying his chessboard (prominent in the film since the beginning). Gunnar Fischer, director of photography in all but six of Bergman's eighteen feature films from 1948 to 1960, has in typical fashion layered the image into four light-and-shade areas, achieving relief and perspective. The bottom third of the image is dark in shadow, extending up through the Knight's body into another relatively dark area made up of shrubs and the Knight's horse. Dividing these two shaded areas is a brighter strip of relatively white light, the meadow itself. And the fourth level, taking up the top two-fifths of the image, is the softly lit sky.

There is no camera movement. Bergman holds the shot for a relaxed ten seconds. The angle of vision is normal, as from our standing eye-level. The image is pleasant to look at, endowed by Fischer's layering with a painterly quality. Nonetheless, everything looks "natural," centrifugal in composition, because the layers stretch beyond the limits of the frame – as they would if one were seeing reality through a window. Thus, on the one hand, Bergman gives us something relaxed and "real," while on the other he has sculpted an image that is highly composed, subtly affecting us as "artistic" or "cultural," a kind of iconic medieval re-creation.

Benign silence reigns, total at first after Raval's moaning that ended the

Shot 2:   8 20/24"

Shot 3:   1 20/24"   KNIGHT: What's his name?

Shot 4:   1 20/24"   MIA: Mikael.

Shot 5:   1 13/24"   KNIGHT: How old is he?

Shot 6:   2 5/24"   MIA: Oh, he'll soon be two.

Shot 7:   2 13/24"   KNIGHT: He's big for his age.[2]

2 Dialogue from the English translation of Bergman's screenplay. See *Four Screenplays of Ingmar Bergman* (New York: Simon & Schuster 1960), 169–77.

previous sequence, gradually punctuated by gentle bird chirruping, a baby's gurgles, and once by soft female laughter. The Knight looks over in the direction of the camera, smiling (a rare occurrence up to now). He sits up, quite charmed.

Shot 2. Cut from the Knight's gazing to what he actually sees. Another relaxed shot at normal eye-level, almost nine seconds, permits us to contemplate (with the Knight) in peace. Framed in slightly longer shot is Mia, the strolling player who is Jof's wife. She is holding her baby, Mikael; and mother and child are centred just below mid frame. The image is less layered than shot 1, the light softer, enveloping the scene with gently varying degrees of intensity. The strolling players' wagon, already familiar to us, fills mid screen left of the frame (as it will through much of the scene), its canvas cover moving with the breeze. Balancing this, screen right and further in background, a plump horse is tethered, its tail switching as it feeds on the grass. In a gentle diagonal the horizon line goes from middle screen right to slightly higher screen left, the soft grey-white sky contrasting with the more shaded glade. No harsh contrasts, no sharp geometric patterns here: gentleness and soft natural contours hold sway.

The still camera permits the Knight (and ourselves) to continue our contemplation of this enchanting scene, made all the more irresistible by the baby gurgles, bird sounds, and a very young mother's soft, happy laughter. Indeed, though the composition may be somewhat less deliberate and less structured in appearance than in the previous shot, once again one is drawn into the contemplation of icon (more about this term later), a *consciously* artistic re-creating of Mother and Child rich in Christian medieval references – and suggesting a lot more as well, as we shall see. By now, it is safe to say, Bergman has totally dissipated the anguished mood of the previous sequence.

Shots 3–9. There follows a series of seven brief shots totalling some fourteen seconds, each lasting a little more or a little less than two seconds.

Shots 3 to 7 are essentially an exchange between the Knight and Mia (in reverse angle from Knight alone in his space, to Mia alone, back to Knight, then to Mia again, and back to Knight) as their conversation begins. The Knight's shots, though lighter, are similar in composition to Shot 1, while Mia and Child are considerably closer and less formalized. Mia, still holding the baby, is in slightly high angle, as we see more of the earth – this is generally the case in Mia's shots – the ground sloping up to the horse and to part of the wagon, leaving a bit of sky lighting up the top right frame. No question now: though still reasonably structured and balanced, the composition is much more "messy" in appearance, neutralizing to an extent the consciously iconic quality of Mia and Child. In Shot 7, the Knight, now at a slightly longer dis-

Shot 8:   1 5/24"   MIA: Do you think so? …

Shot 9:   2 15/24"   … Yes, I guess he's rather big.

Shot 10:   32 17/24"   KNIGHT: You played some kind of show this afternoon.
MIA: Did you think it was bad?
KNIGHT: You are more beautiful now without your face painted and this gown is more becoming.
MIA: You see, Jonas Skat has run off and left us, so we're in real trouble now.
KNIGHT: Is that your husband?
MIA: (*laughs*): Jonas! The other man is my husband. His name is Jof.
KNIGHT: Oh, that one.
MIA: And now there's only him and me. We'll have to start doing tricks again and that's more trouble than it's worth.
KNIGHT: Do you do tricks also?
MIA: We certainly do …

tance (as in Shot 1), rises, the camera obliging him functionally with a slight tilt as he begins to walk over to the two he has been watching with delight.

Shot 8, centred on Mia and Baby, breaks the still pattern of the camera with dynamic movement from the Knight as he moves across the glade, the camera now to his back – from his space into Mia's.

Shot 9, over two-and-a-half seconds, again reverses the angle to Mia's point of view, as we see the Knight walk almost into camera, exiting the frame left. As he looms into the lens, for the first time in the sequence a (very) slightly threatening quality is suggested: indeed, while the Knight's stronger, more formal (metaphysical?) space is yielding to Mia's (and Mikael's) more relaxed, gentle, at-one-with-this-earth world, he does exact a slight price, a touch of the world outside intruding.

Through this series of seven fairly brief shots, then, Bergman has broken the contemplative mood, easing us back into our interest in the narrative. Expeditiously, two spaces, two levels of experiencing – separated by visual cuts and words emanating from their hitherto disparate bits of terrain – reach out to each other. We have been put in readiness for a meeting, a beginning of convergence.

Shot 10. In another reverse angle the camera captures Mia, in close long shot, much as previously but from a slightly altered vantage point. She has risen, leaving the baby on the grass, and she curtsies, the camera tilting up a bit and including more sky. The oval shape of the wagon, darker, now dominates upper screen left, while the sky, lighter, fills upper screen right. The Knight walks into frame left, the camera more active now (but ever so subtly), adapting to the movement of the characters. As shot 10 develops, it seems effortlessly to find its natural position of repose, which also happens to be a position that is obviously aesthetically pleasing: the Knight, in his dark tunic, now framed screen left by the dark grey oval curve of the wagon, stands by Mia, her shoulders and face against the light and sky screen right. The shot lasts over a half-minute as they introduce themselves, Bergman as usual directing his actors beautifully, achieving a naturalness and spontaneity of gesture, movement and intonation that transform what are basically ritualized words and actions into lifelike behaviour patterns. As the shot progresses the Knight crosses screen right, and Mia sits screen left, the camera tilting and panning functionally as they move and sit, finally resting on a high angle two-shot (as from someone's eye-level while standing and looking down). The final composition has abandoned the obvious "aesthetic," having little relief or apparent structure, and no skyline to afford a horizon.

Shot 11: 42 18/24"

... And Jof is a very skillful juggler.

KNIGHT: Is Mikael going to be an acrobat?

MIA: Jof wants him to be.

KNIGHT: But you don't.

MIA: I don't know. (*Smiling*) Perhaps he'll become a knight.

KNIGHT: Let me assure you, that's no pleasure either.

MIA: No, you don't look so happy.

KNIGHT: No.

MIA: Are you tired?

KNIGHT: Yes.

MIA: Why?

KNIGHT: I have dull company.

MIA: Do you mean your squire?

KNIGHT: No, not him.

MIA: Who do you mean, then?

KNIGHT: Myself.

MIA: I understand.

KNIGHT: Do you, really?

MIA: Yes, I understand rather well. I have often wondered why people torture themselves as often as they can. Isn't that so?

Shot 12: 1 8/24"

JOF: Mia!

Shot 13: 17/24"

MIA: What have you done?

Shot 11 moves from the close long shot into a rather close medium shot of the two, the angle more or less reversed. The Knight is now a bit in the foreground of the shot, his upper body filling the lower left of the screen, with Mia, slightly higher, in the centre of the frame. The camera has tilted up, reintroducing the sky in a slight diagonal across the upper third of the image. And though Bergman still sacrifices an overtly formalized structuring, yielding to the desire for closeness, for easier contemplation of facial expression, and for a more spontaneous naturalness, we still have an attractive, nicely balanced, intimate image that is pleasing to the eye. The shot is allowed an even more leisurely rhythm, its duration of almost forty-five seconds permitting us to concentrate on the relaxed, slow dialogue, not up-beat but rendered serene by the pace, the setting, and the general stillness punctuated by the baby and bird chirpings, and now also by the soft sound of the Knight's and Mia's voices.

Mia is the incarnation of naturalness, beauty, friendliness, sympathy, and intuitive insight. She proves irresistible to the Knight (and to the audience) as, freed from the tension evident throughout the previous sections of the film, he finds himself unburdening his soul. He is still the embodiment of existential angst, but now in a more personal, gentle, sad, and perhaps freeing mode.

Movement A has been building to this soul-soothing articulation. And Bergman gives it full value in a language that is at once personal and at the same time characteristic of the existentialist mood and anxiety speech patterns of the 1950s. Shots 10 and 11 are allowed to go on for a minute and fifteen seconds, both shots encompassing the two characters in the same space, communicating – in the formally pleasing reversed images traditional to film language. No threat, no conflict here, as the very texturing and structuring have all the elements converging in creating a mood of sad but sympathetic serenity, in immense contrast to what has preceded.

Shots 12 and 13 end Movement A, or perhaps more accurately, act as a transition from Movement A to Movement B. They are both very brief, 12 slightly over one second, 13 slightly less. Shot 12 shifts the angle over to include the wagon: Jof (Mia's husband), in long shot reminiscent of the early ones in this sequence, appears screen left partially hidden by the wagon, moaning and crying, "Mia" – thereby breaking the flow of the previous exchange. Shot 13 has the camera reversing the angle on Mia and the Knight as they turn around at the sound of the voice. Mia jumps up and runs to her husband, the camera following her in an abrupt functional pan. Once again, of course, Bergman is punctuating shifts in story, feeling, or life experience, with relatively more abrupt cinematic language.

And thus ends Movement A, classically executed by Maestro Bergman.

After the initial two shots (1 and 2), which have been characterized as formalized, pictorial, contemplative, he initiates the main action expeditiously, reaching a new moment of pictorial fulfilment (shot 10B), but one subservient nonetheless to the needs of the dramatic flow, naturalness of tone, and thematic articulation. Two of the film's major characters (thematic poles?) meet in earnest. One might be tempted, within the limits imposed by its modest less-than-two-minutes duration, to entitle this movement "Introduction: The Knight's Existential Anguish Meets Mia's Life Flow," complete with build-up, fulfilment, and interruption.

Shot 14: 1' 25 8/24"

MIA: How are you? Does it hurt? What can I do? Have they been cruel to you?

JOF: Ouch, it hurts.

MIA: Why did you have to go there? And of course you drank.

JOF: Ouch! I didn't drink anything.

MIA: Then I suppose you were boasting about the angels and devils you consort with. People don't like someone who has too many ideas and fantasies.

JOF: I swear to you that I didn't say a word about angels.

MIA: You were, of course, busy singing and dancing. You can never stop being an actor. People also become angry at that, and you know it.

JOF: Look what I brought for you.

MIA: You couldn't afford it.

JOF: (angry): But I got it anyhow.

JOF: Oh, how they beat me.

MIA: Why didn't you beat them back?

JOF: I only became frightened and angry. I never get a chance to hit back. I can get angry, you know that. I roared like a lion.

MIA: Were they frightened?

JOF: No, they just laughed … Mikael! ooh … Mikael!

Husband, wife, and child:
family at love and play

MOVEMENT B

Movement B is made up of two shots, lasting one minute and thirty-six seconds.

Shot 14 takes up almost a minute and a half of that total, beginning with great vigour as Bergman cuts in reverse angle from shot 13, his camera panning to capture Mia as she scrambles to where her husband is moaning. The composition at this point totally forsakes the pictorial: the choice is functionality, to capture movement and naturalness and the main action. Mia bathes Jof's bruises, scolds him, and cuddles him, and he responds as a child. In total innocence, he gives her the stolen bracelet, and Bergman plays out the scene with humour and delight, the accent wholly on the interaction of husband and wife, on spontaneity and uncomplicated love – and on the impish side of Jof's character. This section of the shot is extended in leisurely fashion beyond one minute. By now the camera has reached its point of desired framing, the two in a rather lovely medium long shot as they sit on the ground across the wagon staffs in the bottom two-thirds of the image; the top third is shared by the light of the sky, framing in background the horse and part of the wagon. The baby's gurgles interrupt the play; Jof gets up, walking, arms outstretched, toward the camera, which tilts up and pans minimally to keep him within frame.

Shot 15:   10 17/24"

MIA: Do you notice how good he smells?

JOF: And he is so compact to hold. You're a sturdy one. A real acrobat's body.

Shot 15 captures Jof as he picks up the infant, in medium shot, to be joined by Mia. Again Bergman chooses a relatively "unpictorial" composition, his camera finally resting on the three together on the ground in a high angle shot (surely the Knight's standing eye-level point of view), with a small sloping strip of sky lighting the top right screen. "Unpictorial" perhaps at first glance: but Gunnar Fischer has again layered his image in three tones, progressing from dark shadow to gentle light; and although the shot lasts scarcely eleven seconds, the content is powerful – earth, sky, animals, husband and wife and child celebrating family love, fertility, the life force. It is one of those archetypes impossible to resist, a human experience so deep and universal that no demonstration is necessary, no explanation adequate. And, as we shall see, it is part of a symbolic network working throughout the film, the antithesis of the evil, horror, fanaticism, anguish, and "intellectualizing" permeating most of the film.

These two shots, then, represent precisely what the Knight has lost. They are the incarnation of an idealized vision of life re-created by Bergman. Call this movement: "Husband, Wife, and Child: Family at Love and Play."

Shot 16:   2 1/24"

Shot 17:   34"

MIA: Yes, this is my husband, Jof.

JOF: Good evening.

KNIGHT: Good evening.

KNIGHT: I have just told your wife that you have a splendid son. He'll bring great joy to you.

JOF: Yes, he's fine.

JOF: Have we nothing to offer the knight, Mia?

KNIGHT: Thank you, I don't want anything.

MIA: (*housewifely*): I picked a basket of wild strawberries this afternoon. And we have a drop of milk fresh from a cow …

JOF: … that we were allowed to milk. So, if you would like to partake of this humble fare, it would be a great honor.

MIA: Please be seated and I'll bring the food.

Return to the diegesis

MOVEMENT C

Movement C, made up of three shots (16, 17, 18), is the most literal and prosaic of the five stages of this sequence, lasting slightly over one minute.

Shot 16. A rather abrupt cut (from what is seen to the one who sees) in close medium shot of the Knight, waist up, observing the family scene. There is a relatively dramatic and poignant note to this quick, two-second shot, with, in reverse angle, the "cosmic" elements of earth and sky dividing the image in dark and light. The Knight stands out, his face very pale, his tunic dominating in black except for the greyish-white Crusader Cross in strong relief across the chest. The formal structure makes it quite clear that he is excluded from this kind of reality; and thanks to the lighting and composition and his wistful, timid smile, we feel his sense of not belonging to it.

Shot 17. Reverse angle, a return to the little family (shot 15) sprawled on the ground, unstructured, "natural" in its messiness, in more pronounced high angle and thereby crowding out the sky. Jof and Mia scramble to their feet, he holding the baby, to be joined by the Knight and captured by a panning, upwardly tilting, functional camera that comes to rest in a pleasing, balanced, composed grouping. Jof and the baby are now framed screen left by the wagon's grey canvas arc; Mia is in the centre, backgrounded by the horse further up the little incline and by the sky; and the Knight, his pale face almost lost against the pale light of the sky on the horizon, is half in, half out of the frame – and of this family world. Introductions, politeness, and so on as Mia takes the baby and exits the image to fetch strawberries and milk. In spite of the somewhat shy and awkward formality, this scene of over thirty seconds has a leisurely quality, building (as we shall see) to something special.

Shot 18:   24 9/24"

KNIGHT: Where are you going to next?

JOF: Up to the saints' feast at Elsinore.

KNIGHT: I wouldn't advise you to go there.

JOF: Why not, if I may ask?

KNIGHT: The plague has spread in that direction, following the coast line south. It's said that people are dying by the tens of thousands.

JOF: Really! Well, sometimes life is a little hard.

KNIGHT: May I suggest … *(Jof looks at him, surprised)* … that you follow me through the forest tonight and stay at my home if you like. Or go along the east coast. You'll probably be safer there.

Shot 18. On a matched action cut of the two men in the act of sitting on the ground, this slightly high-angle medium shot has a strong formal tone, the image divided by a strong horizon line created by the light grey sky and darker sea two-thirds up the image, with a further, less even line between sea and ground a bit lower down. The Knight and Jof are in sharp relief: all is solid and functional, real "man talk" as we are brought back to the narrative line, news of the plague, and future plans. Bergman is unwilling to neglect that audience demand. A suitable title: "Return to the Diegesis."3

3 Diegesis, to repeat briefly, is a term from film semiotics generally meaning the actions, incidents, happenings, characters, events, settings, etc., of the "world *within* the story or film."

Shot 19:   8 7/24"

JOF: I wish you good appetite.

KNIGHT: I humbly thank you.

MIA: These are wild strawberries from the forest. I have never seen such large ones. They grow up there on the hillside. Notice how they smell!

Shot 20:   33 3/24"

JOF: Your suggestion is good, but I must think it over.

MIA: It might be wise to have company going through the forest. It's said to be full of trolls and ghosts and bandits. That's what I've heard.

Shot 21:   2 10/24"

JOF: (*staunchly*): Yes, I'd say that it's not a bad idea, but I have to think about it. Now that Skat has left, I am responsible for the troupe. After all, I have become director of the whole company.

MIA: (*mimics*): After all, I have become director of the whole company.

Community and sacrament

MOVEMENT D

Shots 19 to 33, lasting three minutes and forty-eight seconds.

Shot 19. Cut to Mia, initially in that rather close long shot seen so often in this sequence (i.e., shots 4, 6, 8, 10, 12, 14, 17). She is carrying two large wooden bowls, one filled with milk, the other with strawberries. She moves toward the camera, joining the two men, handing the bowl of milk over to Jof and extending the bowl of strawberries to the Knight. In a free-flowing movement the camera pans and dollies down, following Mia as she kneels on the ground between the two, and gradually dollying in on the bowl of strawberries, almost isolating it in large close-up as it rests in extreme high angle upon a white cloth laid on the ground. This introductory shot to what can be called the point of convergence in the sequence lasts close to nine seconds.

Shot 20. Cut to a tight long shot of the three, seated on the ground, in functional, casual high-angle composition, passing the bowl of strawberries, smelling and eating them, talking and laughing. For over thirty seconds we observe the Knight integrated into joyful human companionship as never before in the film.

Shot 21 comes in cued by their burst of laughter. In close long shot, almost reverse angle, the Knight's Squire arrives, followed by the mute woman he rescued earlier on. This is a functional, grey, eye-level shot, divided two-thirds up by the light sky/dark sea-and-land horizon line. A brief, two-second moment, it nonetheless serves to break the previous mood. Bergman thus continues to guide his audience, preparing for his key moment through a rhythm of moving forward, momentarily interrupting that movement, and then leading us forward again – much as in a symphonic progression.

Shot 22: 4 21/24"

MIA: Do you want some strawberries?
JOF: This man saved my life. Sit down, my friend, and let us be together.

Shot 23: 11 15/24"

JÖNS: We accept gratefully.
MIA: (*stretches herself*): Oh, how nice this is.
KNIGHT: For a short while.
MIA: Nearly always.

Shot 24: 12 19/24"

One day is like another. There is nothing strange about that. The summer, of course, is better than the winter, because in summer you don't have to be cold. But spring is best of all.

Shot 25: 23 22/24"

JOF: I have written a poem about the spring. Perhaps you'd like to hear it. I'll run and get my lyre.
(*He sprints toward the wagon*)
MIA: Not now, Jof. Our guests may not be amused by your songs.
JÖNS: (*politely*): By all means. I write little songs myself. For example, I know a very funny song about a wanton fish which I doubt you've heard yet.
(*The Knight looks at him*): Ahem …
JÖNS: You'll not get to hear it either. There are persons here who don't appreciate my art and I don't want to upset anyone. I'm a sensitive soul.

Shot 22. Cut, in almost reverse high angle, to a close medium shot of Jof and Mia on the ground, greeting the two new arrivals and then inviting them to join in the repast. Notice how Bergman gives Jof and Mia the moral dominance here by their relative size in the composition and by the absence in this shot of the Knight.

Shot 23. In almost reverse angle this shot continues shot 21: from those observing (Mia and Jof) to those observed (the Squire and the mute woman). The camera pans functionally, following the two as they join the group, eventually dollying back enough to include all five seated about three sides of the cloth on which lie the two bowls with their benign contents. A flat arc is formed: left to right, the Squire, the mute woman, Jof, Mia (she is lying on the grass), and the Knight. Again here nothing is consciously "aesthetic" in the composition, naturalness and almost haphazard spontaneity setting the tone.

Shot 24. Cut to insert of a close-up of Mia's face and shoulders in total high, vertical angle, diagonally against the grass. The abruptness and off-axis composition are decidedly not an example of Bergman at his best, somewhat crudely obvious as it is in revealing his intention: Mia as living symbol, the one so attuned to the earth, lying full length, expressing her simple, spontaneous joy in the moment, the season, the earth – her at-oneness with it all, with being alive.

Shot 25 returns to shot 23, with the five people seated as before. The shot lasts a leisurely twenty-four seconds; it takes on a slightly more formal aspect as Mia sits up, completing the arc more gracefully. The Squire in his relatively dark appearance, clipped tones, and rigid posture is somewhat at odds with the mood of the setting, his ironic humour – he offers to sing a vulgar ditty – purging any possibility of too-obvious lyricism or sentimentality. Meanwhile, Jof, having risen to fetch his lute, returns with it in hand.

The first seven shots of Movement D take up a minute and a half. For what is really the first time in the film, a small group (five – or six, counting the baby) are forming a benign community built around the sharing of food and drink. The tone is certainly non-solemn (so far), the pace relaxed with comic distractions and wandering dialogue. The audience, in other words, is gently being eased to another level of artistic creation – of experience, really. Bergman magic? It is a question, rather, of mise en scène, a series of choices that seduce the audience into accepting the highly formalized moments soon to follow.

Shot 26: 3 13/24"

Shot 27: 60 4/24"

KNIGHT: People are troubled by so much.

MIA: It's always better when one is two. Have you no one of your own?

KNIGHT: Yes, I think I had someone.

MIA: And what is she doing now?

KNIGHT: I don't know.

MIA: You look so solemn. Was she your beloved?

KNIGHT: We were newly married and we played together. We laughed a great deal. I wrote songs to her eyes, to her nose, to her beautiful little ears. We went hunting together and at night we danced. The house was full of life …

MIA: Do you want some more strawberries?

KNIGHT: (*shakes his head*): Faith is a torment, did you know that? It is like loving someone who is out there in the darkness but never appears, no matter how loudly you call.

MIA: I don't understand what you mean.

KNIGHT: Everything I've said seems meaningless and unreal while I sit here with you and your husband. How unimportant it all becomes suddenly.

MIA: Now you don't look so solemn.

Shot 26. A cut to a medium shot of Jof and his lute inaugurates this "movement within a movement." Jof is seated in his usual central place at the top of the arc, but thanks to the camera angle, he is isolated at sitting eye-level, so that some sky and part of the horizon line can be seen. He is framed against a section of the wagon, with a death mask (part of the strolling players' paraphernalia) hanging on a branch and peering over his shoulder just behind him. A hushed, lovely stillness is transformed into music by the clear, clean, soft notes of Jof's lute as he begins to pick out a tune. Bergman is creating an almost liturgical accompaniment for the solemn and semi-ritualized words and gestures to follow. (This music will continue through the next dozen shots, through almost four minutes.)

We see a transformed Jof, his rascally impishness, whimsy, and clowning no longer in evidence. He is soulful and grave, the seer who sees through and beyond everyday surfaces. In a structural sense, he, the artist (Bergman?), is orchestrating what follows, elevating the cinematic signs to the level of icon, of sacred poetic truth.

Shot 27. Cut to a broader shot, a formal portrait still at sitting eye-level, with the angle a bit lower to reveal a good part of the sky/horizon a balanced halfway up on either side of the frame. The shot, which encompasses the three main characters of the sequence, is a lengthy one, lasting a full minute, and this seen through an unmoving camera. Thanks to its slightly altered positioning, Jof is seen smaller in the background screen left, with Mia in the centre, and the Knight, greyer and darker on screen right, dominating in medium shot.

Jof is humming softly to the pure accompaniment of his lute. It is a song heard earlier, near the beginning of the film, when Jof had his vision of the Virgin Mary and Child in a sunlit forest glade: to Jesus Christ, at midsummer. At times bird twittering can be heard. The soft musical stillness serves as background for the slow, low, clear voices of the Knight and Mia.

The first fifty-three seconds have the Knight sadly recalling his wife in their days of young love. Mia, fairly melting in sympathy, offers berries, but he declines. Without bitterness, almost in a reverie, gently he tells her his pain, his loneliness, his searching: "To believe is to suffer, looking for someone in the dark who never answers."

Then a new mood – call it a new formally articulated theme – emerges. He smiles, takes a wild strawberry and savours it: "But how unreal all this is in your company. It means nothing to me now … " He and Mia are smiling.

Shot 28:   1 21/24"

Shot 29:   23 10/24"

KNIGHT: I shall remember this moment. The silence, the twilight, the bowls of strawberries and milk, your faces in the evening light. Mikael sleeping, Jof with his lyre. I'll try to remember what we have talked about. I'll carry this memory …

Shot 30:   23 10/24"

… between my hands as carefully as if it were a bowl filled to the brim with fresh milk. (*He turns his face away and looks out toward the sea and the colorless gray sky*) And it will be an adequate sign – it will be enough for me.

Shot 31:   7 1/24"

Shot 32:   7 20/24"

Shot 33:   5 4/24"

Shot 28. A quick cut to Jof playing his lute (just as in shot 26), without dialogue. In two seconds it re-establishes the role of the artist/seer/creator and serves to punctuate the shift between the Knight's two moods, or rather, it helps highlight the new formal affirmation of meaningfulness about to begin.

Shot 29, a three-shot, cuts back to shot 27 but in slightly higher angle. Now begins the Great Speech: "I shall remember this moment," says the Knight, describing the people, the place, and the hushed beauty. This shot lasts almost half a minute, and especially strong individual lute notes magnify the mood. The camera eventually dollies back to include all five people seated together. The angle of shooting now has the Squire in left foreground, and the others behind him to an extent, including Mia and the Knight. The Squire, ever sombre, is on the alert, looking off screen right. Meanwhile, the Knight, having accepted the bowl of milk from Mia, has begun his speech.

Shot 30. Cut to the Knight, matched action, but now framed alone in medium shot, almost in close-up, with the camera at his eye-level. This is probably the most abstract shot of the sequence, the background stylized à la Gunnar Fischer in three layers of light: top quarter light, bottom three quarters the grey earth, the right half of which is relatively darker, the left half setting off the Knight, his hair glowing white in a halo effect. A smile of serenity and joy lights up his face. He raises the bowl of milk and in a priest-like gesture in exact parallel to the ritualized action of Offertory, Consecration, and Communion of the Mass, drinks deep and hands the bowl back to Mia: "And it will be an adequate sign – it will be enough for me." (See sketch on p. 151.)

This almost close-up shot, in its reverential tones, solemn pacing (the few words are stretched over twenty-one seconds), ritualized action, and soulful musical accompaniment on the lute, is indeed a crucial moment, not only a blessed relief and release for the Knight (and for the audience) after the anguish that has so recently preceded – and that so soon will follow – but more, a moment of revelation, a kind of answer, however short-lived, to the Knight's quest. One senses a formalized, conscious extension into the sacred, or at least into traditional Christian iconography and ritual representing what western tradition calls the sacred. The earth's offering – strawberries and milk – has become sacrament.

Shots 31, 32, and 33 end this sacred movement within a movement. *Shot 31,* lasting seven seconds, returns to the composition of the end of shot 29. The Knight rises, and through matched action into shot 32, moves toward the camera. This is a far more distant shot, with the little group, the wagon, and the horse now dwarfed by the surrounding land, which covers the bottom three-

fifths of the frame, the sky filling the other two-fifths, with its sloping horizon line. The Knight strides obliquely toward us (the camera) and left, finally exiting screen left, abandoning the blessed space. Cut to shot 33, to Jof (as in shots 26 and 28). He is still playing the lute, the scene he has been orchestrating now completed. The notes will continue being heard, nevertheless, in background for a few more shots. The birds are still chirruping, but their whistles are sharper, perhaps in warning. For the tone is shifting: is there another presence lurking? And Jof, with that far-away look: is he seeing something?

And so Movement D, one of the crucial points of the film – and, as we shall see, perhaps a pivotal moment in Bergman's evolution at that time – comes to a close, but not before having brought the Knight and the audience to a moment of wholeness and meaningfulness, built on such notions as community and sacrament. Big, mystical concepts, these, growing out of the Christian tradition. But more than that: there are overtones here suggesting the existentialist debate raging through western Europe since the 1940s, as we shall see.

Shot 34:   15 14/24"   DEATH: I have been waiting for you.

Return to the struggle:
from affirmation back
to angst

MOVEMENT E

Sequence 8 comes to a close with this movement (shots 34 to 41), which lasts a minute and a half (or just over that, if the dissolve into sequence 9 is included).

Shot 34, lasting a charged fifteen seconds, changes the mood radically. Jof's lute-playing and humming maintain the aural background for a while, but everything else veers into another kind of filmic expression. With the much darker hues, harsher contrasts, grainier stock, and spectacular compositions, one may indeed refer to "expressionistic heightening and distortion."

Through a brief ellipsis in time from the previous shot, the Knight is now seen, slightly screen left, in medium shot against a curving horizon line dividing the extremely dark ground, more dominant on screen left, from the sharp white sky, more dominant on screen right. At the beginning of the shot the Knight's face is unnaturally white, almost absorbed by the sky and decapitated by the sharp, curved horizon line, his white Crusader cross standing out in contrast to the dark tunic and black ground. He looks about dramatically as he walks toward the camera into a tight facial close-up, his face and neck now greyer, in interestingly varying skin shades. As he exits screen right, the land and skyscape is left empty for a few seconds (which seem to last an intense length of time precisely because of the emptiness). The soundtrack suddenly is invaded by a brief non-diegetical[4] outburst of deep woodwinds sounding the "Dies Irae," part of the old funeral mass, followed by high, wailing "cosmic" voices as the camera pans left and down into almost total blackness (the

4 Courtesy (again) of semiotics, this means that the music does not come from a person or source *within* the action or story of the film but is added "from the outside," for whatever wished-for effect.

Shot 35:   1 23/24"

Shot 36:   11"   KNIGHT: Pardon me. I was detained for a few moments. Because I revealed my tactics to you, I'm in retreat. It's your move.

Shot 37:   40 13/24"   DEATH: Why do you look so satisfied?
KNIGHT: That's my secret.
DEATH: Of course. Now I take your knight
KNIGHT: You did the right thing.
DEATH: Have you tricked me?
KNIGHT: Of course. You fell right into the trap. Check!
DEATH: What are you laughing at?
KNIGHT: Don't worry about my laughter; save your king instead.
DEATH: You're rather arrogant.
KNIGHT: Our game amuses me.
DEATH: It's your move. Hurry up. I'm a little pressed for time.
KNIGHT: I understand that you've got a lot to do, but you can't get out of our game. It takes time.

ground), finally moving up what we eventually recognize as the black cowl surrounding Death's artificially white face in tight close-up. Dark eyes glittering,
"I've been waiting for you," he says softly.

Shot 35 lasts a brief two seconds, from a totally different angle, at standing eye-
level, of the Knight in medium shot, waist up, with Gunnar Fischer capturing
more or less five layered levels of light encompassing background sky, sea,
earth, a rock fence, and trimmed trees or bushes. This is far removed from the
dramatic expressionism just seen, back to nature, with its pleasant, balanced,
restrained composition and lighting. The Knight wheels about at the preceding words, presumably facing Death.

Shot 36 cuts back to Death, his white oval face in medium close-up screen right
in a rather high angle, as if he were seated, and the Knight (and ourselves) were
standing, looking down. His face seems suspended in nothingness, with all the
rest of the image drowned in black. Jof's soft music is still heard as the camera
tilts down, panning left, to capture, in extreme high angle close-up, the chessboard in off-axis composition, its network of black and white squares and figures
in sharp contrast. The pan continues left and up, to capture the Knight's head,
side view, in extreme close-up, his white face covering almost two-thirds of the
frame, the rest almost all black. The distortion in texture and contrast is less pronounced than it was in shot 34, but Bergman is once again flirting with expressionistic effects. The Knight seems buoyant, to Death's quiet amusement.

Shot 37 restores the balance, achieving an equilibrium beyond that of any other
shot in this sequence. One might call it a true establishing shot – at many levels: in the centre background, in distant long shot, and framed by the two figures in the foreground, is the little band (sans Knight, of course) in their space
by the wagon and the horse. In the foreground, seated in medium shot on either
side of the chessboard are the Knight, screen left, and Death, screen right. The
bottom third of the image, in true Gunnar Fischer style, is extremely dark, as are
the dark borders extending up either side (the two bodies), especially on Death's
side, what with a dark bush or tree right behind him. The curved horizon
between them has almost half the image in greyish-white light, broken up in the
middle by the wagon, horse, and little band who are in intermediate dark grey,
almost the same shade as that of their patch of ground.

   The scene is one of static repose, with the camera still and the small chess
moves restrained. It works its way at a quiet, sedate pace, lasting some forty
seconds; and it is during this shot that Jof's music, now ever so soft, finally
fades out. The Knight seems eager and re-energized for the game, and Death,

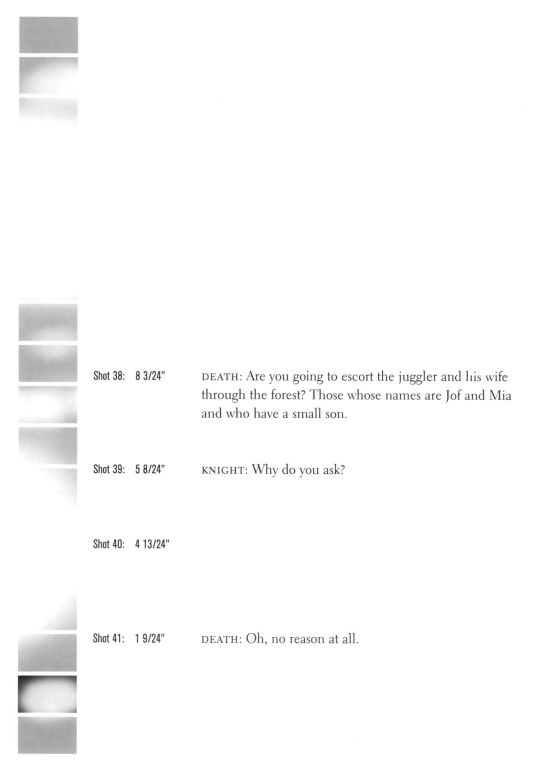

Shot 38:   8 3/24"   DEATH: Are you going to escort the juggler and his wife through the forest? Those whose names are Jof and Mia and who have a small son.

Shot 39:   5 8/24"   KNIGHT: Why do you ask?

Shot 40:   4 13/24"

Shot 41:   1 9/24"   DEATH: Oh, no reason at all.

somewhat bemused, is in an observant, almost friendly mood. They face each other, the Knight with his white chessmen, Death with his black ones, conversing quietly.

Here is self-conscious, deliberate, beautiful, "artistic" composition, Bergman obviously wanting us to relate consciously to this medieval (symbolic? metaphysical?) icon. We are brought back to the famous image at the beginning of the film, with this significant variation: the background that separated the two then was sea and sky; now it is the little band and the sacred place. So it is still a struggle between man and death, but in some mysterious way other humans, other realities are, willy-nilly, now involved: the Knight is not alone, and both a communal and a certain spiritual dimension have been added to the cosmic.

Shots 38 to 41 shatter the mood and the touch of something approaching camaraderie: they break up the symmetry of shot 37 with a series of four brief, alternating, close medium, over-the-shoulder two-shots of the Knight and Death, almost in reverse angle. They become progressively briefer, totalling not quite twenty seconds (or twenty-two, if the dissolve into the next sequence is included in its entirety).

Shot 38 shows the side and back of the Knight's white head in the left foreground, an oblique angle shot as he towers over Death, who faces us in the right foreground, with extreme contrasts of black and white. No at-oneness here: the struggle is renewed.

Shot 39 is in partial reverse angle, with the Knight still a bit higher in the frame but now facing us screen left, and Death, side and back to us, placed screen right. The background is more natural, rolling ground and trees.

Shot 40 returns to shot 38 for four-and-a-half seconds. In the most traditional of filmmaking strategies, Bergman has brought us back to the metaphysical battle. Via relatively expressionistic composition, lighting, and editing, the Knight (and humanity), still nourished by the moment of communion and meaningfulness, savours some kind of victory over Death.

But the experience is short-lived: *Shot 41* returns to shot 39, ending the sequence very quickly. The feeling of repose is gone, with brief and abrupt shots having jumped back and forth in increasing momentum, and the dialogue, synchronized to the speaker facing us, equally firing back and forth, as Death, in calm cat-and-mouse enjoyment, reveals his "interest" in the little family. In reaction, the Knight's composure disappears, as once again he is victim to anguished concern.

191

Shot 41:
Dissolve
into sequence 9
        2 3/24"

Shot 1 of sequence 9

The shot and sequence end on a two-second dissolve into sequence 9, from the Knight's expression to the object of his solicitude, the little family. They are now in the nearby village, enveloped in a darkness punctured here and there by harshly burning torches. Mia is clutching baby Mikael, as Jof scurries about worriedly.

The moment of revelation has ended, signalling a return to the bitter, cruel, suffering world. Movement E might well be called "Return to the Struggle: From Affirmation to Angst."

CHAPTER TEN

THE BERGMAN MAGIC

Once the digging in the trenches was completed, the promise went, we would be free to gambol in the fields of cultural appropriation. To a limited extent we have done our job of delving into the sights and the sounds, into the way they are textured, structured, put together. Not without a certain amount of cheating, it was freely admitted: even at this stage, there was some straying beyond strict description/analysis. With Gimli (to shift into a Tolkienesque mode), I could not resist adventuring into Legolas's magical world, emerging from the digging to explore the giddy elevated regions of poetry, culture, interpretation. That occurred, however, most discreetly, and only at those moments when Bergman creates signs that are meant to be recognized immediately as having further significations or connotations obvious as such in our culture. The prime effort in chapter 9 was given to pointing out what is there at an obvious first level of denotation.

Now, however, is the time to reveal the "Bergman text" in those multi-levelled riches that build on and may well soar beyond the simple recognition and enjoyment of beautiful images and sounds and so on. That inevitably brings in a highly subjective, or personal, dimension. And so the writing, here especially, depends on my own appropriation of our culture – in this particular context, my own formal knowledge of film and of those other areas of the culture that I feel attuned to, and, finally (and perhaps most mysteriously), those experiences in life that have taught me "what it's all about." So for the writer, and so for each viewer and each reader.

In *Film in the Aura of Art* Dudley Andrew goes about this sort of revelatory task in very neat fashion. In his chapter entitled "The Turn and Return of *Sunrise*"[1] Andrew comes to the film (*Sunrise*) from a particular point of view, then returns to it from another, and yet another, and so on. In a way (but not *his* specific way) I use a similar strategy, approaching the sequence just

---

1 Dudley Andrew, *Film in the Aura of Art* (Princeton, NJ: Princeton University Press, 1984), 28–58.

described from different perspectives and levels, hoping with each return to unearth something culturally broader, deeper, or at least *other*. The repeated "returnings" to the same materials can verge at times on the repetitious, but it permits the revealing of any number of aspects of Bergman's film text, by that very exercise demonstrating its remarkable richness at the aesthetic level and at the level of cultural relevance in general.

OVERALL UNITY

Many have pointed out Bergman's eclecticism, his penchant for mixing styles and themes with a theatrical bravura – a point, I believe, that is very well founded in Bergman's films. But Bergman's eclecticism rarely gets in the way of our aesthetic enjoyment, and that is because of the very tight organization of his materials, which is in evidence through every aspect of those films. And so the forty-one shots of our chosen scene, lasting not quite ten minutes, witness to a cultivated, conscious imposition of unity: the sequence does indeed make up a "perfectly balanced, self-enclosed unit" in the inner workings of the segment. But it also fits in beautifully as part of the entire functioning film text.

The scene opens with the Knight reclining on the grass by the chessboard, pondering over his next move; it ends with a return to the chessboard, this time with the Knight on one side, and a very visible Death on the other, framing the sacred space where the rest of the sequence has taken place. Without question that sacred-space scene is one of the most positive and life-affirming of the film; but Bergman contrives to suggest Death's presence throughout in a number of ways, thereby making the scene that much more poignant and fragile but also more integrally one with the rest of the film. For example, the Squire, whose presence seems clouded with the consciousness of death, is often blocked so that he is seen looking off somewhere left, as if half-expecting the dreaded visitor. And Jof, as he plays his lute, has that far-away look, seeing beyond us, seeing … what? Over his shoulder, suspended on a tree branch, sure enough, is a player's mask of death, visually intruding upon the liturgy-like music he is playing. In other words, this little oasis may be only that, an oasis in a death-enshrouded world.

But the chess motif and Death go far beyond this one scene: they are, as already stated, framers for the rest of the action as well, enclosing it, punctuating it between its various segments. Shot 37 is indeed a direct recalling of the opening of the film (see chapter 9). The all-but-final Dance of Death is strangely in keeping with the spirit of the chess motif, a game in its own way, a cultural and metaphysical (and plot-ending) one.

MOVEMENT: SPACE, TIME, AND OTHER WORLDS

So the carefully chosen, knit-together, controlled nature of Bergman's film-making leads to a profound feeling of underlying unity. And this is felt in many other ways, some of them far less obvious. Some, for example, we tend to translate into abstract notions such as space, time, other levels of experience, other worlds – even though they are communicated to us by Bergman through very concrete cinematic strategies.

As soon as we give ourselves to such notions, however, other possibilities of simultaneous experiencing open up to us, interweaving, deepening. Most movie sequences, to be sure, contain surface plot incidents structured into a narrative line, along with the sights and sounds – all of it potential for excitement, involvement, enjoyment. But, as Francis Fergusson[2] pointed out some forty-five years ago, there is another kind of underlying action, a deeper movement of the spirit, or, better, of reality itself, equally at work. We may encounter it, in varying degrees of our own consciousness and intellectual appropriation. This holds eminently true for the "strawberries and milk" segment. It is fascinating to see how Bergman orchestrates this "deep" action through his organizing of time and space in what becomes a very significant soul journey.

We go back, then, to the site of the chosen scene, the meadow, one end of it (we call it screen left) running down to the sea, the other (screen right) gently inclining upward into the horizon line. From our vantage point – that is, as we organize the film space into a coherent left/right, up/down pattern – Mia is screen right, seemingly near the centre of the glade. Certainly she is the central radiating force of a benign world hitherto beyond the Knight's reach. He is screen left.

Bergman's mise en scène here seems extremely simple, its methods and clarity firmly entrenched in traditional film usage. On the surface, the Knight joins Mia and her child, they chat, are joined by others, have a meal of strawberries and milk, and the Knight leaves to continue his chess game with Death.

But so much more, in the Fergusson understanding of "action," is happening. Bergman sets up different worlds, visions, levels of experience with dazzling ease, through a series of progressions achieved by the way he organizes different "spaces," and by the way, through his editing, he moves from one space to another, or from one dimension to other dimensions within the same space. The accompanying diagram (figure 1) sketches out those kinds of movements or progressions in all their simplicity. But it is a simplicity that structures

2   *The Idea of a Theatre* (Garden City, NY: Doubleday Anchor, 1949). Fergusson, of course, was referring to theatre, not film. But the insight holds true with even greater force for cinema drama.

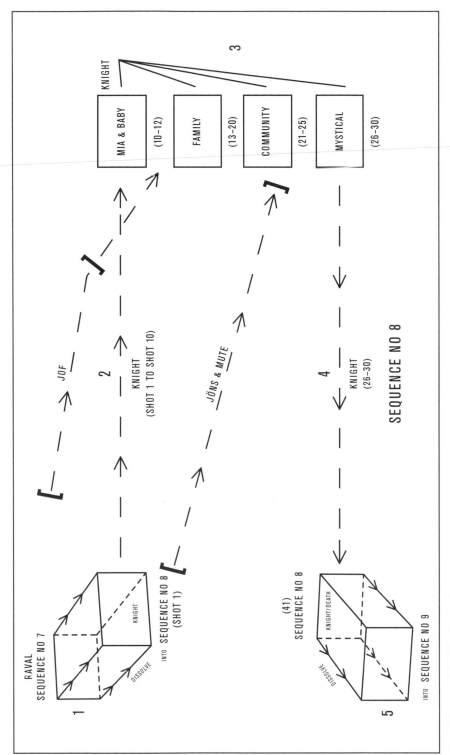

Fig. 1 Diagram of the Five Progressions

a metaphysical exploration/revelation which can indeed be seen as cinematically extraordinary.

First Kind of Progression: "Depth Dimension"

The Knight emerges from one incarnation of our world into another via a dissolve. We are not dealing here with anything resembling the literal passage of time or the reality of screen space within its horizontal and vertical limitations. True to the effect typically associated with the editing technique called the "dissolve," time and space become, so to speak, mystically indeterminate: the tavern (sequence 7), with its fire, smoke, dirt, and noise, symbolizing a death-infested, cruel world on the edge of madness, dissolves into the glade (sequence 8), where all is natural beauty and blessed silence. True, there is a compositional paralleling going on between Raval (end of sequence 7) and the Knight (beginning of sequence 8), each reclining in the same part of each one's own frame; but the action has, as it were, moved forward in space, from one time/place/human condition to another, its very opposite, the evil symbolically yielding to the benign.

Second Kind of Progression: "Horizontal Lateral Right"

In leisurely fashion the "real-life" space of the glade is established for us, the Knight in his section, reclining by his chessboard presumably at the "left" end of the glade, and Mia and her child, presumably in the centre. Back and forth we are led by the editing between Knight and Mother and Child, two separated realities but reaching out to each other. Finally, the Knight moves laterally right, from his section to Mia's; and Bergman ends the series of the opening ten shots by framing them together, *in Mia's space*. Clearly the Knight has entered into another level of human experiencing, something beyond his reach thus far into the film.

Third Kind of Progression: "Vertical Exploration of Mia's World"

The "mystical" movement in time and space from an evil world to a benign-nature one and the more literal move from the edge of that benign world to its very life centre have been completed. Bergman stops his lateral moving: now he dedicates his next series of shots (from 10 to 31) to an exploration of that vital reality. One might describe the movement as "vertical," digging down, examining this reality in its various manifestations or levels or component parts, ever deepening, ever broadening.

But before going into those manifestations, it is probably useful to remind the reader that I am proceeding in extremely schematic manner, limiting myself here – as indeed through most of the different parts of this section – to the particular perspective under exploration. I do not go into, for example, the formal dialogue, which makes far more explicit much of what I am suggesting. Moreover, the mise en scène does not permit things to be nearly as unilinear and logically precise as the analysis might suggest. On the contrary, Bergman plays with us: there are shifts in rhythms and intensities, in the tonal quality and the degrees of seriousness or playfulness. The Knight moves forward, hesitates, moves again. And so on. The many elements making up the total mise en scène, of course, tend to appear in one form or another in the next two divisions of this section. The reader (again) should refer back to pages 156–93 for the specifics.

The four components/levels/manifestations:

1   *Mia and Baby*. The first group of shots (10 to 12) has the Knight relating to Mother and Child, the first level of the life force, surrounded by stillness, beautiful nature, bird sounds, fertility and joy. Sharing their world, he responds by confiding in the young woman.

2   *Family*. Shots 13 to 20 extend this into the Knight's experiencing the family unit: Jof, Mia, and Baby, the spontaneity of love and fruitfulness.

3   *Community*. Shots 21 to 25, with the arrival of the Squire and the mute young woman, celebrate community, hospitality, the sharing of food.

4   *Mystical*. Shots 26 to 30 extend the moment into its mystical, religious dimension, the final reality that encompasses the life force, bringing with it respite, insight, meaningfulness, fulfilment.

The Knight has thus made a huge journey, into experiencing a life force he had felt was no longer meant for him. And the film has clearly established one of its essential poles.

Fourth Kind of Progression: "The Return"

From shots 31 to 41 the Knight retraces his "second progression" by a lateral movement left, back to his opening chessboard position. His area may be the same as at the opening of the sequence, but the level of existence is not: he is back to his mythic/allegorical/symbolic chess game, the struggle with Death, beyond this world yet within it, unseen by any of the others – except perhaps by the poet Jof, and vaguely intuited by Jöns the Squire. Shot 37, which frames what is left of the little group with a foreground of the Knight on one side and Death on the other, the chess game lower down between them, makes it quite clear: this is where questions of (literally) life and death are settled for common mortals.

Fifth Progression:
"Back to the Suffering, Sick World"

Sequence 8 ends as it began, with a dissolve, leading – via a "depth dimension" movement as in the "first progression" – the protagonists into sequence 9, a return to the harsh, evil world of sequence 7 and of most of the action of the film. It is a world tragically lacking, precisely, in meaningfulness and the experience of the life force.

Sequence 8, then, is indeed a rich unit complete unto itself and essential to the "deep action" of the whole movie. Its clear, strong underlying structure is able to translate a complex metaphysical vision into simple, natural moments familiar to our culture – indeed, to human nature, one might claim. And its control is such that the veritable hodgepodge of mixed levels of reality, comedy, irony, lyricism, metaphysical discussion and the like can be accommodated without any aesthetic problem. On the contrary, the viewer delights in its dazzling "unified/simplified complexity."

CLASSIC YET BAROQUE

A few years after the appearance of *The Seventh Seal* the "Nouvelle Vague" was launched in France, proclaiming its manifesto in favour of a kind of renewed film language that would be free and open to communicating any kind of experience, with, say, the suppleness, freedom, and sophistication of the novel. And indeed the 1960s were subsequently to witness in many parts of the world efforts espousing this aesthetic (and what many insisted was an ethical) option. This was hardly new in the history of the cinema: the German expressionists, the Soviet formalists, the neo-realists, and many other movements can from this perspective be understood as also seeking to renew film language.

The Ingmar Bergman of the mid 1950s can in no way be considered as sharing this preoccupation, not if film language is taken in the strictest sense of film grammar and syntax growing out of certain practices in film scripting, editing, camera movement, composition, use of light and shadow, manipulation of sound, and so on. Any familiarity with his sixteen previous features reveals that by now Bergman, a veteran of twelve years of film involvement before the making of *The Seventh Seal*, had acquired a mastery of established film technique which translates into what is called traditional film language. Not for him, *at that time*, the deconstructing of the tried and true.

Returning to our sequence in an effort to situate his filmmaking from this vantage point reveals two fundamental characteristics which might at first appear contradictory: on the one hand, he adheres to the basic, traditional, classic usages of already existing film language; on the other, he has a very free-wheeling attitude in combining in the same film what are often different film styles. Not for him the austerity imposed by strict adherence to a particular method or aesthetic or school to the exclusion of another (as Mikael Timm points out convincingly in his essays).

The classic approach is in evidence at every step of the creative process. For example, the fact that the overall structuring of the sequence lends itself admirably to a division into five movements, building as it does to an eventual fulfilment and then receding, is in the finest classical tradition. The small movements themselves also reflect the same spirit, as we recall the pacing, with the quick interruptions and then resumptions, advancing to the key moments, all of them building to the essential revelation.

But that is only part of the story, as we have seen. It is fascinating to note in our chosen scene the varying degrees of "liberty" Bergman permits himself in the use of film language. Summarizing from this point of view some of the data contained in chapter 9, one can conclude that, for example, the first twenty-five shots (lasting almost six minutes) are contained within a style permitting only a limited range of variation: from the natural, relatively informal and "unstructured" style of most of the mise en scène to those slightly more consciously aesthetic, formalized, "iconic" moments of repose often laden with an obvious richness of connotation. Then, however, there is a change: from shot 26 to shot 30 and beyond – when Bergman reaches the moment of revelation – the style shifts daringly into a more formalized, liturgical mode: music, soft and lyrical, played by Jof, now enters as a key element of heightening and poeticizing; and the spoken language takes on a more recitative tonality. The visual, in its composition and pacing, as already described, shares in the creating of solemnity. Bergman is not through, however: the shift is yet more dramatic from shots 34 to 41 (the end of the sequence). Non-diegetical, highly theatrical "Dies Irae" music intrudes upon the soundtrack, with corresponding visual harsh contrasts, looming close-ups, a nervous, space-disorienting editing, converging into what I have been calling a mitigated expressionism (seen at other times in the film, to be sure). And so we have gone from twittering bird sounds and soft laughter to a cosmic-doom choir, from understated natural flow to confrontational editing and composition.

However – and this bears repeating – these shiftings by no means signify that Bergman has "invented" a new use of film language. In his cinema of the 1950s he is unashamedly working within existing systems that serve his purposes: the patternings/figurations/styles, with their elements converging according to well established codes, create the desired effect. And Bergman is true to them, in his own way.

But that way, as we have seen, is the dedication to a structural control and a sense of direction so strong that it permits Bergman in the same film, even in the same scene, to shift from one system, one set of stylistic conventions, to others. In the hands of a lesser artist, this would be courting disaster, to what ultimately is empty, showy mishmash (shades of some of the worst examples of contemporary postmodernism). But not so with Bergman: the aesthetic miracle, it seems to me (if not to all of Bergman's critics), is that he succeeds in pulling it off, thereby creating a work of art of amazing complexity and, yes, artistic prestidigitation. As applied to him, "eclecticism" is by no means a derogatory term. It is of the essence, a source of added richness.

This all legitimately leads us to two broad conclusions about Bergman's kind of film art at this stage of his development. Seen from the perspective of the actual making of the work of art, it testifies to an artist at the height of his mastery of existing film language, exulting in exploiting that language to the full, in shaping his materials so that all the elements – all "the sights and the sounds and their structuring and texturing" – converge in creating powerful effects, moments, in the service of clarity, impact, and the ability to move deeply. In the manner of many great theatre directors, Bergman emerges as the artist/prestidigitator behind it all, his art creations proclaiming his belief in the exercise of art-making, as understood above. Classical adherence to established film language there certainly is, with supreme skill, good taste, and discipline – but also with a good dose of baroque exuberance.

As for the audience, the very nature of its aesthetic experience is thereby profoundly affected. Bergman may actually be achieving the artistic dream of having the best of both worlds. On the one hand, his audience "believes" in the scene, in its natural, deep humanity; it is lulled into a relatively easy and comfortable acceptance, thanks to the familiarity of the film language. Simultaneously, however, that same audience, seeing the obvious shifts in style, the obvious creating of recognizable symbols and cultural connotations, is made aware of the nature of the event in which it is participating: it *is* art, spectacle, artifice, the artificial communication of the artist through his artifact. And that, of course, becomes an essential part of the fun, putting the audience in the position of a mature, conscious, responsible party sharing in the benign complicity.

And so for (merely) one aspect of the whole complex business. If one extends the investigation into other aspects, including those facets of film language beyond the strictly filmic, the richness of the text continues to grow … as we shall see.

WORDS, DIALOGUE, IDEAS

Words, words, words – and how the cinema has struggled over their role, their validity, as part of film language. History has revealed every possible attitude and subsequent practice: from movies being little more than filmed theatre to film as the elimination of words (and ideas as communicated through words) from the soundtrack, in the name of "pure cinema" communicated uniquely by the "free flow of image and sound totally divorced from the tyranny of the theatre and the novel."

The question of the autonomy/non-autonomy of words in film surfaces in many different contexts; and each movie is a reflection of the attitude/practice, conscious or not, of the people/industry producing the film. The sanest approach, it would seem, is to understand film as a functioning system, made up of myriad elements of film language, of both the visual *and* the audio kind. This latter sound category itself can be divided into three sub-categories: noise, music, and words. Just what is the role of words?

For Bergman that role is an immensely important, essential one, and nowhere is this more in evidence than in *The Seventh Seal*. Just how he goes about using words and fashioning dialogue in this film is indeed fascinating.

A first characteristic: the words are tailored to the "essential nature" of each particular character. In our scene, for example – and this is typical of the whole film – the Knight often speaks sententiously, making philosophical statements; Mia speaks spontaneously about how good life is; the Squire is ever abrupt, cynical, witty; Jof's words are playful, ingratiating, and then solemn and lyrical; and Death speaks little, giving nothing away, signifying nothing-ness.

The words naturally fit into a dialogue, though at times, as in the Knight's ritual offering, they take on the form of a kind of solo *recitativo*. Generally, however, the dialogue is tailored to the needs of a particular film moment, with a rhythm and tonality in keeping with the mood and the particular signification. To a great extent everything is shaped in keeping with the traditional dramatic mode, its essential theatricality nonetheless wholly adapted to the nature of the cinema. The dialogue, for example, is subjected to a greater number of pauses and ellipses, thereby becoming subservient to the total complex nature of filmic communication and permitting the visual aspects their full play. In other words, the "film" does not stop in order to allow the dialogue to inhibit the camera.

However, the words and dialogue do indeed attract immense attention to themselves. Unlike, say, most painting and music, words tell specific stories, and they communicate specific ideas. They also have their own privileged domain, literature, and they occupy a most privileged place in all developed cultures. In *The Seventh Seal*, those words are very special: as a matter of fact (as already claimed in the preface), one of the key reasons for this particular movie's popularity with its audience over the years has been its overt, explicit word-treatment of its subject matter. There is as never before in a film an almost formal existentialist philosophical debate going on – in words, of course. And at times the words emanating from various characters are almost direct quotations, albeit in simplified form, from that debate as it was being waged (and taught) in writings and discussions in the western world during the preceding decade.

Through much of our sequence, and especially when leading up to what I have been calling the moment of revelation, the Knight's words reflect this, both in their content and their style. The same might be said of some of Mia's more understated and apparently spontaneous comments about life. Bergman's film is indeed obviously steeped in *culture*, and it contains "intellectual" ideas and words that themselves have become icons within that culture.

And so, another dialectic of sorts, similar to the classic/baroque one described above, informs the scene, alternating from the spontaneous, natural flow of everyday conversation suitable to the relaxed friendliness of a given moment to the enunciatory style and content just noted. That means that the educated viewer is pulled in by the natural attractiveness and charm of the scene; at the same time, he or she recognizes what are almost quotations from a well-known philosophical point of view. Chunks of pre-existing cultural artifacts (the ideas or "themes") are here recognized as such, part of the film material Bergman is using, working on, commenting on. As film elements they either confirm or are confirmed by the other elements, or they subvert or are subverted by these elements within the context of the whole functioning film text.

Thus the words increase natural credibility (that was one of the results of the advent of sound to the cinema), while at the same time proclaiming their being borrowed from the culture. The ideas too are part of the game, the overall game that is art, Bergman's complex, culture-conscious communicating with his audience and his culture.

By his choices of words and dialogue, then, Bergman's highly sophisticated, self-aware attitude to cinema is revealed. In its way – and one might say not in spite of but because of the overt traditional theatricality (the philosophical/literary mode, etc.) of some of the words – *The Seventh Seal* represents a new kind of movie making.

CLUSTERS

At the most basic level of what is actually seen and heard in a movie – the sights and the sounds, in the various aspects and modalities under which they are communicated to us – *The Seventh Seal* reveals opposed clusters that are the result of a most systematic series of choices.

An anguished, cruel world dominates most of the film, and Bergman establishes a network of sights and sounds to communicate such a world. That network is extended into even the strawberries and milk sequence, for all its eminently life-affirming qualities. Bergman maintains the presence of certain images and sounds, as we have seen above: Death is there, the chessboard as well; and even during Jof's beautiful sacred music, a player's death mask is looming – ever so discreetly – over his shoulder. Jons's gruff, cynical presence itself is almost a death-of-the-spirit motif. And the way in which so much of this is presented, Death quite naturally being surrounded by somewhat expressionistic effects – the extreme contrasts, the dark costumes, the disorienting of space into the more or less abstract, complemented by confrontational editing, and of course the added "Dies Irae" motifs – makes the negativity inescapable. Even the closing nature scenes, because of the harsh contrasts and absence of fertile aspects, become menacing, a kind of "cosmic" warning when Death is around. One could go so far as to suggest that this pattern is reinforced in far more subtle fashion by the Knight himself, given his grey aura, his being torn between the death and the life forces: he longs for Mia's world, but he brings into her world his own tired, tormented aura, complete with strained looks, weary speech patterns, and whatever else that results from his contact with Death and an evil world. The dark cluster of images and sounds is indeed present in this most benign of sequences, though relatively reduced in breadth and intensity from its powerful representation in most of the rest of the film.

But it is of course the life force that dominates our chosen segment. And it is in this sequence, probably, that Bergman's clustering of positive images becomes most coordinated and meaningful. He has generous amounts of pleasant earth, sea, and sky in many of the shots; the meadow has its shrubs and trees gently affording visual perspective. There is a beautiful young woman, a delightful baby, heartwarming shots of mother and child, and of husband and wife and baby at play: a contented horse grazes, plump and at peace. And of course there are strawberries and milk. Add to that the gentle tone of the human voices, the soft laughter, the baby's gurgling, the twittering of the birds, and you have a communication of the goodness of the earth. Even the usually anguish-ridden characters who are welcomed into Mia's world fit relatively well into the reality of hospitality and friendship.

The rituals of human interchange that are consistently chosen are the loving ones: baby cuddling, husband-and-wife teasing and hugging, the postures of relaxation, sitting on the good earth, Mia lying on it. A very young Bibi Andersson is a marvel to behold as Bergman iconizes her into the incarnation of life, tenderness, loving care. How could the Knight possibly resist such a manifestation of natural and spontaneous goodness and love?

The final element in the clustering is Bergman's communion ritual, when the Knight offers everything up and shares it in communion. Everything converges into oneness – earth, fertility, life force, friendship, hospitality, religious ritual. The richness of connotation here is dizzying in its possibilities of expanding interpretation, certainly a statement about life not too often matched in the history of the cinema.

It is not merely a question of the intellectual understanding of cultural terms of reference. The rhythm and texture of the sequence is a loving gift to the audience, an inviting to universal convergence. Except for the reappearance of Death at the end, sequence 8 has practically no jarring cuts, no cultivated dialectical effects: almost all is benign synthesis. Bergman gently gives us time to feel and to understand. His compositions please the eye, his soundtrack soothes the ear. His rhythm keeps us pleasantly on the alert as we are led from one level to the next in an ever-deepening sense of oneness. There are times, as previously shown, of relaxed progression, then interruptions, and then further progression, until we attain fulfilment. The very texture and structure of the scene, then, express and make us share in the sense of worshipful serenity.

A more complete exploration of *The Seventh Seal* would reveal how this benign network operates throughout the film, surfacing and all but disappearing in a constant ebb and flow from beginning to end. The same can be said about the network of death-and-evil sights and sounds, with greater insistency and consistency, though that network may operate in slightly more complex fashion. The "negative" forces can well be divided into two clusters that intertwine, become one, yet maintain a certain diversity: the cosmic/metaphysical images and sounds surrounding Death, and the evil/suffering images and sounds associated with our plague-ridden earth.

Now is not the time to engage in exhaustive demonstration of the above. Suffice it to say that *The Seventh Seal* becomes a battlefield whereon the forces of evil and death and the forces of life and love struggle over the fate of human beings; these forces are expressed by opposed clusters made up of carefully chosen, consciously interrelated images and sounds expressed through the appropriate film language.

This gives the work of art an amazing consistency and power. The tapestry – if we can use that as our figure – is made up of these recognizable strands and motifs, constantly grouping in new configurations thanks to variations in the elements, and constantly being renewed. In this artistic strategy each element is endowed with added richness and signification because of its converging with the other elements within its cluster. The whole work becomes a dynamic, evolving entity, with multi-levelled meaningfulness at any given moment. The interplay of these filmic signs rewards repeated viewing with constantly deepening awarenesses. This works at the emotional level as well, if not even more powerfully. For example, whenever we see Mia and Mikael, we also experience the medieval rendition of Madonna and Child (Mary and Jesus), because the first time we encounter them in the film, Jof has a (ravishing) vision of Mary and Jesus in a forest meadow and (along with the audience) is blessed with the insight that in some mystical way Mary and Jesus participate in the reality of Mia and Mikael and his love for them.3

The same phenomenon operates, naturally, within the negative cluster(s). The dying, filth, ugliness, religious fanaticism, plague, corpses, torture, flagellations, witch-burning, the hideously agonizing crucifixes, the "Dies Irae," Death himself – all become one, each element progressively bearing the burden of meaning and emotion borne by each of the others.

Anyone familiar with the critical work, especially in the second quarter of our century, devoted to the study of imagery and sound in poetry and drama (above all in Shakespeare4) will realize that Bergman did not invent this way of creating art. Far from it. In so structuring his work, he has given us a movie steeped in the ways and riches of poetry. *The Seventh Seal* is simply not your average, cause-and-effect, literal film narrative. It centres on the great metaphysical questions with the breadth, depth, heightening, and indefinitely expanding complexity that are the domain of poetry. As such – and this has been a problem shared by a number of great movies – it may prove somewhat befuddling for first viewers; but the rewards are immense. One can go back to it again and again, as I have said, ever renewing, ever deepening, ever broadening the experience. And this can be the occasion for mature aesthetic delight. Are we entering here into the mystery of the "magic" of art? At any rate, as Dudley Andrew might say, here is one movie that certainly stands up to multiple returnings.

3 This becomes clear through Bergman's use of film language, particularly the composition and the music, in the most lyrically beautiful moment of the film, near the beginning. Given space limitations, my statement will have to be taken on faith, without the rather obvious textual demonstration.

4 In the kind of work done, for example, by Caroline Spurgeon, Wilson Knight, Cleanth Brooks, L.C. Knights, Kenneth Muir, and Middleton Murray.

REALITY, ART, SYMBOL

All through this section devoted to the description, analysis, and interpretation of one Bergman sequence, I have been referring to "signs," and to certain moments as "iconic," and to others (or, at times, to the same ones) as "natural," "informal," "unstructured." A return to these notions in more systematic fashion helps in furthering the understanding of the riches of this scene, or (borrowing the jargon of semiotics, since we shall be advancing, however timidly, into semiological territory) in revealing the complexity of the functioning of this cinematographic text.[5]

5   What follows is in great part indebted to the work of Peter Wollen. In his *Signs and Meaning in the Cinema* (London: Secker & Warburg, 1969 and 1972), especially 120–54, Wollen shapes some highly ingenious semiological – or semiotic, which means the same thing, at least for our purposes – tools to help us understand how film language works. His point of departure is pure semiotics: film is a system of signs. Adapting the work of Charles Peirce, he divides these signs into three categories.

This is all terribly complex matter, and it has been discussed at great length, especially in the 1960s and the '70s. While studiously endeavouring to avoid the intricacies and jargon of semiology, I nonetheless believe I am being true to the spirit of Wollen's insight when I give the following extremely brief description of the three kinds of film signs (or of film styles), skipping over, I admit, what should not be omitted for any adequate understanding of Wollen.

The three categories:

The indexical. The film language used makes us feel "we are there," actually observing a real event or place – at least that is the convention we are asked to share. And indeed there seems to be some kind of direct connection between the scene and reality, or, to put it into more properly semiotic terms, between the signifier and the signified aspects of the sign. Think of neo-realism, or of a television on-the-spot report.

The iconic. This may "resemble" reality, but that is only the starting point. One feels the presence of the art maker, the emphasis being on stylization, heightening, poeticization. We are conscious that we are dealing with a "work of art" inspired by, say, a school of painting or some artifact of culture, communicating an *essence*, the soul of something.

The symbolic. What we see and hear immediately refers us to something else, but without any basis in ontological reality. Thanks to cultural convention, growing out of a common usage, we accept that transposed meaning of the sign, even though in reality the connection is gratuitous. For example, the American eagle, or (to use something less bellicose) Bergman's wild strawberries: they symbolize other realities with which they have no direct connection.

It is important to know that the richest signs often work at all three levels simultaneously; and it is often difficult, almost impossible, even, to classify a sign clearly as belonging to one category or another.

The thing to remember, of course, is that we are dealing here with an analytical tool, nothing more – but one that can prove truly enlightening.

Let's look more closely, then, at the strawberries and the milk from a more semiological vantage point. In shots 19 and 20, for example, Bergman shows Mia bringing a bowl of milk and a bowl of strawberries to the Knight and her husband. They are all sitting on the grass, they chat, Mia mimics Jof, they laugh – and eat some of the strawberries. The composition, let us repeat, is very informal, free of any apparent effort to achieve conscious artistic effect. The main lines of composition seem to follow nature and a normal "you are there" sort of perception, at least up to a point. Prior to and immediately after these shots, a clear horizon line obviously stretching both sides beyond the frame destroys any possibility of centripetal "picture" composition. No, the whole feel is of the spontaneous capturing of life in its sprawl and naturalness. Careful attention, of course, reveals that the shots are well composed and that Bergman actually ends shot 19 with a close-up (unaggressive) of the bowl of strawberries. But no matter: the dialogue, editing, and the little incidents only confirm the feeling of spontaneity. As Wollen would say, the signs here are (relatively) indexical: it all seems real, it has the feel of the rhythms of natural living.

But if we go to shot 30, when the Knight, in a very close medium shot, raises the bowl of milk in a kind of offering, the effect is totally different. The moment glows with what one might term an iconic aura. One is struck by a resemblance, one recognizes the Offertory and Consecration from the Christian Mass; and when the Knight drinks with joyful reverence, it is, of course, the Communion of the Mass. The whole style and rhythm of filmmaking has changed, as already shown: spontaneity, sprawl, the mundane have been banished. Jof's music, the perfectly balanced composition in almost close-up, and the obviously ritualized action do indeed cry out icon, a sacred stylization from the Christian tradition.

But it goes further. At least for many viewers, the transposition is inevitable: through a convention of the culture, we understand that what we are witnessing is a *celebration* of the mass. Part of our mind is telling us that the strawberries and the milk are standing in for bread and wine, that the Knight is exercising a priestly function, that he (like Christ) is offering up his own life as sacrifice (which will soon follow); and that the beautiful realities of humanity and earth he has just experienced and enumerated (in a kind of recitative manner) are themselves part of that mystical offering and transformation. In this sense the iconic sign (at least for some part of the audience) is also a sign "spontaneously" meaning something else, some other kind of reality. We are now at the third level of film language, what Wollen calls the symbolic.

This kind of shorthand, whereby one thing or sign means something else with which it has practically no real physical connection, depends, of course, on a shared culture. Sometimes the understanding is shared by only a (privileged?) few. For example, that "innocent" close-up of the strawberries in shot 19 means just that, a bowl of strawberries (indexical sign). Well, no, not for those who know Bergman's work. In the Bergman films of the 1950s, wild strawberries were to take on a rich, specific connotation, beyond the dreams of even the wildest of strawberries – young love, the mystical Swedish summer, the brevity of beauty, the life force.

That, surely, is one of the great joys afforded an aware viewer in this sequence. Bergman, one might insist, manages to have his strawberries and eat them. His cinematic text is replete with signs shifting back and forth from the indexical to the iconic to the symbolic (again as Wollen would understand it). And this makes for a very rich and delightfully challenging viewing experience, the richness deepening with the growing awareness of the viewer.

In summary – and here a return to the description/analysis part of this chapter might prove useful – much of the sequence gives us the feel of reality, of life and nature as they are. We are comfortable: we feel, yes, that we are there. But, consistently, another kind of awareness is appealed to: those opening shots of the Knight alone by the chessboard, and Mia with her baby, are beautifully framed: they smack of medieval paintings. And those almost haphazard little series of apparently spontaneous actions or movements have the tendency, time and again, to find their moment of repose in an almost archetypal structuring. For example, shots 12 to 15, for all their sprawl and movement, eventually end with a glowing portrait of mother and father and child – an icon, an idealized vision, an obvious poeticization of a certain "truth." This is the way the entire sequence and indeed the entire film operate. At times, finally, the signs – the offertory ritual, the strawberries and milk, but also the Knight and Death at the chessboard, the "Dies Irae" – immediately point to something else with which they have no "real" connection. They are operating at that third level, the "purely symbolic," as we have seen.

The Seventh Seal, then, can be the occasion for an extraordinary kind of experiencing for an audience. This is a film text that is indeed very complex, affording delight to mind and heart, profound in its feel for reality, and rich in its cultural terms of reference. In his exploiting of all three levels of film language, Bergman is enabled to communicate with his audience in most sophisticated and nuanced fashion. The possibilities for the artist are broadened. And the spectators are given a challenging, active role, delighting in the depth of insight, awareness, and complexity, and in their own voyage(s) of re-creating.

SPONTANEITIES

"Profound in its feel for reality" – here is a loaded phrase, and one that might occasion a fundamental debate among film theorists. The disagreement surrounding the assumption underlying this kind of statement reveals a deep philosophical divide. For a good number of theorists, film has no connection with "reality out there," for the simple reason that we cannot really know anything about such a reality, not even that such a reality exists. Thus film can only be an adventure in film language gymnastics, the result of the "vertiginous interplay of signs forming, disintegrating, re-forming into ever shifting figurations and significations."[6] And "really" signifying nothing, except maybe how language functions in creating meaning, that sort of thing. In other words, the filmmaker, the industry, or the system, or the culture, *create* meaning, impose it on phenomena that in themselves have no intelligibility. A Peter Wollen might well agree with this proposition, as would an Eisenstein (and other Soviet film theorists of the 1920s in quest of a cinema imposing a Marxist-Leninist understanding of whatever is relevant, i.e., the social/ideological/economic context). In this kind of framework Bergman becomes a superb manipulator of film language, no more, no less.

The opposed view holds that film in fact can reflect, even reach, "reality." For reality does exist, and it does have at least a degree of intelligibility: it is attuned to our antennae and decoders, which exist precisely to enable us to know and understand. André Bazin is generally given credit for being one of the chief articulators of this understanding of film, given his belief that the camera in fact receives an "imprint of reality."

Obviously a philosophical or even religious conviction underlies this position, one that might well be highly sympathetic to Thomas Berry's notion of "spontaneities."[7] Berry, condemning what he sees as western culture's divorce from reality (which has led to the suicidal impasse we have almost reached in polluting the earth), affirms that the possibility of a return to sanity, that is, of coming back into contact with the reality that is our earth, lies in the recognition and acceptance of human spontaneities – deep fundamental things and experiences that we know and feel, and that we *are* – which are not the product merely of *cultural* coding. They are pre-rational, coming before the invention of culture, arising from our *genetic* coding, which itself grows out of its source, the earth. The earth in turn is already coded by the universe which

6 As Roland Barthes, in his heyday, used to put it concerning literature.

7 Mentioned earlier on in this section of the book: see his *The Dream of the Earth* (San Francisco: Sierra Club Books, 1988), especially chapter 15, 194–215, "The Dream of the Earth: Our Way onto the Future."

gave it birth. Finally, that very universe is but an emanation from its "numinous source," a thinking, willing, primordial and ultimate entity (that western tradition generally calls God).

Once we start giving attention to the signs chosen by a director, a very different kind of understanding of the film may well emerge. In the strawberries and milk sequence, for example, Bergman consistently turns to images and sounds and experiences incarnating what Berry calls spontaneities. It is not a question necessarily of Bergman's being conscious of this in the specific Berry sense. Essentially, however, spontaneities is what he is about in this scene. And what are these spontaneities? There are things all human beings spontaneously react to, without having to reason about it, without the need, or even the ability, to prove or disprove. They simply correspond to what we are. For example, people love to experience nature: something about certain settings of earth, sea, sky "does something" to us; a beautiful, life-giving young woman (Mia), a mother and baby communing, husband and wife and child playing, the sharing of a meal in community, rituals of laughter and of joy and of feeling at one with the universe – these things we spontaneously resonate to. As we do also for certain scenes of desolation, loneliness, conflict.

We resonate to such things in real life. And we often resonate to them when experienced through the cinema. Bazin would affirm that their profound power (in movies) grows out of a particular reality that the cinema can capture. The cinema truly can permit us, through a cinematic sign anchored in the real, to reach that real. It is fundamentally a spontaneous process: we react because that real in a sense is part of us, in our genetic coding. Understood in that context, the "mystical way" is nothing else but a response to that which has been genetically transmitted into human nature.

At least at this phase of his filmmaking career, Bergman seems intensely in touch with these realities and with their power over us – to these spontaneities deep within our nature. Seen from this point of view, the strawberries-and-milk sequence represents an extraordinary pattern of choices in the moments Bergman chooses to bring to the screen. It represents nothing less than a roll call of experiences that Berry would include among the spontaneities. No wonder, then, that many cannot resist reacting spontaneously to them. We are indeed dealing with a cinema laden with great potential – a power able to reach the viewer back then in the mid 1950s, but the audience today as well, because it is reaching into what is always deepest within us.

Thus this scene, in its achievement of at-oneness, comes as a life-affirming release from the ultimate insanity and immorality of war (the Crusades? World War II?) and the threat of cataclysm (the Black Death? nuclear holocaust?) and the whole catalogue of human barbarism (cruelty, ignorance, perversion of religion). So for the Knight at the close of the Middle Ages and for Bergman at mid-century. And as for us today in the year 2000, the Edenic scene of communion with nature coming as a resounding antithesis to the contemporary folly (the violence and starvation, lust for power and wealth, earth's pollution and our culture's contempt for natural creation).

We react as we do because it is part of our nature, of our coding, going all the way back to the "numinous source." And what more *natural*, therefore, than that the climax of the scene be reached in an act of worship to that source, in the form hallowed by the West's Christian tradition?

Caught up as it is in its endless plot repetitions, banal concerns, and penchant for commercial trivialization, the cinema rarely explores these dimensions so overtly, and certainly not with such explicitness.

RELIGION

What most astounded people when *The Seventh Seal* was first released was its overtly religious character. Never had a movie treated the "religious question" so directly, so intensely, and in such contemporary, not to say urbane, fashion. *The Seventh Seal*, in fact, inaugurated a whole series of Bergman films, from 1956 to 1962, in which religion took the stage (or screen) front and centre, something unique in the history of film. It is not, as previously noted, unreasonable to affirm that those philosophical and theological concerns are what first hurtled Bergman into international prominence. And certainly they became the occasion for numerous writings and discussions on "Bergman and the God problem."

What seemed somewhat bewildering when the film first came out now appears relatively clear and simple, especially if one addresses the film from a knowledge of its clustering of images and themes. On the one hand, *The Seventh Seal* is ferociously anti-clerical, a severe condemnation of Christian practice, as pictured by Bergman, in the dying Middle Ages: Death is clothed in black monk's garb, and detestable, hate-filled, fanatical religious figures are strewn all through the film. "Religion" tortures and burns young women for witchcraft; it encourages processions of self-lacerating flagellants; it is intoxicated with fear, punishment, and hell-fire; it creates hideously tortured deformations of the crucified Christ figure. The most loathsome character in the film, Raval, is a renegade seminarian. No doubt about it, official clerical religion in the film is firmly on the side of Death as it masochistically intones the "Dies Irae." And in that the film reflects in systematic and intense fashion what had, in a much milder and more scattered way, been appearing in many previous Bergman features.

But at a far deeper level *The Seventh Seal* is an extraordinarily complex, ultimately religious movie. It asks the questions that have always been at the heart of religious concern, those metaphysical probings about life and death, faith, hope and love, evil, suffering, and despair. And it does so drenched in the sensibility of its own times. The spectacular re-creating of medieval iconography cannot mask its decidedly mid 1950s existentialist anguish and doubt.

The quest has a powerful affirmative side. In the sequence under scrutiny, as we have seen, the film achieves a religious synthesis seldom matched in the history of the cinema. The life force is identified with human love and beauty and fertility; human community is its social extension. The earth itself, and all created beings, are viewed as holy. But more: Mia, the heart and centre of this life force, has from the beginning of the film been extended into a medieval Mary figure; and she and Jof and Mikael take on the hues of Christianity's Holy Family. With the introduction, through the Knight's liturgical act of offering, of the central act of Christian worship, the mass, the life force itself is given a Christian rendering, and this in the most positive sense. The movie even proclaims, in the Christian existentialist mode of the 1950s (as we shall see), that *this* is the true meaning of existence.

All of which represents a new synthesis for Bergman at that time. In his previous movies of this period he had created a dazzling vision of the Swedish summer paradise, setting it up as the real life force, inimical to religion, almost its antithesis. But with *The Seventh Seal* the opposition disappears: nature, life force, religion become one ... at least for a time.

Well, it is not quite as simple as that. And here the opposed clusters already analysed help clarify matters. There is a side to religious belief and practice and institutions that belongs to the forces of Death and evil – and we have seen its manifestations as parts of the dark cluster. But true religion is something else, at the centre of the goodness of life – and our sequence has shown us that. So Bergman is exorcizing the notion of religion, freeing it of what he sees as its perverse manifestations. Once we understand this, once we experience life consciously as opposed clusters, the choice becomes clear. Of course this is no easy task, a fragile enterprise at best, subject to the doubts and contradictions of our times – as Bergman's later films will amply demonstrate.

IRONY: THE CONTEMPORARY AWARENESS

As I reread these words I realize that another "return" to the Bergman text is inescapable. What has been written, I believe, certainly has its basis in the movie; but something is missing; it all sounds too simple, too uncomplicated. Even within this most positive of sequences, for example, the tranquillity and confidence are seriously threatened by suggested outside intrusions (the Squire, for example), above all by Death's arrival. And one must not forget the overall tone of the film: what immediately precedes our sequence is the tavern torture scene, and what soon follows is the witch-burning, in which the Knight's new-found sense of meaningfulness is all but annihilated. At a more harmless and charming level as well, Bergman plants little details that help derail us from too unequivocal a reading track. For example, our poet/seer (Jof) has just stolen the bracelet which, in our scene, he "innocently" gives to his wife, happy to make her believe that he bought it for her. This is the man who has the visions, remember. And the looming presence of the chess game at the beginning and of the Dance of Death at the end, with its somewhat predictable result, casts a troubling metaphysical shadow.

In other words, the Bergman text has a built-in quality that subverts any simplified reading: there is complexity, perhaps ambiguity and ambivalence. Each character may clearly espouse or represent a philosophical view-of-life option, and each has his or her moment. But in each instance the character or moment is severely tested by a kind of ironic awareness. Bergman is creating a medieval tapestry shot through with contemporary concerns; and – what is most important – we are conscious of the film as precisely that. *The Seventh Seal* is decidedly a work of self-conscious art; all kinds of distancing devices "protect" Bergman from being totally identified with any one option or meaning. Among them is the very iconography, which bespeaks medieval *re-creation*. And just in case we might miss that point, the whole film is contained by a chess game, itself framed by "cosmic" prologue and epilogue. One could go on indefinitely listing these devices: and indeed many have already been pointed out (more than once) in the description and analysis and interpretation of this scene.

The Seventh Seal, to put it rather sententiously, is drenched in the sensibility of modernity, sharing in modernity's openness but also in its lack of conviction, in its desire for meaning but also in its cynical awareness that maybe all is indeed futility, in its quest for knowledge but also in its loss of direction. A "believer" understands and even deeply feels the thrust to affirmation and fulfilment experienced in the sequence; a non-believer is in no way offended, understanding it as merely one among many possibilities presented in a brilliant piece of self-aware art-making. Bergman has respected the freedom – and the bewilderment – of the times in which he lives.

MAGIC?

So what should one's final words be on the "Bergman magic" as exemplified in this sequence? One thing the magic would not seem to consist in is the re-inventing of cinematic technique and film language. As we have seen, Bergman's mise en scène is traditional in this film: he achieves his effects by recourse to tried and true methods. It is a "user-friendly" cinema of converging elements, the composition, lighting, movement, pace, editing, sounds, dialogue, music, costuming, acting style, locations, and so on reinforcing one another, coalescing as a whole, converging into clear and intense moments (even if the "content" may be extremely complex or multi-layered). There may be a mixing of styles; but there are no radical departures here. Instead, what we have is sheer mastery, taste, and intelligence in their utilization.

Where Bergman's power explodes upon the audience is in his specific choices of story, so different to those of mainline commercial cinema; of a spoken language reflecting a level of culture (one could even say philosophy) by and large excluded from that cinema; and of images and sounds that are ravishingly beautiful or awesomely frightening. Above all, that power resides in his courting of the "spontaneities" described above. In his cinema, he unashamedly reflects those sights and sounds that bring us to the basics we all share; in so doing he is restoring an enchanted world that was part of the natural mind for most of human history (we are told). He brings all the resources of the cinema to bear on these, making them at once recognizably real but also poetically or dramatically heightened. There is a soaring, here, while digging into the depths below the surface mundane.

Not only that: Bergman's cinema reflects an amazing breadth of contemporary awareness – he sees the moment, the person, the situation from so many points of view. While seeming to do everything to create as much impact as possible, he manages to subvert simple, non-judging acceptance at face value: you cannot escape the awareness, the ambivalence, the irony, and above all the deliberate insistence that his movie is just that, a show he has put together. So much of his filmmaking revels in this aspect of spectacle – and spectacle as fun both, it would seem, for the filmmaker delighting in his obvious tricks, and for the spectator responding to them in what is at times almost a mischievous complicity.

There is indeed much of the traditional in this conception and practice of film art. But, as we have seen, it is tradition infused with the spirit of modernity. More than that, this cinema feeding on culture, tradition, ideas, and contemporary currents demands the individual, engaged interpretation of viewers treated as intelligent and free adults. Precisely because of the complexity of Bergman's filmic text, and the many levels of its cinematic signs, the members of that audience bring a vitally personal reaction to their experiencing of the film, and to the act of finding signification – which of course often produces vastly differing interpretations.

Finally, one might add, the Bergman of *The Seventh Seal* and of his other 1950s' movies may be creating a cinema often immersed in rather grim realities; but the very exuberance in his use of cinema probably serves as the most potent antidote – a celebration of art and of creativity, and therefore of life, which transforms whatever grimness or neurosis or pessimism may be portrayed on the screen.

One may use the word "magic" to describe all of this, but it is not magic at all, except in the sense of something wondrous with the power to enchant. It is rather a question of choices exercised at every level of filmmaking, served by mastery, intelligence, insight, and heart. What results is an aesthetic/cultural/human experience which offers delight and insight because of its complexity, its ever-renewing possibilities of discovery and recognition, its depth and dazzling display, its amazing ability to be simultaneously a searingly personal and sincere communication and a disavowing act of cinematic entertainment and prestidigitation – all of it profoundly contemporary in sensibility. To what degree Bergman was and is aware of all this, and especially of what everyone will make of his films, is hardly the point.

A concluding caveat: the fairly complete but, in terms of scientifically controlled precision, modest general description of one sequence can thus be seen as leading pretty far in the exercise of cultural appropriation. I readily admit that some of these latter conclusions, enriched by my viewing and studying of all of Bergman's films (some of them many times), venture beyond the strict limits of the one strawberries and milk scene I have been discussing. To be sure, when situated within that broader context, the scene becomes even more poignant, a bearer of a far more complex, dialectic-ridden significance. As has been already strongly suggested, even within its own film it is not the most typical, or perhaps the most obviously powerful: one need but recall the witch burning, or the procession of the flagellants, or the torturing of Jof in the tavern – out of many more possible examples in *The Seventh Seal*.

The strawberries and milk scene, then, gains still more in intellectual and emotional significance when seen as part of Bergman's feature-film evolution. It represents a brief, fragile moment of resolution and fulfilment built up through his previous sixteen features (1945 to 1955). It symbolizes a formalized high point of affirmation in the religious dialectic that will dominate most of his nine features between 1956 and 1962. And it represents what is all but rejected in the succeeding final feature films from 1963 to 1982.

To understand that, of course, demands an overview of all the films: one must ascend high enough to discern the trends and evolution – and by that very fact to risk giving in to broad over-simplification, and a breathtaking cultural pretentiousness.

Which is precisely what the first section of this book has attempted.

A post scriptum. It is always nice to end where one began. For this section, that means returning to personal anecdote. I have to admit not everything written here about the strawberries and milk thing occurred to me during that Lidingö brunch of rather long ago. Years of film study and other things have intervened; and one does reflect on one's memories, re-*creating* them, I suppose, more often than not. Anyway, real-live Bibi Andersson re-enters the picture. Some twenty-five years after doing that particular scene with Bergman she came to my film class to talk to the students (they too, of course, bedazzled). As part of an introduction, I showed this particular sequence; and she was enthralled. "I haven't seen that since then … I was so young, I'm amazed how good I was! How could I do that at that age?" But Bergman, methinks, had a pretty clear notion of what he, and Bibi, were about.

SOME OF THAT OTHER WORK

CHAPTER ELEVEN

NOW ABOUT TELEVISION

The Rite, After the Rehearsal, Scenes from a Marriage, The Magic Flute, Face to Face, Fanny and Alexander, and the two *Fårö Documents* – all of these were included (some more, some less) in section 1 of this book, dedicated to the study of the feature movies directed by Ingmar Bergman. Yet in varying degrees, they are works primarily created for television.

That leads us to the inescapable: the Bergman and television question. No easy matter, this, especially for a foreigner, like myself, who has not had the opportunity of seeing the majority of Bergman's work in this medium. There does not yet exist, to my knowledge, a single systematic study of this aspect of his work, which has grown so much in importance in the latter part of his career.

But that I feel will change before long. As a matter of fact, Jannike Åhlund, former editor of *Chaplin* (then Sweden's official film journal), recently (1998) wrote an article for *Dramat*, a special issue of the magazine published by the Royal Dramatic Theatre to honour Bergman on the occasion of his eightieth birthday.

The article is entitled "Confessions of a TV Freak," and it opens a new area for Bergman study: his television output. Åhland in no way pretends to be doing the final, scholarly job, and still less is her point to tackle the question of Bergman's philosophy of life, and similar topics. Her significant contribution rather is to gather the materials, show the complexity of the phenomenon, and create a historical context – and in so doing she adds rather delightfully to our understanding of the man.

What follows is hers; and I am deeply grateful for her permitting me to use it.

CONFESSIONS OF A TV FREAK

Jannike Åhlund

If you take a closer look at Ingmar Bergman's television productions – a large body of work, often overlooked in the overall context of Bergman's dramatic *œuvre* – you realize that it covers a huge range of styles, methods and approaches. Ingmar Bergman is a person who does not like to be put into a corner. On a personal as well as on a professional level he detests and defies categorization.

His television work, which comprises some twenty-one works (see list at the end of this chapter) – plays, chamber plays, "theatre-in-TV," mini-series later shortened as cinema movies – really does not have much of a common denominator, from an aesthetic point of view. Each and every one of these productions, ranging over a period of thirty years – from the technically utterly primitive *Mr Sleeman Arrives* in 1957 to the utterly sophisticated artistic swan song *In the Presence of a Clown* in 1997 – have been dictated by the specific purposes and needs of the time of its creation. Therefore, trying to create a sort of chronological coherence or even a line of development in the list of Bergman's TV work is a futile ambition. All you can say, categorically speaking, is that fifteen works were conceived and made for television exclusively, while six works had a prior and/or posterior life on stage or in the cinema. Best approach it with the same carefree detachment as the director himself.

The variety and the complexities in Bergman's TV work more often than not reflect the director's mood or whim, his curiosity or his vision of the world at a specific period in his creative life – be it 1957, when he simply wanted to toy with the newest gadget around, or 1997, when he felt the urge to sum things up, without the strenuous workings of a film shoot. Researching Bergman's TV work, it is not advisable to walk in *his* footsteps. Ingmar Bergman has an excellent memory, but his sometimes contradictory statements can be very confusing; and when the conversation tends to turn into the analytical, he is likely to veer.

The only thing that has ever mattered, according to Bergman, is that his creation – be it television, theatre, or film – take on a life of its own and that it matter to the people who give themselves to it. He prides himself only on one thing: being a craftsman. And it is only in the quality of your craftsmanship that you can tell the quality of the product: "I make commodities (artistic utilities). Everything else is completely insignificant." Well, let's stay at that level for now.

In the very beginning of things – at least from the vantage-point of Swedish television history – Ingmar Bergman directed five productions in the pioneer era, the late '50s. They were based on plays by his favourite Swedish authors,

221

Hjalmar Bergman (no relation) and "the titan" August Strindberg.

At that time Stockholm had only one television studio, a gym in the old regimental barracks on the outskirts of the city. Bergman had to share it with Ria Wägner, a popular Swedish TV cook. "We were shooting *The Woman from Venice* and had constructed a set of bridges, gondolas – the whole works – a perspective view of a street that sort of faded away in the distance. And at the end of that street you could see Ria Wägner preparing sliced reindeer meat together with a little old Lapp man, making the entire Venetian street reek of it. Most bizarre."

In these early days when Ingmar Bergman first tackled the infant medium, every performance had to be broadcast live – videotape did not make its appearance until several years later. In practical terms, it meant that everyone was on location at the same time, and shooting was done in one fell swoop, no mistakes, no slips of the tongue, no post-production editing: "It was extremely primitive, it just went straight on the air. I don't see how we had the nerve."

Mr Sleeman Arrives was Bergman's TV debut. In this tragi-comic marionette piece (by Hjalmar Bergman), a young, sweet girl living with her elderly aunt is married off against her will to an older, sickly gentleman. She is in love with a hunter but feels constrained by circumstances and fate to comply with her aunt's wshes. Bibi Andersson and Max von Sydow as the young lovers are surrounded by a magical aura of indomitable youth – in heartrending contrast with the actress Naima Wifstrand as the stern old spinster and Yngve Nordwall's character, one foot already in the grave. "The problem was that Naima was unable to memorize her parts. The other actors were terribly afraid that she would falter – it is rather embarrassing in a live TV broadcast. But Naima floated serenely like a swan, she was the only one who did not forget her lines."

The Woman from Venice followed next year. It is a love divertimento in which the female character is a scheming mistress and the lover becomes his own victim. Despite sound levels that vary wildly, noisy props, and shadows from the mike boom that travel across the television image like threatening storm clouds, *The Woman from Venice* has kept its freshness. In *Mr Sleeman Arrives* Bergman experiments with a moving camera and close-ups, while in *The Woman from Venice* the camera is static and there is no attempt to separate the viewer from a classical theatrical setting with elements of *commedia dell'arte*.

"When I made these first few plays for television, I was at the Malmö City Theatre. We rehearsed the ensemble in Malmö, then we travelled up to Stockholm. There we had a day's rehearsal in front of the camera, and the following day we had a dress rehearsal with makeup and costumes – and then we went on the air without further ado! That included camera movement and all, there wasn't a chance to change anything. Scary, but fascinating" – and a lot of fun, according to Bergman.

What was the one thing that made you decide to turn to TV? You started at a time when production costs in film were soaring at the same rate as movie audiences were dwindling. Did that influence you?

"No, the main reason was that I loved – and still do – watching TV. Technically it was completely different from film and theatre. It was exciting to use three cameras, an entirely new challenge. The flip side of the coin was the difficulties, the akwardness of the cameras and the extremely short time at your disposal. There was simply no room for improvization, every setting, every cut was figured beforehand, all you could do was to hope that things would not go completely to hell."

Bergman produced five plays for television during that initial period, 1957–60. The two dramas by Hjlamar Bergman were followed by two by Strindberg, *Storm* and *A Dream Play*. In between he made *Rabies* by the lesser-known Swedish author Olle Hedberg.

It was not until *The Rite*, his next effort in 1969, however, that Ingmar Bergman felt comfortable with the technical aspect and expressive potential of the new medium. You could say it ushers in a brief interim TV phase, *The Rite* being followed in 1970 by a minor work, *Sanctuary*. "*The Rite* was my first experiment with form, even though it was not made with television technique but on film." Made on film: in that sense it was to be a precursor to a magnificent new Bergman TV decade beginning in 1973 with *Scenes from a Marriage*.

In the 70s, Bergman used television to capture a completely new audience. It was primarily his TV series *Scenes from a Marriage* and Mozart's opera *The Magic Flute* that mesmerized viewers.

We must not think, however, that videotape and the electronic immediacy of television, now common facts of life, were things that Bergman found altogether desirable. "To be able to visualize the finished product right away is a frightening thing. It is completely different from carrying around a finished picture that you can look at now and then until the film receives its final form on the editing table. You don't want to see this beloved picture ruined by the cold objectivity of a TV screen."

Even though Bergman now felt at ease in the TV studio, exploring the artistic possibilities of the new medium, he did, in a manner of speaking, turn to the film medium: all of the TV productions from this period and onwards to the present day were transferred from videotape onto film stock, there to be edited.

Even after the introduction of non-linear, digitalized computer editing, Bergman preferred this slightly unorthodox method of making television: "I hate those bloody AVID-submarines," he says, referring to the state-of-the-art editing systems. "I want to be able to physically feel the texture of film, to be surrounded by film. The editing table is an erotic piece of equipment!"

Erotic or not, after 1982 and the writing and directing of his last "movie" (*Fanny and Alexander*), Bergman has made very sure that all the television work transferred onto film stock remain only that, i.e., "*work* copies." "I didn't like the idea of my TV productions suddenly appearing at this or that festival, announced as Bergman's last *movie*," he explains.

He is referring here to a certain amount of confusion surrounding yet another category, works shot on film but written as television mini-series and first shown that way, and then, in a considerably shortened version, projected around the world in regular theatres as movies: *Scenes from a Marriage*, *Face to Face*, and *Fanny and Alexander*.

Scenes from a Marriage Bergman describes as his "first quality TV production: the others had just been warm-ups." The series was not only a powerful demonstration of the potential of the medium but also brought in its wake, if not a revolution of married life, then a wave of marital reappraisal. "That's what I liked about it, getting a new audience. Of course, I had to change my phone number to avoid turning into a marriage counsellor. Then *Scenes from a Marriage* hit the world – it was great!" Bergman edited his TV series from six hours to just under three "for reasons of sheer greed." In the U.S. and Canada, the film was first distributed as a movie before becoming a TV series. "I really liked writing *Scenes from a Marriage*. Knowing that it would be made into a televison play, it came about very naturally. We were a small production team, there was a kind of gypsy-like quality about the whole thing, a fun project. And we moved like the devil!"

The Magic Flute, *your next TV success, was actually made for free?*
"Yes, there was a hell of a lot of whining and complaining at the Swedish Television Network. *The Magic Flute* was entirely my idea, but they thought it might be too costly and too complicated (2.6 million Swedish kronor – $U.S. half a million). I like it when people lose face. And that is precisely what happened when I said I would do it for free. Making *The Magic Flute*, a project close to my heart, was a tremendously enjoyable period. And it is still shown, still bringing people pleasure ... The kids who played the children are now bearded men, taller than I."

After his German exile in the late 1970s and after having finished the monumental task of directing *Fanny and Alexander* (1982/3), Bergman shifted gears once more, returning, more often than not, to the TV studio model, often transposing plays he had previously directed for the theatre into his own TV versions – something he had long been arguing for as a means of extending the Royal Dramatic Theatre's expensive productions to a broader popular audience. In 1982 he directed a TV version of the Molière play *School for Wives*. Interestingly enough, though he had directed the play himself at the Royal Dramatic Theatre in 1966, this one was an adaptation of the theatre production directed by Alf Sjöberg. Adapting the play for television was a real treat: "It was fluid and easy. It was so extroverted. There is never any doubt in the spectator's mind that he is at the theatre. And what a spectacular cast! I made it as a tribute to Sjoberg, whom I admired greatly. And I wanted to preserve the performance of the decade: Allan Edwall as Arnolphe."

In Ingmar Bergman's book *Images* we can see how his motivations for directing for television shift. *From the Life of the Marionettes* was born "out of a therapeutic feeling that it might be healthy for the *esprit de corps* at the Residenz-Theater in Munich to do a play together." With *Scenes from a Marriage* the ambition was to produce "a quality everyday product for TV" without the crushing weight of making a feature film. *After the Rehearsal* arose "from the pleasure of making it with precisely those actors."

Were there other important reasons for making TV?
"As far as adapting plays goes, it is the feeling of being able to bring out new aspects, nuances, and angles by translating it to another medium. Transmitting or televizing it the way it stands on the stage doesn't interest me. With an opera or a ballet, yes, it may be possible – and sometimes quite rewarding – just to mount cameras and start shooting, sound and image techniques are so incredibly sophisticated these days. But in the case of traditional theatre, you usually have to move the set, the actors and everything into a studio.

"On the other hand, the acting technique called for in an intimate space, such as our small stages here at the Dramaten, is not very different from that of a small television studio – a performance like that is easy to transfer to TV."

Do you make any difference – dramaturgically speaking – between what you write directly for television, and stage plays adapted for this medium?
"They are completely different! When you transfer a play to television, the rehearsal work is already done. But in moving from the stage to the studio camera the actors may suddenly become very nervous since they have to use

completely different means of expression. In television, the audience is as close as you and I are to each other this very moment, but from a stage you have to project into the distance – a situation that also might give rise to other nuances."

So this calls for a different approach to directing?
"Yes, in a way. It makes no sense to keep on rehearsing; instead you have to change settings and provide extremely brief and concise directives."

Is everything you have written for television purposes with the intimate aspect of the medium in mind – or are your contemporary chamber plays simply unusually well suited to the medium?
"I write specifically for TV; it calls for a certain technique and certain conditions. The audience is in another receiving situation and mode, the distribution of images is different. It is possible to do things that you don't want to do on film – some films are not well suited for TV. But in the case of *Fanny and Alexander* I never thought about whether it was for film or TV, I refused to consider television as the medium. I simply made a five-hour feature film with no restraints at all. I thought I would be able to cut it down to the two hours and forty-five minutes called for in the contract for the cinema version. But it could not be done. It was a terrible professional miscalculation on my part and a horrible mistake. The distributors were not very happy about that extra half hour. It meant they could not fit enough screenings in during an evening. And I could not make any more cuts. Had I done so, I would have mutilated the very spirit of the film."

A director in full control of the means of production – what would that actually mean with regard to television?
"The same thing as in the case of cinema. From 1955 and the success of *Smiles of a Summer Night*, which took everyone by surprise, I have had full freedom to do whatever I want. Of course I had to come up with some cost calculations and keep to a budget, but that was the only condition. Total freedom – which I have enjoyed also by staying away from the American market, where I suppose only Spielberg and a few other guys are given free rein. No one has ever peered over my shoulder. No one has offered their opinion on anything … It can get a bit lonely at times, you know."

Maybe you could have used a bit more creative resistance?
"Yes, I could definitely have used someone to bounce my ideas off. Because of this I have always valued my collaboration with Ingrid Dahlberg [former head of drama production at the Swedish Television Network, now director of the

Royal Dramatic Theatre in Stockholm]. She has always been outspoken and has never been afraid to voice her opinion. I felt I could show her different alternatives and things I felt doubtful about and work on them if needed.

"Erland Josephson is another person who has always spoken his mind. I have always shown my work to Erland before I let go of it, and he has told me precisely what he thinks of it. It is very comforting to have a person like that, that you trust 100 per cent."

In the Presence of a Clown *is about theatre as a miracle: is it not ironic that it is being done for television?*
"No, why? I think it is fun to make a real witches' brew of TV, theatre, film, and music."

Childish magical tricks and exalted mysticism under one and the same hat?
"Exactly. Terrible dreams and beautiful music … I wasn't sure myself when I wrote it whether it would work. First I planned it as a stage play for one of the small stages at the theatre. But then I reconsidered and realized I couldn't take all the production complications that that would entail. That being the case, it became very tempting to stage the whole thing, complete with winter blizzards, exploding fuse boxes, and all: so it had to be either film or television. The long scenes were better suited for TV and that's the way it is!"

Your principal actor, Börje Ahlstedt, has called In the Presence of a Clown *a swan song of your life and career. Do you agree?*
"Yes, *In the Presence of a Clown* is definitely outside the "program" I seem to have set for myself. I am basically done with studio work. I was simply scared stiff that I would not have the physical strength to go through with it, after the emotional depression following my wife's death. But then I remembered Georg Tabori, whose play *The Goldberg Variations* I have staged. In it the director says that the only sensible alternative to the stage is the morgue."

And you prefer the stage, I take it?
"Sure as hell. *In the Presence of a Clown* was actually something I decided to do, whatever the outcome, even if I were to die in the process. I might not manage, I said to myself, but I sure wanted to try. Working hard was a way to survive."

I presume that all the references to and borrowings from other films and all the recurring motifs in In the Presence of a Clown *carry a great deal of weight for you, on a personal level?*

"Yes, they actually do. After sixty years in this profession, the past naturally keeps intruding. There are obvious and conscious quotations from earlier works, especially the audience that we first saw in *Winter Light* – that they should be allowed to participate and to take part in a more earthly and concrete communion during that stormy night at Grånäs. I enjoyed including them and having Lena Endre appear dressed as Ingrid Thulin … When I set about writing *In the Presence of a Clown* I truly had the feeling that Death was looking over my shoulder. As author Göran Tunström puts it: "I had a sense of always having a silent man behind me, measuring me for a suit." It was a very strange experience, and it very much became a factor in urging me on to write it. Then it turned out it wasn't me he wanted, but my wife."

At one level, In the Presence of a Clown *is about individuals and their redeeming encounter with art. And at another, about your "cinematographic endeavours." Are they basically one and the same?*
"Well, what is this thing really about? Maybe about the fact that you have to be mad in order to accomplish something."

Understanding In the Presence of a Clown *is highly contingent on an understanding of your earlier works. In your opinion does that exclude those who do not have access to the Bergman codes, who are unfamiliar with your world? Or is there even a risk of a point of saturation – "Now we are tired of Bergman and his family business" … ?*
"No, I don't think so at all. Those who are familiar with my world and my way of expressing myself, well, that's just a bonus, I guess. Those who have never seen any of my earlier works, however, and then discover something … either they take it to heart or they remain unaffected. A certain tone or emotion may strike a responsive chord in one person and leave another totally indifferent. Surely, that's the way it is."

In the script you describe your Uncle Johan/Carl in these words: "Afraid, nice, anxiously pedantic, keeping extremely clean, very ambitious. All this interspersed with the occasional outbursts of rage." It does sound like a latter-day descendant of Uncle Johan.
"Who? Me? Is that meant to be me, you mean? Oh no, never! It is a great and loving tribute to one of my great loves, my Uncle Johan, whom I really adored. A genius he was, completely mad, of course. There is so much discipline, normality, and talent in those two families I stem from, the Bergmans and the Åkerbloms, so much propriety and so many bourgeois virtues. Uncle Johan had to bear the burden of all the remnants of asocial behaviour, madness,

violence, and anarchy. He had to bear them and spend the rest of his life in the loony bin. So it certainly is not a self portrait! If I were to be terribly profound – which I don't like to be, just as I don't like to analyse my own works – I could say that if you combine the play's Uncle Carl, Professor Vogler, and Pauline Thibault, and add a touch of the teacher in Grånäs: maybe they are me! You might actually say that.

"Without Pauline's sensibility and tolerance, her willingness to house those two madmen … well, that is the combination in which I lead my life. I realized quite early on in my life that if I did not impose an ironclad, professional discipline on myself, I would have to live my productions, rather than stage them."

TELEVISION PRODUCTIONS BY INGMAR BERGMAN

1957   *Mr Sleeman Arrives*
1958   *The Woman from Venice*
1959   *Rabies*
1960   *Storm*
1960   *A Dream Play*
1969   *The Ritual*
1970   *The Sanctuary*
1974   *Scenes from a Marriage*
1975   *Face to Face*
1975   *The Magic Flute*
1976   *From the Life of the Marionettes*
1981   *Don Juan*
1983   *Fanny and Alexander*
1983   *The School for Wives*
1984   *After the Rehearsal*
1986   *The Blessed Ones*
1992   *Madame de Sade*
1994   *The Bacchae*
1995   *The Last Cry*
1995   *Harald and Harald*
1997   *In the Presence of a Clown*

EPILOGUE

LARGE SECOND THOUGHTS, OR, IT DID NOT END IN 1983

The first section ended on a mixed note of admiration, affection, a touch of sadness. And that was supposed to be the conclusion to this study on Ingmar Bergman. But inevitably I was suffering all kinds of misgivings. For example – and as has been made clear from Jannike Åhland's TV overview – had I not violated my own "rules" (of dealing with only the *movies directed* by Ingmar Bergman) by feasting also on TV/film hybrids, especially *Scenes from a Marriage*, *The Magic Flute*, and, of course, *Fanny and Alexander*? More importantly, what about all the other (ignored) TV work, the prodigious quantity and quality of Bergman's theatre output, and all the rest? Once you create parameters, you risk cutting off what may prove essential.

There is another spectacular fact of life I have alluded to more than once: in his native Sweden today, Ingmar Bergman is, if anything, even more dominant a cultural figure than he was in the past. This study's cutoff date, to all intents and purposes, was 1982–83. As I write these lines in the summer of 1998, consider his artistic output *since* 1983: nineteen theatre productions as director (including his own *The Last Cry*); one opera; eight television productions; three feature film scripts; two major autobiographical books on his life and works; numerous published treatments or novels of his movies or television and theatre plays. Add to that the occasional print articles and a series of lengthy and important TV interviews. And, finally as a sort of background, there is his apparently unrelenting (and notorious?) involvement in the politics of Sweden's cultural institutions – the funding, the choosing of who is to run what, the policies.

This is hardly the image of one who has ceased to have ideas about a whole lot of things. Could, then, my own closing image from *Fanny and Alexander* (Little Ingmar/Old Ingmar curled up safe and sound on his Granny's lap) serve adequately as metaphor for Bergman's outlook today? Isn't there the strong possibility that in all this ferment, Bergman has still been evolving through these last fifteen years, indeed continuing his job as "prophet of his times" –

his times, that is, as still continuing right now?

One might have thought that 1995 would have put an end to his artistic activity. The death of Ingrid Von Rosen, his wife since 1971, was a devastating loss, his soul mate and the talented companion who managed the practical aspects of their life. Nearly eighty years of age, how would he survive? Bergman's way of coping with his grief was, on the one hand, to live almost as a recluse on Fårö, not seeing his friends, using only the phone as a link, and, on the other, periodically (and progressively) to plunge with even greater intensity into his artistic endeavours.

Those endeavours have indeed been going on ever since. No surprise, then, that the Cannes Film Festival awarded its all-time Palme des Palmes to Bergman in 1997, and fêted him again in May 1998 in prestige showings of his latest Swedish television success, *In the Presence of a Clown*. And that Stockholm, chosen as Europe's Cultural Capital for 1998, has made Bergman the focal point: retrospectives of his work, special publications, seminars, major TV interviews … "Bergman" everywhere, with, as the highlight, the national celebrating of his eightieth birthday on July 14.

Typically, in a press conference held a few days before Cannes began (1998), Bergman announced that he was working on a new film script (*The Faithless*), to be directed by Liv Ullmann in the summer of 1999, and starring Sweden's wondrous Lena Endre.

Thus, indeed, some of my misgivings.[1] And what about his recent film

---

1 Had I wished to include, for example, Bergman's theatre activities in this study, how could I (who have seen barely a half-dozen of his plays) have gone about it? Research difficulties abound here. As I indicated briefly in the preface and at the end of chapter 1, ambitious studies in this area are still extremely limited. But they are growing. Sweden's Drottningholms Teatermuseum have listed Bergman's theatre productions, while expressing (to me) certain reservations about their findings, ever seeking greater accuracy and completeness. The museum has also begun the far more difficult task of gathering pertinent information on individual Bergman productions. At another level, although some excellent critical comments exist concerning this or that Bergman undertaking – see, for example, the recent collection in English, *Ingmar Bergman, an Artist's Journey on Stage, Screen, in Print*, edited by Roger W. Oliver (New York: Arcade, 1995), and the earlier, more systematic works of Lise-Lone Marker and Frederick J. Marker, *Ingmar Bergman: Four Decades in the Theatre* (Cambridge: Cambridge University Press, 1982) and *Ingmar Bergman: A Project for the Theatre* (New York: Frederick Ungar, 1983) – we are still far from any kind of complete synthesis of Bergman's approach to, and treatment, editing, or changing of, the plays he has directed. To begin with, how can such work be done satisfactorily in the absence of the *living* productions? I did mention insights arrived at by writers such as Peter Cowie and Frank Gado (chapter 3) concerning some of the plays Bergman wrote in the earlier days; but the fact

scripts? After completing *Fanny and Alexander* as both writer and director, Bergman wrote two feature film scripts about his parents (with himself as infant in the womb, then as a young boy). He chose Denmark's Bille August to direct the first, *The Best Intentions*; highly respected, that film went on to win the Cannes Film Festival's Palme d'Or in 1992. For the second "family script," he turned to his own son Daniel, for whom this would serve as feature film directorial debut. The ensuing movie (*Sunday's Children*) I find fresh and captivating. Both of these films certainly have their intrinsic merits, and especially when coupled with Bergman's two "autobiographies," they tell us a good deal about Ingmar's early private life.[2] Dare I recall here, however, that film, being a most complex art form, cannot be reduced to script alone? Quite convinced – most of the time, at least, and when dealing with quality work – that *directors* are the real *auteurs* of their films, I chose not to include even these latest Bergman scripts as part of this study. Having seen both movies, I really felt that they added little substance to the basic argument. And, so went my thinking, that surely would prove equally true of the *third* (and most recent) "Bergman family" feature film script, *Private Confessions*.

So I thought. But then, enter Liv Ullmann. It now became obvious that writing this epilogue was not only desirable but unavoidable.

Spring 1995. Liv Ullmann, Norway's distinguished film and theatre actor, author, and UNICEF Good Will ambassador, was directing her second feature film, the most ambitious movie yet undertaken in the history of the Norwegian cinema – her own adaptation of the first volume of Sigrid Undset's masterpiece, *Kristin Lavransdatter* – when she received a call from Ingmar Bergman: would she be willing to direct his latest film script, *Private Confessions*? How could she not accept: before the end of summer, with *Kristin* barely finished,

remains that much, much work remains to be done. A most interesting approach right now is that of Mikael Timm (cf. my preface and the Oliver collection above), as, piecemeal, he presents a more pan-cultural, more holistic portrait of the total artist as he moves eclectically from one medium to another.

2 Just how reliable all of this may prove, of course, remains highly problematic – as I pointed out towards the end of the introduction. Hubert J. Cohen's *Ingmar Bergman: The Art of Confession* (New York: Twayne, 1993) is a lengthy, highly intelligent, well-researched study of Bergman's films, scripts, and other writings and interviews considered as ongoing bits of personal confession by Bergman. Cohen's book certainly can be recommended, but a worrisome and fundamental question remains: How do we know to what extent this or that element reveals the real "private" Bergman and is not, in fact, Bergman's yielding to the story's need to invent for the purposes of the artistic creation at hand?

she plunged into the script written by the film legend who had shared her personal life for some six years and her professional life for considerably longer.

Shortly after beginning the shooting of *Private Confessions*, and having known for some time about my book-in-the-works, she informed me, "If you're really intent on capturing the evolution of Ingmar's thinking *right up to today*, you'd better see this film." "Why?" "Because Ingmar's back into the religious question – with a vengeance!" I was more than intrigued. According to Liv Ullmann, it was not merely a question of updating, but rather of a profound change, so much so that my way of concluding (in chapter 8) might not be true of the Ingmar Bergman of "today."

Well, books tend to take longer than one might hope. *Private Confessions* had its television première in the winter of 1996–97, in two episodes totalling three hours and seventeen minutes. I saw it in that format soon after. Some months later, in May 1997, it had its world première as a shorter, two-and-a-half hour feature movie at the Cannes Festival, adding a fitting note to the awarding of the special Palme des Palmes to Ingmar Bergman.

Joy and consternation: I was forced to conclude that Liv Ullmann was in no way exaggerating, and that a mitigated return to Bergman's work was necessary. I do not propose to critique all his creative output since 1983, nor to submit any of it to the kind of "complete text analysis" applied to all the movies he directed as I did, to an extent, in the first section of the book. But by concentrating on a few aspects of *Private Confessions* and of the subsequent TV production he has written and directed (*In the Presence of a Clown*), I shall attempt to capture the shift in Bergman's thinking and to resituate him in contemporary culture – and by so doing, perhaps, to correct some of my previous oversimplifications. In other words, the fifteen years since *Fanny and Alexander* have had a dramatic impact on his way of encountering reality.

Private Confessions centres on Anna, wife of a Lutheran pastor. To what degree the story contains true-life biographical material it is difficult to say, but behind it loom unquestionably the real-life figures of Bergman's parents. Pernilla Wållgren August and Samuel Fröler reprise the roles that they played as the parents in *The Best Intentions*.

Anna is having an affair; in her distress and moral confusion she turns to her Uncle Jacob, also a Lutheran pastor (played by Max von Sydow in, most agree, one of his greatest performances). So much for a radical plot summary. And the heart and soul of *Private Confessions*? Try good old-fashioned Bergmanian specialties such as a woman's soul life, her spiritual death, her desperate struggle for new life, hope, meaningfulness.

The longer television version is divided into six sections, and in all of them

Anna is the central figure, interacting with, or, really, confessing to one person, be it Uncle Jacob, or her husband, or her lover, or her friend (a Lutheran missionary sister), or her mother. Bergman's script moves backwards and forwards in time: with hindsight, one can sketch out the time-line extending from 1907 when Anna was eighteen and preparing for her Confirmation with Uncle Jacob through various moments from (roughly) 1925 to 1927, until 1935, when the now forty-six-year-old Anna is visiting her dying uncle. Bergman's writing freedom extends into shifts from "real reality" to thought or imagination or dream projection.

The structure, rhythm, and feel of the work make it impossible to pontificate as to what medium it is ideally meant for: film? television? theatre? Is it some hybrid variation of spoken drama? Liv Ullmann does a remarkable job in respecting the Bergman text and its choose-your-medium nature. With the collaboration of her cameraman and former mentor, Sven Nykvist, she reveals the glowing, sometimes austere, sometimes resplendent world in which these people live – Uppsala, Stockholm, the Swedish summer in the country, the sea and Molde (in Norway), the exteriors and interiors of their homes. Above all, however, Ullmann insists on extremely lengthy (and beautifully lit) medium close-ups of Anna – and, one is tempted to say, of Anna's soul. Because of her exceptional talent, Pernilla August is up to the formidable task.

Words, words, words. Indeed, Bergman *says* everything, explains all, recounts other things that have happened (essential plot details?). And Ullmann, her technical team, and her actors, serve those words magnificently, intelligently, and with depth. Here is human suffering, human striving, and human beauty. A discreet lingering on a physical detail, a special quality of light, silence, some sacred moment of music from Bach or Shostakovich … *Private Confessions*, in its austerity, paradoxically shines with spirit.

Here is one dramatic work, the antithesis of commercial film or TV, that makes demands on its audience. One may (legitimately?) regret its literal explaining of everything.[3] But then, is that not its unique challenge, a courageous trust in what the film is actually saying and in its profound implications – and it its audience's ability to share in this noble flight of the human spirit?

With immense power Bergman returns to what he is perhaps best known

---

3 The movie version lasts two hours and fifteen minutes, one hour less than the television. Overall, I find the television experience richer, especially when seen in two separate sections, as it is meant to be. It is not only because the dialogue, or, perhaps more accurately, its aggressive dependence on words, become less demanding when separated into the shorter halves but also because everything becomes better interrelated, more meaningful. And above all because certain superb moments are not sacrificed.

for: the portrayal of the suffering interaction of human beings, the anguishing complexities that surround human love.4 Ah yes – and guilt, dryness of the human soul, condemned yearnings, frustrated hopes … It is as if the great brooding Swedish film artist were coming back without self-conscious reserve to something he never truly abandoned.

But it does not stop here. Perhaps more astonishingly, and in spite of many of his statements made in his later periods, Bergman pitches his tent in yet other familiar territory: love and suffering, but also sin and the need for forgiveness, the possibility of new life, and the question of God's existence – and of the nature of the Divine, and of the role of Christ. One might say as never before.

My intention is not to point out an endless series of examples: indeed, *Private Confessions* is nothing if not an unrelenting communication of these kinds of human concerns. But for the special purposes of this epilogue, I shall limit myself to two moments, following this up with an attempt to situate matters in the context of contemporary culture.

The final scene has been translated in its entirety to the screen in the television version, but only partially in the movie. Forty-six-year-old Anna has been visiting her Uncle Jacob, summoned by him because he is approaching death. The old man is still hounded by the fear that his advice to her long ago to tell her husband the truth about her love affair may have proved destructive. Anna tries to reassure him, telling him truths which we, the audience, already know are masking the whole truth. Indeed, Anna is a ravaged woman, distressed and unhappy. More or less forced to share communion with Jacob, his wife, and his old friend, the bishop, she flees into the next room when Jacob has a fit of vomitting, unable to digest even the host. While the others are tending to him she looks at an old photograph of her Confirmation group.

It is then that the "Sixth [and final] Conversation" begins. In a flashback to the days when that picture was taken (1907), when Anna was a teenager, on the eve of her Confirmation day, she is telling her uncle that she cannot go through with it, since she lost her faith and cannot receive Communion. What will she do?5

The scene is bathed in a muted, rather understated loveliness, glowing lights illuminating parts of the great church in Uppsala. It is obvious that uncle

---

4 The entire "Third Conversation" has been dropped from the movie version, to its loss. It is a reprise of sorts of the mother/daughter love/hate complexities experienced in *Autumn Sonata*. Swedish theatre's extraordinary Anita Björk plays the Ingrid Bergman role.

5 The script is available in English, in Joan Tate's translation (New York: Arcade, 1997). What follows, though seriously shortened in the movie, appears in its totality in both script and television versions. It is well worth going into.

and niece share a great affection, a kind of shared complicity of trust – and that Bergman, too, loves them.

For brevity's sake, I paraphrase those parts of the segment that serve my purpose. After the others have left the rehearsal for tomorrow's Confirmation service, Anna at last can talk to her uncle: "I can't believe all this anymore. Do you really believe in a loving God, Uncle Jacob?" Harking back to films Bergman directed thirty, forty, fifty years ago, the questions have a familiar ring. Good heavens, are we back to *The Seventh Seal*? But this Lutheran priest is a different kind of defender of religious affirmation: Jacob *understands* what he is about, and he explains to his niece his belief in God "because of an unfathomable, incomprehensible, magnificent miracle" – a factual one. Not the resurrection, not the stories told for the consolation and joy of the believers, but the *fact* of the *coming back to life* of the dispirited apostles after Christ's death. Instead of clinging to what is left of their wretched little lives, as Jacob sees it, they suddenly turn their lives "to a useful purpose: to live Christ's message of invincible love, of unfathomable solicitude; to get out of the darkness and go into the light and tell everyone that *love exists* – love, that disregarded reality in our lives – and that they have been called by Christ to do this. And the miracle? The *fact* that within two years, Christendom spread like wildfire over the Mediterranean world, as millions and millions prepared to endure torture and persecution for this conviction." Pastor Jacob proclaims aggressively, "And *that's* where I stay." (This long, formal explanation of faith, in great part, is what I have already referred to as having been dropped in the final editing of the movie version.)

The scene from the Bergman script and both television and movie versions concludes with Anna in a confused state, on the verge of tears, trying to break through to a certain autonomy. She understands her uncle up to a point, confiding in him that she has decided to become a missionary nurse in order to help others. Jacob encourages her: "Yes. You don't have to talk love, you can love by carrying out deeds of love."

The Swedish darkness of early winter evening bathes Uppsala as they walk. They stop on a bridge over the river Fyris, now a veritable torrent. Anna deliberately removes her recently bought ornate hat, and drops it into the waters. Impulsively, she embraces her uncle. Jacob tells her to go home, go to her room and think things over. Yes, she will have a good cry. And then she will know what she must do – and then "phone me tomorrow morning to let me know your decision."

The two part, their ways pointing in opposite directions. Opposite directions, two voices, two *Bergman* voices, one is tempted to say, one in affirmation, the other at least in uncertainty … with matters left unresolved. The End

… well, not by a long shot, as we shall see later.

The other scene occurs much earlier in the film, near the beginning, during the "First Conversation." It is 1925: Anna is in her twenties, married with three children, and, willingly/unwillingly, she is confronting her beloved uncle in Stockholm. This part of the "First Conversation" takes place in the rectory inhabited by Anna, her pastor husband and the children, and she is telling her uncle about her infidelity. The priest insists she must tell her husband the truth; but she feels that such a solution will oblige her to continue to live her life with him, a life indeed that is anything but the truth, a pathetic masking of reality. Jacob insists that the truth will give her strength. "Don't you believe God concerns himself with your misery? Don't you believe any longer?" "No." And Anna turns the question onto her uncle: "Do you really believe in God, Uncle Jacob? A 'Father in Heaven'? A God of Love? A God with hands and heart and watchful eyes?" And once again one hears distinct echoes of past Bergman films, belonging to an era that Bergman had later disowned.

Uncle Jacob's answer: "All that is unimportant to me." This unexpected beginning of Jacob's response actually reflects some Bergman statements made in that later era (the 1970s) which I have already quoted (chapter 8). But Jacob continues in another mode, reflecting a kind of attitude not at all at odds with some strands of recent Christian theology as it seeks to find a language capable, in contemporary terms, of appropriating the reality of God: "Don't say the word 'God.' Say the Holy One. The Sanctity of Man. Everything else is attribute, disguise, manifestations, tricks, desperations, rituals, cries of despair in the darkness and silence" – with decidedly Bergmanian overtones, one hastens to add. Jacob (my paraphrasing) continues: "You can never calculate or capture the Sanctity of Man. At the same time, it's something to hold on to, something quite concrete. Unto Death. What happens thereafter is hidden. But one thing is sure … we are surrounded by events we do not grasp with our senses, but which constantly influence us. Only the poets, musicians and saints have given us mirrors of the Unfathomable. They have seen, known, understood, not wholly, but in fragments … It is consoling to me to think about the Sanctity of Man and the mysterious Immensities surrounding us.

"What I am saying to you now is not a metaphor, for it is *reality*. Inscribed in the Sanctity of Man is the Truth. No one can commit violence against the Truth without going wrong. Without doing harm."

The scene, as described in Bergman's script and in both the TV version and the movie, ends with Anna and Uncle Jacob seated in chairs on either side of the hall door. "The lights from the wall brackets officiate sleepily. It is dark beyond the open windows of the dining-room. A lone song-thrush concealed in the foliage heralds the as-yet invisible dawn."

If one stands back, and, from the vantage point of this study's preoccupations, attempts to fit *Private Confessions* into the overall Bergman evolution, the script (most unexpectedly) signals a spectacular *return* to a time in Bergman's life when theological considerations were very much a relevant part of the culture as he understood it. And, more than that, it can be seen as pointing towards a new synthesis. The *contrast* at that level with, say, *Fanny and Alexander* of the early 1980s is astonishing.[6] With *Private Confessions*, indeed, one witnesses a decided departure from the postmodern stance I was describing as marking Bergman's final period as a film director.

To begin with, there is an overt return to the traditional Great Questions, without clever or playful distraction and the protection afforded by a mocking, self-conscious referring to his own previous images, symbols, "themes," figurations. *Private Confessions*, on the contrary, is fuelled by an intense moral concern, growing out of a renewed sensitivity to the metaphysical dimensions of existence, that dimension as relating to and dependent on the ultimate reality generally signified by the West's use of the word "God."

But it goes beyond this. In the film-ending flashback, Bergman's pastor becomes even more explicit in the return to a kind of "Christian way" of positing values and realities. He appeals to Christ's revelation of Love as the force that empowers human beings and brings meaningfulness and joy to their lives. He is now able to understand the "infamies occurring in the name of love" as the results of the misuse of human freedom. For some idea of how far Bergman has progressed in his portrayal of Christian pastors, compare Uncle Jacob with, say, what we see in *Winter Light*.

Going back to my 1970 interview with Bergman (chapters 5 and 6, and especially the beginning of chapter 8), one may recall how I situated his position at that time by resorting to a certain classical theological jargon. Bergman seemed to be ridding himself of the notion of the transcendent God he had grown up with (the God-out-there or -up-there) while remaining attuned to the immanent notion (humanity's inner wholeness, a sort of God-within-us). But in any case (and he was insisting on this), he was coming to the conclusion that the question of God/non-God was no longer a concern of his, no longer relevant to his life. And this was borne out in his subsequent films

With *Private Confessions*, however, the God-question is once again of immense concern, the very heart of the film. One hears strong formal echoes from, for example, *The Seventh Seal* and *Through a Glass Darkly* – the same

6 Let it also be noted that neither of the two more recent "Bergman family" scripts preceding *Private Confessions* ventures into areas similar to what I am describing. On the contrary – and this even though they are dealing with a Lutheran pastor's family, the family Ingmar was born into.

kind of fundamental questions are raised. But now there are clarifications, at least differently worded answers, at once extensions of the 1970 position and changes from that position. *Private Confessions* now permits one to sketch things out in the following fashion:

1   The immanent God, while never specifically defined, is still strongly affirmed ("the Sanctity of Man," etc.);

2   And the discarded transcendent God? Bergman now appeals rather to a transcendent *reality* "the Unfathomable, mysterious Immensities that surround us, the fact that we are surrounded by events we do not grasp with our senses, but which constantly influence us";

3   Bergman is now able to take a further step: what is *rejected* is "God," that is, the cultural notion of God, which he experiences as a human reduction, precisely, of "the Unfathomable." He rejects, as we have seen, the very word "God," because of all the cultural accretions clinging to it, whether it be in the officially formulated church credos, the theological conceptualizations, or the pietistic images and practices of some religious adherents.

Uncle Jacob's words to Anna most certainly are not what is habitually used in the language of Christian orthodoxy. Yet the words can, at least to a large extent, be accommodated to a long tradition of attempts in Christianity itself to demonstrate the impossibility of describing God adequately in human language, a tradition rejecting a kind of human over-confidence in circumscribing "God" with specific words, formulations, descriptions, rationalizations. I have already referred to the "God Is Dead" theology of the 1960s (note 6, chapter 7). Simon Weil puts it this way: "There is God, there is no God." Long before that, St Bernard, trying to describe God, cries out: "I know not, I know not." Meister Eckhart affirms that God must be loved as He is, "a sheer pure absolute One, sundered from all twoness, and in whom we must eternally sink from nothingness to nothingness." St Gregory sees the paradox in this fashion: "Then only is there truth in what we know concerning God when we are made sensible that we cannot know anything concerning Him." Less controversial, perhaps, are the much more recent words of Graham Greene:7 "In January, 1926, I became convinced of the probable existence of something we call God, though now I dislike the word with all its anthropomorphic associations, and

---

7   See Huston Smith's *The Religions of Man* (New York: Harper & Row, 1965), 358, for more quotations and a more extended discussion of such matters. Indeed, the whole book is rich in insights pertinent to this kind of intellectual probing. The Graham Greene quotation is from his autobiography (A Sort of Life, London: Bodley Head, 1971), 225.

prefer Chardin's *noosphere*."

The point to all this is fairly obvious: in large measure, the words put by Ingmar Bergman into the mouth of Uncle Jacob are not foreign to Christian theological tradition. One could extend the discussion of similar paradoxical affirmations made in Hindu, Buddhist, and other great religious traditions. Which leads to another, far less exalted kind of conclusion: this epilogue could, in the hands of the appropriate specialists, easily be expanded into another book, or other volumes, belonging more properly to the field of theology than to the cinema. But when inserted into the cycle that governs the cultural mix of the classical, the modernist, and the postmodernist that I keep coming back to, they are keenly relevant to this study.

Admittedly, I have been working mostly from the words of one character, Uncle Jacob. However, given the nature of this study, and what was originally planned as the final summation in chapter 8, the treatment that Uncle Jacob enjoys from *Bergman's* writing, *Ullmann's* direction, and *von Sydow's* acting merits special attention. To repeat, this priest is radically different not only from any previous Bergman spokesman about the religious or philosophical but also from all the other male protagonists in the extended Bergman movie catalogue. Uncle Jacob seems to have none of the anguish, desperation, or doubt-ridden semi-paralysis of his predecessors. One need only think back again to *The Seventh Seal, Through a Glass Darkly, Winter Light,* or to minor characters such as the priest in *Cries and Whispers,* to be struck by the contrast. Nor is he a clown figure in the manner of Gustav Adolf Ekdahl in *Fanny and Alexander,* who indeed might be seen to be saying some fine things incarnating the life force but who is ironically reduced by his buffoonery.

No buffoonery here, and still less tortured semi-affirmations or mere wishful sighing for what might be. Max von Sydow's priest is rich in humanity, gifted with intelligence, lived wisdom, a loving spirit, and even what one might call a God-blessed humour. And his words have the ring of truth, the power to convince. But more than that. Bergman's protagonists, to put it mildly, have never been noted for dynamic epic qualities. That is why I felt it perfectly fair, in what I thought was to be the conclusion of this book, to focus on that warm, tender, and slightly pathetic closing image of *Fanny and Alexander* (Alex on his Granny's lap) as a kind of archetype revealing a dominant part of Bergman's poetic inspiration and what, in the early 1980s, Bergman seemed to understand as his own soul state: life as a dream, the only safety consisting in a return to the womb.

That was not to be the final word. In *Private Confessions,* Uncle Jacob sounds a call, however discreetly, to *action*. Forget the smallness of self-absorption, come alive in the great Reality of Love, bring *that* to the world. By the same token a profound meaningfulness is now restored to human existence: we do not have to live in the world of so many of Bergman's latter films, one that in spite of its moments of beauty is ultimately a wasteland of meaninglessness posited by a certain systematic deconstruction, with only a few precious moments and maybe our cleverness to make it bearable.

Overstatement is a danger, and here one must be wary. *Private Confessions* does present another point of view: indeed, the two scenes I have described have a poignancy precisely because Anna, in her great suffering and desolation, can not share her uncle's vision. I refer now to the *script as written by Bergman* which, after all, does leave us in a state of *inconclusivity*, with two loving yet divided people walking off in opposite directions, in the dark of evening, on a bridge over threatening waters.

What can we conclude from all this? *Private Confessions* certainly signals at least a return to the God-and-meaningfulness question. Indeed, even if it seems to end on an open, inconclusive, and rather divided note, the whole film can still be said to be organized and energized by a life-and-death struggle growing out of that question.

At the script level, I hasten to add. For there is significantly more – and here I move into an area rather personal to Liv Ullmann and Ingmar Bergman. One wishes to tread softly. But with Liv Ullmann's permission, or should I say encouragement, I shall paraphrase what she related to me.

In the making of any movie, the director, of course, will, for any number of reasons, bring minor changes to the script, and so with *Private Confessions*. But Liv Ullmann, in shooting the ending of the film, made what was far more than a minor emendation. It occurs at the very ending of both movie and television versions, in that final flashback scene between the young Anna and her uncle as they part on the bridge.

If Bergman's script had been followed to the letter, the last shot of the *forty-six-year-old* Anna would be the one in medium close-up as she contemplates the photo, hanging on the wall, of her Confirmation group. Her face, to repeat, is tense, weary troubled – grieving, really. Then the script flashed back to her teenage conversation with her uncle, as described in the first excerpt above. But instead of ending the movie then and there (with the flashback as in the script) – the two figures ever moving away from each other, in darkness, with the noise of the onrushing river, and Anna on the verge of tears – director Liv *extends* both movie and television versions by *adding* a shot, *returning* to the forty-six-year-old Anna as she walks out of her dying uncle's parsonage after her visit. The camera slowly dollies back, allowing her as she moves forward on the dimly lit street to get closer and closer to us. Finally, the camera, in medium close-up again, holds her face, deeply troubled, lost in thought. And then comes *another* (brief) flashback, to the teenager again in conversation with her uncle. They are animated, joyful, talking as they walk away along the winter street. Young Anna looks back toward older Anna (and us) as the flashback rapidly dissolves back into the close-up face of the mature Anna we have just left, that older, unhappy face we are so familiar with.

A wonderful, long-awaited thing begins to happen. Slowly, the mature Anna's face loses its tense and almost bitter expression: Uncle Jacob's words from those earlier days seem to be striking home – precisely what had eluded the teenage Anna when, on the bridge, she had parted, semi-lost, from her uncle. *Now* perhaps it makes sense, now she begins to understand. And at long last, life seems to be returning to her face … the beginning of a smile. It is all terribly understated, and ever so fragile; and Liv Ullmann has left each one of us free to understand as we will. For me, the Ullmann ending brings substantially different tonality, meaning, sense of affirmation. The *whole film* – not only Uncle Jacob's words – is pointed in Jacob's direction. Admittedly, this is not the overwhelming kind of close-up that forty years before had totally regenerated Isak Borg in *Wild Strawberries*. But Anna now has at least a chance, there really may be a meaning in Uncle Jacob's words, *for her as well* (and dare one say for Bergman's mother and for Bergman himself and for ourselves).

What we see, then, in the ending of both movie and television versions, is sufficiently moving in its own right. But just how that new ending came into being adds an additional note of human poignancy, and perhaps adds as well to our understanding of the space occupied of late by Ingmar Bergman.

A number of the film's key people were gathered at a meeting with Bergman concerning the new ending which Liv Ullmann had already filmed without Bergman's knowledge. It is safe to say that Liv was not looking forward to this session. And, sure enough, Ingmar was furious: no, he could not, would not tolerate that change. Enough was enough, yes, all along he had felt uncomfortable, embarrassed even, by all the God-talk and morality talk he had put in his script. After all, had he not settled all that kind of thing long ago … and now Liv was adding *this*!

Reliving the moment as she told me the story, Liv's eyes were brimming with tears. The public Liv Ullmann, of course, is known for her fearless speaking out on human issues, a tigress, one is tempted to say, who has not hesitated confronting Pentagon generals and worse in the struggle against international arms dealing. But to her surprise, all she could do was stand there, looking at Bergman, tears running down her cheeks. "I had to tell him that the film could not *end* as it did in the script, with nothing resolved, heading nowhere. There had to be a point to it all." Bergman, however, was unyielding, very angry, still indignant about the ending.

"There are too many of us here, come with me to the next room." Liv followed him. And suddenly, the anger was gone. He was looking at her, holding her by the arms. All she could see now was the vulnerability of this man she knew so well. Quietly he asked, "It's for *me* you did this, isn't it?" Pause. "Of course, yes, I did it for you," tears still streaming down her face. "It's my act of love for you." All that well-known past, Ingmar's anger at his mother, at his father, at God, the inability to forgive any of them …

Ingmar's face changed back into its normal everyday expression. "All right. We'll do it your way. Come." They returned to the others, and Bergman announced that, yes, he would go along with the proposed changes. Concluding our conversation in Stockholm, Liv added that in the two or three week interim since then, Bergman had really come round, now (as she spoke to me) actually preferring the new ending to the old.

Later, when *Private Confessions* was released, Bergman would simply state to the media that Liv, being the more religious person of the two, was better suited to directing the work, doing things he might not feel capable of doing.

Just how far one should wish to include this story in a new attempt to situate Ingmar Bergman is open to discussion. The essence of Bergman, as we have seen, seems to consist in being the uneasy, imperfect, living and changing synthesis of conflicting tendencies. And I feel no inclination whatsoever to attempt some kind of obvious psychological probing. But in terms of the overall understanding of Bergman's journey, personal and cultural, his acceptance of the new ending makes a case even stronger than that already made by *his* script of *Private Confessions*. Indeed, the evolution does not end with the postmodern detachment that was my "final word" in chapter 8. And it brings an important corrective to what I assumed was Bergman's final acquiescing to that Strindbergian "dream reality" and that Freudian "return-to-the-womb" wish. The Big Metaphysical (and personal) Questions are back – and along with them a new and more dynamic attitude.

This does not mean that Bergman is simply returning to the possibilities of understanding offered by the classic theology of the past, that which informed his young years. The new understanding is almost a new language, a new synthesis capable of accommodating a more complex world view.

In this, amazingly, Ingmar Bergman once again assumes the prophetic mantle. It is as if, with *Private Confessions*, he were bringing a corrective to one of the ways I have been characterizing contemporary culture. All through this book I have been subscribing to a limiting kind of meaning to "postmodernism." And that, it is important to stress, is its negative side, that which, as we have seen in its most radical manifestation, ultimately exposes all beliefs, symbols, or thought systems as mere cultural constructs incapable of "really reaching reality" – if such exists.

Some – they tend to call themselves positive postmodernists – employ the term in a profoundly different sense. They share with deconstructionists the conviction that humanity must expose – deconstruct – the tenets and general ways of thinking both of the classic or premodern stage of culture and of the succeeding modernist era, at least in what has become stultified. But unlike the radical deconstructionists, positive postmodernists do not create a vacuum out of which emerges an alienated, distanced sensibility verging on the nihilistic. Rather, they return to modernism in a *constructive* spirit, discerning what within that world view is positive, life nurturing, and hence to be retained and built on. Science, for example, may have contributed to the soul-withering impoverishment of human culture, but it has brought, and can go on bringing, tremendous benefits to humankind. And so for the premodern or classic culture: whereas certain systematic thought systems and rigid social structures were tending to block off many aspects of the study of the universe, at times displacing reality with ritualistic superstition, still, that culture was immensely rich precisely in what tended to be ravished by modern rationalism – the numinous aspect of the universe, closeness to nature and to the mysterious, the poetic, the spiritual.

Underlying this positive aspect of postmodernism is the recognized need of belief in life, a sense of at-oneness with the universe, without which, precisely, humankind suffers desolation of the spirit.[8] Much of the literature on this aspect of postmodernism does indeed have the ring of optimism; but the complexity of the task by and large is recognized, banishing what might be seen as a certain naiveté when compared with the sophistication and often cynicism

---

8 For expanded treatment of this positive version of postmodernism, see, for example, *Spirituality and Society: Postmodern Visions*, edited by David Ray Griffin, 1988, and *Primordial Truth and Postmodern Theology*, David Ray Griffin and Huston Smith, 1989, both books published by SUNY (Albany, NY: State University of New York Press). Thomas Guarino's article, "Postmodernity and Five Fundamental Theological Issues" (*Theological Studies* 57, no. 4, Dec. 1996, 654–89) receives my vote for the most brilliant and enlightening synthesis of recent writings on the positive aspect of postmodernism (philosophy, cultural studies, communications theory, theology) that I have yet encountered. I would dearly love to incorporate it into this text, but that would prolong the book unduly and shift the focus overmuch.

of tone characterizing its opposite, deconstruction.

There is no denying, however, the call to hope, to affirmation of life. In a far different context, a review of Karl Barth's critique of Mozart,[9] John Updike's words might be used to summarize this spirit of ultimate affirmation: "This ideal man, Mozart, carrying the full baggage of human woe and of temporal convention and restraint, possesses his freedom through a triumphant turn out of Nay into Yea ... a turning in which light rises and the shadows fall through without disappearing, in which joy overtakes sorrow without extinguishing it, in which the Yea rings louder than the ever-present Nay."

Constructive postmodernism, then, is not a mere return to the ancient in an effort to replace the modern but rather a judicious, discerning, wary return to what is humanly enriching in (both) previous traditions, in an evolving new synthesis. In that kind of context, though admittedly in a subdued, not to say muted tone, Ingmar Bergman's evolution is indeed revealed as prophetic: consciously or not, he is very much a vital part of the ongoing conversation. And one can see in *Private Confessions* his emergence from the spirit[10] of negative deconstruction, into what characterizes the positive side of postmodernism.

Which is not to suggest that the above is meant to encapsulate the "total Bergman" today. In 1992, for example, Bergman wrote and directed for the theatre *The Last Cry*, a play on Swedish film pioneer Georg af Klercker, which he later (1995) adapted and directed for television. His latest theatre involvement this past year (1998) had him directing *The Image Makers*, Enquist's play about an imaginary meeting in 1920 between Sweden's Nobel Prize novelist Selma Lagerlöf, and Victor Sjöström, over the making of what would become the great film classic *The Phantom Chariot*. He is presently at work on a version also destined for television.

In the Presence of a Clown, a two-hour TV drama written and directed by Bergman and released in early 1998, fits in perfectly with Bergman's increased formal absorption with a topic central to his work: artistic creativity in all its complexity. The story, inspired by his uncle, Carl Åkerblom, is about an inventor who in 1925 wants to bring sound to the silent movie. It might be described as a *television* play about the *movies* that finally reaches fulfilment in the *theatre*.

Private Confessions never forsook high seriousness, its human suffering and aspirations leading inevitably to the Great Questions. *In the Presence of a*

9 In *Odd Jobs: Essays and Criticism*, (New York: Alfred A. Knopf, 1991), 229.
10 Linn Ullmann, daughter of Liv and Ingmar, is a journalist working in Norway. In an interview with her father in 1997 she relates how, during the session, he suddenly asked her: "Tell me, do you know anyone in your generation who believes in anything?"

Clown certainly explores those regions; but it helps round out the Bergman picture, resolutely courting the theatrical, the tragicomic, the absurd, madness, quasi-buffoonery. Loaded with references to earlier Bergman work – names of characters, familiar actors and situations and figurations – it is steeped in his themes and concerns: the agony of artistic creation, to be sure, its truth and power, or lack thereof, and (of course) mystery, love, death. Forty-two years after *The Seventh Seal*, Death actually appears again (played by Dramaten's Agneta Ekmanner), this time as a nasty, enigmatic female clown.[11]

We find ourselves in very familiar territory, familiar and yet without the peculiar power and magic of the earlier films. The charm and delight here is of a different nature. It is as if Bergman need no longer overwhelm us with cinematic splendour and prestidigitation: because of the unique and consistent film world he has created over so many years, he has won the right to explore and nuance it further, confident that in a shared complicity we delight in following him. What is his wisdom now, what have the years of incomparably intense probing and reacting brought to him? Because it is so important to him, it becomes important to us as well.

In other words, Bergman now enjoys a position of immense artistic privilege. And he is aware of it, grateful for his incomparable freedom. Repeatedly he insists that nowadays, when initially he sits down to write something, he cares not one whit what artistic medium it is destined for. He is free: he has something to communicate that he feels is worthwhile, and that gives him the joy and energy to vanquish his laziness – the "laziness," of an eighty year old whose quantity and quality of artistic production remain astonishing. It is only later that the final work will evolve as it should, becoming a novel or a script for a movie or television or the theatre. For him it is the communicating that is of the essence.

In some ways *In the Presence of a Clown* with its doses of absurdity, suffering, madness and frustration might seem to be populated with characters indeed helpless and pathetic, flirting with the *ingenting* of the semi-nihilistic *Persona* period. Not so: Uncle Carl does create art, art that transcends its own medium of expression, and he does touch people. He can, and does, communicate. And in spite of all the failures and humiliations and the fact of death, he is surrounded by love. The film ends, one could say, on two notes, one with the familiar image of the weary male seeking absorption in woman, and the other celebrating the power and validity of art, celebrating communication and love. We are here far removed from hopelessness and helplessness; but the dialectic between life and death goes on.

11 The drama is in part motivated by Franz Schubert's death. A musician friend of mine finds Bergman's use of Schubert's music spell-binding.

In that sense, and in the midst of its profound ironies, *In the Presence of a Clown* signals a return to the possibility of the life force, to meaningfulness, much as did *Private Confessions*. And both are experiences of bitterness vanquished. On 14 July 1998, to help celebrate his birthday, Swedish television premièred an interview of Ingmar Bergman by Jörn Donner, the novelist and filmmaker who was producer of *Fanny and Alexander*. For the first time Ingmar speaks about his wife Ingrid's death in 1995. All but paralysed by grief, he tells us, he was convinced that he could never work again. Leading, on the one hand, a semi-hermetic life on Fårö deliberately dominated by excessive order, he managed to survive, gradually returning to the theatre, greatly comforted by the presence of the actors, though still living in the felt need for Ingrid, and in the frequent consciousness of her presence. Now his life varies between semi-isolation on his beloved island and intense creative activity with others.

Repeating the experience related in chapter 8, he explains to Donner how, back in the 1960s, he had lost his fear of death, convinced that simple extinction was our human destiny – and "thereby feeling an enormous sense of security." But Ingrid's death, he continues, changed that feeling of security. He finds it unbearable to believe she simply no longer exists, that they will never meet again. And so he remains on Fårö, feeling close to nature … the sea … the infinity … the indescribable, the inconceivable. As I listened to these words, I was hearing the short version of Uncle Jacob's profession of faith to Anna in *Private Confessions*, those "other realities that surround us, the feeling of being part of a bigger scheme of things which we cannot analyse, understand, or take in. You feel that sometimes [my paraphrase of Bergman's words to Jörn Donner]."

And so, Ingmar Bergman, so long considered the quintessential film *auteur*, now is the freewheeling poetic communicator, talking almost directly to his audience, whatever the medium, his work overtly a sharing with us of experience and insight. The searching, the joy, the doubts – affirmation, rejection, denial, rebirth, re-involvement – what a journey it has been. And it continues, never totally resolved, never finalized, with its shifts and turns, intensely personal and yet always resonating to the rhythms of our culture in its different manifestations.

And surely it is precisely that ceaseless striving for truth, and that fragility and openness, that make him so relevant to those with eyes and ears and minds and hearts – and a sense of that culture. Time seems to have rewarded him with a relative serenity, but the most astonishing aspect in all of this is the vigour of the ongoing quest in an artist in his eighties, a quest reflecting, illuminating, and poeticizing the quest of the culture at large.

FILM LIST

Ingmar Bergman's work, it bears repeating, appears in many media, many forms. There are the various kinds of writings, and radio, theatre, opera, cinema, television. This book contains no detailed listings. Very little of this kind of work has been published concerning his *radio* work. *Theatre* and *opera* are better served, serious data, though incomplete, already having appeared, led by Sweden's Drottningholms Teatermuseum. Jannike Åhlund gives us a list of the titles of his *television* work (seen on page 229).

Many excellent, rather complete and detailed *filmographies* have already appeared in numerous works on Bergman. I refer readers to these. What appears below is a simple list of the English titles (sometimes two for the same film) of the works that Bergman has *directed*, and which have been released as movies (sometimes after an initial television release), along with the dates of release.

Crisis, 1946
It Rains on Our Love/The Man with an Umbrella, 1946
A Ship Bound for India/The Land of Desire, 1947
Music in Darkness/Night Is My Future, 1948
Port of Call, 1948
Prison/The Devil's Wanton, 1949
Thirst/Three Strange Loves, 1949
To Joy, 1950
This Can't Happen Here/High Tension, 1950
Summer Interlude/Illicit Interlude, 1951
Waiting Women/Secrets of Women, 1952
Summer with Monika/Monika, 1953
Sawdust and Tinsel/The Naked Night, 1953
A Lesson in Love, 1954
Dreams/Journey into Autumn, 1955
Smiles of a Summer Night, 1955

The Seventh Seal, 1957
Wild Strawberries, 1957
Brink of Life/So Close to Life, 1958
The Magician/The Face, 1958
The Virgin Spring, 1960
The Devil's Eye, 1960
Through a Glass Darkly, 1961
Winter Light/The Communicants, 1963
The Silence, 1963
Now About These Women/All These Women, 1964
Persona, 1966
Hour of the Wolf, 1968
Shame/The Shame, 1968
The Rite/The Ritual (TV play), 1969
The Passion of Anna/A Passion, 1969
The Fårö Document (documentary), 1970
The Touch, 1971
Cries and Whispers, 1973
Scenes from a Marriage (TV miniseries), 1973
The Magic Flute (TV opera), 1975
Face to Face (TV miniseries), 1976
The Serpent's Egg, 1977
Autumn Sonata, 1978
The Fårö Document (II), 1979
From the Life of the Marionettes, 1980
Fanny and Alexander (TV miniseries), 1982
After the Rehearsal (TV play), 1984
In the Presence of a Clown (TV play), 1998

N.B. The following screenplays were written by Bergman in the 1990s for others to direct:

The Best Intentions (director Bille August), 1991
Sunday's Children (director Daniel Bergman), 1992
Private Confessions (TV miniseries, director Liv Ullmann), 1997
The Faithless (TV play? director Liv Ullmann), in progress, 1999

INDEX

110, 120, 123, 130, 132, 233–47
Undset, Sigrid, 234
Updike, John, 247
Uppsala, 236–7

vampire, 96
Variety, 132
Vietnam war, 94, 108
Visby (Gotland), 118
The Virgin Spring, 46, 64–8, 133

Waiting Women, 32, 35–7, 39

war, 107–9
Wifstrand, Naima, 43, 222
Wild Strawberries, 46, 57–61, 104, 244
Winter Light, 70, 77–80, 107, 120, 228, 240, 242
Wollen, Peter, 208–11
The Woman from Venice, 222, 229
World War II, 108, 119

Young, Vernon, 23, 25